PESTICIDES
and
FRESHWATER FAUNA

PESTICIDES
and
FRESHWATER FAUNA

R. C. MUIRHEAD-THOMSON

1971

Academic Press
London and New York

ACADEMIC PRESS INC. (LONDON) LTD
BERKELEY SQUARE HOUSE
BERKELEY SQUARE
LONDON, W1X 6BA

U.S. Edition published by
ACADEMIC PRESS INC.
111 FIFTH AVENUE
NEW YORK, NEW YORK 10003

ISBN: 0–12–509760–3
LIBRARY OF CONGRESS CATALOG CARD NUMBER: 73–149702

Made and printed in Great Britain by
William Clowes & Sons, Limited, London, Beccles and Colchester

PREFACE

The study of the impact of pesticides on animal life in fresh waters is only one aspect of the much wider problem of chemical contamination of the environment in general, but one which nevertheless is of direct concern to biologists of widely diverse interests and activities.

Pesticides may reach the fresh waters of rivers, lakes and streams in a variety of ways. They may be applied deliberately to water bodies for the control of undesirable aquatic fauna or the aquatic stages of insects of public health importance. They may also make an incidental impact as a result of aerial application of insecticide for control of terrestrial pests in agriculture and forestry in surrounding areas. They may also reach lakes and rivers by aerial drift or by run-off from the land. Finally, gross impact of pesticide may occur from time to time as a result of accident or carelessness involving chemical concentrates.

The object of this present survey is not simply to record or summarize the vast amount of relevant data published in recent years. The emphasis is not so much on the recorded facts and observations, but on the methods and techniques which have been used or designed to provide the facts. Whether pesticides are studied in their role of chemicals in the service of man, or in their role as dangerous contaminants of the natural environment — freshwater bodies in particular — all investigators share a common interest in that they are trying to achieve a correct and scientific evaluation of the impact of pesticides on particular freshwater organisms.

The methods used by public health biologists in their continuing search for selective pesticides — which ideally would control the target pest in question while at the same time having only minimal effect on other freshwater forms — are in many cases unknown to those who work in different spheres of interest such as freshwater fisheries and conservation. Similarly, applied biologists faced with the harsh practical realities of pest or disease control can seldom find time or opportunity to enquire further into the wider ecological effects of the chemical dosages they apply regularly to water surfaces.

Because of the wide range of specialists interested in the many different facets of this problem, evaluation techniques and standards tend to be equally diverse, and to have developed independently of each other. In this book an attempt will be made to assess these evaluation techniques, to compare them critically, and to try and judge the extent to which each phase of evaluation from strictly controlled laboratory tests to plot or field trial, assists in building up a true or complete picture regarding the effect of that particular pesticide on the aquatic environment.

It is felt that each of the many different groups of specialists concerned with this common problem have still got a great deal to learn from each other, and that in few other fields of research can there be a more urgent need for closer coordination of effort.

This present book, by a single author, should be regarded merely as a first step in bridging the gap between groups of workers not normally conversant with each other's interests and objectives. While the literature cited is extensive and representative of the many interests, it is only quite a small proportion of the information on record from all countries of the world. For this kind of critical review and assessment, papers must be studied in their entirety — the brief summaries in English of publications in other languages are quite inadequate and often misleading. For this reason, limitations of time and linguistic ability have made it impossible to do justice to numerous pertinent publications in Russian and Japanese, for example. It is hoped that this introduction to the subject will stimulate others better qualified to delve into this untapped literature and produce a more comprehensive review which can truly claim to be more international in outlook and in application.

ACKNOWLEDGEMENTS

I am greatly indebted to a number of colleagues and correspondents who have all been most helpful in providing me with reports and up-to-date information about particular aspects of pesticide impact on fresh-water ecology.

To Dr. J. R. Anderson of the Fishery Research Board of Canada's Biological Station, I am grateful for various reports, published and un-published, bearing on the activities of the Station and on the classic work on DDT contamination of salmon streams in New Brunswick.

To Mr. John Howell and Mr. E. Louis King of the Hammond Bay Biological Station, Michigan, I am indebted for a full set of reports and publications dealing with all aspects of the Sea Lamprey Research and Control programme in the Great Lakes.

To Mr. R. Lennon, Director of the U.S. Fish Control Laboratories, I am very grateful for full documentation regarding their research pro-gramme, and the use of Antimycin and other chemicals for the control of undesirable fish populations.

To Mr. W. Dill, FAO Department of Fisheries, I am also greatly indebted for information concerning FAO's interests in fisheries and fish culture, and for drawing my attention to Russian work on the chemical control of fish populations.

Mr. A. J. A. Pearson of Woodstock Agricultural Research Centre, and Mr. N. O. Crossland of Shellstar, very kindly put at my disposal reports and unpublished information regarding the use of the molluscicide Frescon for control of an intermediate host snail of a fish parasite in England.

May 1971   R. C. MUIRHEAD-THOMSON

ACKNOWLEDGMENTS

CONTENTS

1*

CHAPTER 1

INTRODUCTION AND GENERAL SURVEY

The role of chemicals in controlling insect pests of crops and forests, as well as the insect vectors of human and animal disease, has been recognized and accepted from the beginning of this century. Over a long period this chemical armament was based essentially on a comparatively small range of inorganic copper and arsenic compounds, or on naturally occurring insecticides such as Pyrethrum and Rotenone. Over many years the rate of progress in the development and more effective use of these chemicals was steady but unhurried up till the period of the Second World War, when, quite suddenly, the development of a new synthetic organic insecticide, DDT, introduced entirely new concepts into pest control and initiated the period of intense development and expansion which has characterized the last twenty-five years.

Until that time, the particular pesticide which probably made the greatest direct impact on natural freshwater bodies in many parts of the world was Paris Green — copper aceto-arsenite — which was applied extensively both from the ground and from the air to a wide variety of mosquito breeding places, particularly in malaria control. For example, application of Paris Green to small pools, water collections and other likely breeding places of *Anopheles gambiae*, the principal mosquito vector of malaria in Africa, was the basic method used in the successful eradication of that mosquito following its invasion of Brazil in 1940 and Egypt in 1945 (Soper, 1966). These and other country-wide applications of Paris Green to water surfaces were never considered to have had any major impact on freshwater life other than the mosquito larvae concerned, and more recent work in the United States has confirmed that there is no evidence of any accumulation of arsenic in the soil following repeated applications of granular Paris Green to the water surfaces of impounded salt marshes (Rathburn, 1966).

The realization of a synthetic pesticide, which combined not only unusually high toxicity to a wide range of insect enemies of man, but also hitherto unheard of persistent properties enabling deposits to remain toxic for months or even years, stimulated the search for other synthetic chemicals with similar properties. This stimulus has led to a remarkable proliferation of new organic chemicals for pest control. Initially, efforts were concentrated on the particular group to which DDT belonged, namely the organochlorine or chlorinated hydrocarbon group, and produced a whole range of new equally familiar names — dieldrin, endrin, gammexane, methoxychlor, etc. Continued research revealed the potentialities of two other chemical groups, namely the organophosphorus compounds such as parathion and the carbamates such as Sevin. More recently quite new chemical groups of insecticides, including the synthetic pyrethroids allied to natural pyrethrins, have been the subject of the same intense exploration.

In other spheres of pest control, apart from insects, the last twenty years has also been marked by phenomenally rapid progress in the development of new synthetic organic chemicals. In the control of the aquatic snails which form the intermediate hosts of the worm parasites of human bilharziasis, this period has marked the replacement of copper sulphate by a series of progressively more effective molluscicides, quite unrelated to insecticides, culminating in the two dominant chemicals at the moment, Bayluscide, a product of Bayer Chemicals, and Frescon, a product of Shell.

This period has also been marked by striking progress in the chemical control of undesirable fish populations, leading to the outstandingly selective compound Fintrol or TFM, for the control of larval sea lampreys, and antimycin for controlling populations of undesirable and competitive fish of no economic value.

Looking back, it is difficult to understand how the initial dramatic successes achieved with DDT and its allies managed to obscure the possibility that powerful biocidal chemicals applied indiscriminately on a vast scale must inevitably have some undesirable effect on the environment and on wild life ecology. The cautious and in many cases accurate forecasts by a comparatively few far-seeing biologists prior to 1950 were nevertheless ignored, and it was not until nearly ten years after the introduction and widespread use of DDT that the impressive accumulation of evidence swung the pendulum in the direction of re-appraising pesticides in the role of environmental contaminants. In recent years this aspect of pesticide use and application has attracted the long-overdue attention it merits and has led to a great deal of careful scientific research and to a vast amount of published work in a wide range of journals (West, 1966; Westlake and Gunther, 1966; Middelem, 1966; Dykstra, 1968). Understandably, the increasing appreciation of pesticides as possible contaminants has also given rise to strong feelings, prejudices and emotions which have on occasion gone beyond reason and established fact.

A general discussion of pesticides in relation to contamination of the environment as a whole is outside the scope of the present review, and the reader is referred to Mellanby's "Pesticides and Pollution" (1967) as an example of the way that subject is reviewed against the background of other environmental contaminants such as soot, smog and radioactivity.

The present review is concerned with the impact of pesticides in general on animal life in fresh water, particularly on freshwater fish and aquatic invertebrates which live in lakes, ponds, rivers, streams, irrigation canals and other water bodies. The review includes on the one hand the great amount of information and experience which has been gained in the deliberate chemical control of a wide variety of undesirable aquatic fauna such as larvae of mosquitoes, blackflies, midges, aquatic snails, as well as undesirable predators and trash fish. It also assesses an equally varied wealth of information on pesticide impact on water bodies brought about by incidental, indirect or accidental methods.

Some of the most outstanding examples of direct contamination of rivers and river systems occurred in North America and Canada as a result of blanket aerial spraying with DDT over extensive forest areas for control of such forest pests as the spruce budworm. The heavy dosage of up to 2 lb of DDT per acre adopted in the early fifties evidently had a catastrophic effect on stream ecology in many of these areas, and stimulated a great deal of research which has added considerably to our knowledge.

As a result of this new information, DDT dosages were subsequently reduced to 1 lb/acre, or down to 0·5 lb/acre where fishery interests were directly affected. However, despite increasing awareness of the insidious cumulative effect of DDT in the environment, and evidence of its persistence up to nine years after a single treatment, DDT continued to be used for aerial treatment of spruce budworm up to and including 1967 at least (Dimond et al., 1968). The indiscriminate use of DDT itself in such a manner has now been reduced or suspended in many countries; nevertheless, aerial application of other pesticides for the control of agricultural pests and for the treatment of extensive areas of mosquito breeding, still continues as vigorously as ever. Despite improvements in the design of aircraft and the technique of application, it still appears almost impossible to ensure that the pesticide will not extend beyond the strict limits of the target area, unless the situation permits the use of types of granular formulations which fall directly onto the target without drift. In many of the cotton growing areas of the southern United States and Central America, aerial application of insecticide is carried out on an almost continuous basis throughout the growing season, during which time extensive areas of the environment, including rivers and streams, may be exposed to a whole assortment of available chemicals and their formulations.

In general, pesticides which impinge on streams and river systems in the course of spraying operations directed against crop or forest pests, only make a periodic impact producing high concentrations of the chemical in the water for a comparatively short period, followed by periods of several days or weeks of freedom from contamination. With the increasing replacement of the residual and persistent DDT with the comparatively short-lived organophosphorus compounds and others, the periodicity of such impact becomes more marked and consequently might be expected to have a rather less drastic effect on freshwater ecology and freshwater organisms in the area under spray cover.

From the point of view of evaluating pesticide impact, the examples above do provide one advantage in that in most cases the exact nature of the chemical pesticide applied is known, and interpretation of findings is less liable to be confused with other possible sources of contamination. In contrast to these intermittent or periodic impacts of pesticide on fresh water by known agricultural pesticides are those occasional and unpredictable cases where rivers in particular become accidentally polluted by high concentrations of chemical pesticides, not always immediately identifiable.

In June 1969 sudden high pollution of the Rhine in West Germany produced high kills of fish and obliged the Netherlands Government to cut drinking water supplies from the Rhine to the main cities, and to switch to emergency reservoirs. The contamination in this case was attributed to endosulfan, an organochlorine insecticide used for control of certain agricultural pests. Nearer home, a pesticide spillage killed thousands of fish in the South Holland Drain, a water cut running between the Lincolnshire rivers Welland and Nene. The pesticide was identified as Thionazin which is used for bulb dipping to control eelworm. A similar spillage in the previous year was reported as killing 50,000 fish in the same waterway. Even some of the most carefully protected angling rivers in England, well away from the industrial zones, may still be exposed to the devastating effect of such occasional accidents, as happened in the River Frome in Dorset a few years ago.

As these occasional occurrences of exceptionally high pesticide impact on fresh water are quite unexpected and unpredictable, and usually of comparatively brief duration, it is rarely possible to carry out any worthwhile scientific studies on the reactions of different groups of freshwater biota to the pesticide in question, especially when the identity of the chemical is not always immediately known. Apart from the obvious fish kill, and the fact that conditions in the polluted rivers appear to return to normal quite quickly, very little of scientific value emerges from these sporadic instances of gross contamination.

In contrast to such comparatively short exposures to very high concentrations, many of the large rivers in countries where agricultural pesticides are widely used are now recording the almost continuous presence of one or other major insecticide at low but

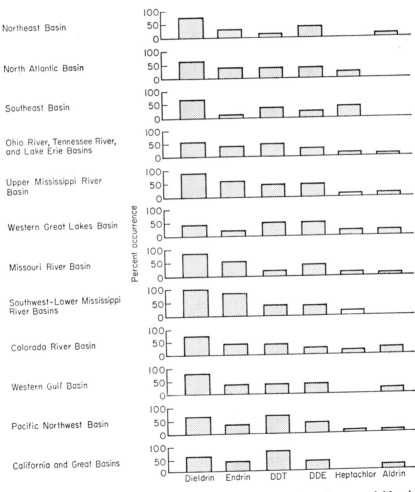

FIG. 1. Frequency of occurrence of six chlorinated hydrocarbon pesticides in twelve water basin areas in the United States (after Weaver et al., 1965).

continuous dosage. Many of the major rivers in the United States of America record almost chronic contamination with such organochlorine compounds as DDT, dieldrin and endrin, usually at concentrations of less than 1 part per billion (1 ppb), i.e. 1 part per thousand million by U.S. standards (Weaver *et al.*, 1965; Novack and Rao, 1965) (Fig. 1). Curiously enough, despite the apparent predominance of DDT, dieldrin emerges as the pesticide most frequently found in the main rivers of the U.S.A. Even in Great Britain, pesticide residues of DDT, gamma BHC and dieldrin have been determined in numerous spot samples of sewage effluent and river water (Holden, 1965; Holden and Marsden, 1967; Water Pollution Research Laboratory, 1967). Very little is known about the effect on freshwater organisms of chronic exposure to these very low, and presumably sub-lethal, concentrations.

In recent years knowledge about the presence, amount and distribution of pesticide in the environment in general and in freshwater ecosystems in particular, has greatly advanced due to the development of increasingly sensitive and accurate physico-chemical techniques, in particular the method of gas-liquid chromatography. These methods are especially sensitive in the case of pesticides in natural water bodies, being able to detect concentrations in the range of 0·1 ppb, as compared to a range of 10 ppb in soils and 100 ppb for fauna and flora. The availability of these refined techniques has stimulated a great deal of research on pesticides in the environment to such an extent that we are now passing through a phase where the ability to measure smaller traces of chemicals is outrunning the ability to interpret the importance or harm of these traces in the environment (Warnick *et al.*, 1966).

Improved chemical methods for detecting and measuring pesticides in various components of the environment, as well as in the tissues of fish and other aquatic organisms, have now convincingly demonstrated one of the most far-reaching repercussions of pesticides in their role as contaminants, namely, the rapidly progressive build-up of DDT and its metabolites within food chains of aquatic organisms. Within the freshwater ecosystem this reaches its climax in the tissues — the liver in particular — of freshwater fish, but outside this freshwater environment the build-up continues firstly in the birds feeding on these fish, and secondly in the tissues of the raptorial birds which prey on these birds in turn.

Biological concentration of a pesticide within the aquatic ecosystem was first demonstrated in studies carried out in Clear Lake, California to investigate the effect of the periodic application of DDD (TDE) in midge control (Hunt and Bischoff, 1960) and led to similar investigations in other moderately sized lakes (Hunt and Keith, 1963; Walker *et al.*, 1964) and in larger lakes (Burdick *et al.*, 1964), all of which revealed the accumulation of DDT, via food webs or food chains, in the tissues of lake trout. A similar build-up in much larger lakes was demonstrated in Lake Michigan (Hickey *et al.*, 1966). It should be pointed out that while the existence of such a build-up of DDT and its analogues was first demonstrated in a moderately-sized lake in which pesticide — DDD — had been deliberately applied in pest control, in the majority of lakes, particularly the large ones, the DDT does not originate from deliberate application but finds its way into the lake water from a variety of sources. It may be brought in by rivers and streams carrying insecticide from agricultural or forest land exposed to pesticide treatment; or it may come from run-off or rain. The detection of traces of ppDDT, DDE and Dieldrin in watershed soils and stream sediments prior to any known treatment of that area with these insecticides, also indicates that aerial transport — perhaps in the form of particles adhering to dust from remote treated areas — must play a part in contaminating extensive areas of lake surface (Cole *et al.*, 1967).

The extent to which this biological concentration occurs within the freshwater ecosystem is well illustrated by these studies in North Pennsylvania where it was found that in watershed soils and stream sediments, DDT usually occurs at concentrations of a few parts per billion. In trout, the concentrations were found to be 20–100 times higher, while in white suckers the concentration was 6–15 times higher than in trout; these residues in fish increasing considerably in the month following area treatment for agricultural pests, but return to pre-treatment levels after four months. The extreme example of biological concentration revealed in this investigation was found to occur, not with DDT, but with dieldrin. The concentration of dieldrin in stream sediments was found to be 0·003 ppm, while in white suckers in the same stream the concentration was 1·80 ppm, i.e. a 600-fold increase.

In the United States nationwide studies have been initiated to sample water, soils, plants and animals, including humans in an effort to determine pesticide levels in all areas, and already there is a large number of publications dealing with this aspect alone. The studies on freshwater habitats include rivers, streams, creeks, canals, ditches, ponds, marshes, drainage areas, as well as springs and wells. Many of these were potential mosquito breeding areas with known records of insecticide application. These studies have shown that although commercial DDT as applied in the field is composed mainly of the para para isomer, this is the least abundant form in water and bottom muds, where ortho para DDT and the metabolite DDE predominate (Warnick *et al.*, 1966). Although DDE is a chemical which is not produced commercially and is not readily available, it is widely distributed throughout the environment as a stable metabolite of DDT and has a half-life in excess of ten years (Risebrough *et al.*, 1968; Keil and Priester, 1969).

The further history of DDT accumulation in tissues of birds and animals outside the aquatic environment is strictly beyond the scope of this present review, but brief mention must be made of some of the more significant recent advances which can be traced back ultimately to the contamination of natural water. The general findings in that direction have been sufficiently dramatic as to be familiar not only to ecologists but to a large section of the lay public as well. These investigations have revealed not only the global nature of DDT dispersal and contamination, which extends to the fauna of the antarctic, but also that the fish-eating and carnivorous birds which represent the extreme apex of a complex food chain or food web, may be exposed to such concentrations of organochlorines as to lead to aberrant egg shell formation leading to a drastic decline in population (Bitman *et al.*, 1969; Heath *et al.*, 1969).

In simple food chains like fish to seal, fish to guillemot, fish to heron and fish to white tailed eagle, the increase in DDT (and DDE) residues is at least ten-fold in both whole tissues and fat. In the eagle and heron the increase is up to 100 times.

Analysis of pesticide residues in animal tissues has recently disclosed a quite unforeseen complication in the isolation of previously unknown contaminants of the group polychlorinated biphenyls (PCB) (Jensen, 1966; Holden and Marsden, 1967). PCB is used almost exclusively in industry and appears to be more persistent than DDT (Reynolds, 1969). Chemicals of this group have now been recovered in many countries including the United States and Great Britain. In Sweden they have been found to occur in the natural environment to the same extent as the chlorinated hydrocarbons (Jensen *et al.*, 1969). At the moment, PCB has been recovered from marine animals in the Baltic, but little is known about its presence or distribution in fresh water. The situation fully endorses the opinion expressed by one authority that improved chemical methods for detecting and identifying trace residues have outrun our knowledge about the biological effects of these chemicals. Not only is a vast new field of experiment indicated, but until much more experimental work is done it may be difficult to define whether such new compounds can really be classified as pesticides or pesticide metabolites, or whether in view of their industrial origin they must simply rank as toxic chemicals.

The chemical analysis of samples from freshwater habitats has also revealed the important part played by certain plants in acting as concentrating agents for DDT. Some aquatic plants evidently have a greater capacity for taking up DDT than others, and in this respect *Cladophora* appears outstanding. In irrigation canals in areas normally treated with organochlorines, the highest residues — up to 19 ppm — were found in *Cladophora* as compared to the next highest in *Potamogeton* (9 ppm) and *Oscillatoria* (Ware *et al.*, 1968). The use of DDT containing radioactive chlorine has also demonstrated that following DDT-treatment at the comparatively low dosage of 0·2 lb/acre a much higher concentration of DDT occurred in *Cladophora* than in any other plant or animal. Furthermore, over nine months after treatment, *Cladophora* still retained 1·62 ppm DDT, being the only one of fifteen plant species to retain a residue in excess of 1·0 ppm (Meeks and Peterle, 1967).

In contrast to the retention and persistence of the organochlorines in various freshwater plants and animals, extensive chemical analysis of samples has shown that the organophosphorus compounds have a comparatively short life in water, and there appears to be little indication of either persistence or build-up. In areas under mosquito control by organophosphorus compounds only, such as parathion, dursban and abate, concentrations in the water have been found to vary from maxima of 0·3–70·0 ppb depending on the method and amount of treatment (Ludwig *et al.*, 1968; Bowman and Orloski, 1966). The latter figure is considerably in excess of the 3 ppb which is considered necessary to kill mosquito larvae. Lethal concentrations were found to last 3–4 days, and thereafter until 8–12 days, after which no chemical could be detected, even after a heavy original treatment. The same short-term life occurred in the soil, in plants and in the fauna itself, as compared with the steady concentrations of DDT and DDE which were maintained throughout the year (Warnick *et al.*, 1966).

The disclosure about the widespread dispersal and accumulation of DDT in animal tissues, together with the fact that only now, at this comparatively late stage, has realization come about of the irreparable damage that may already have been produced by chronic or delayed effects of DDT residues already in existence, has produced a strong body of opinion in favour of placing severe limitations or even a complete ban on further use of this pesticide. Already a ban has been placed on DDT by the Scandinavian countries and by certain states of the U.S.A. such as Michigan and Arizona. A similar ban is proposed in New Zealand and there is a possibility of similar strong action on the part of Canadian Natural Resources Authorities. In contrast to this, overriding public health considerations of immediate import still permit DDT to be applied regularly to many of the large rivers of Africa for control of the larvae of the *Simulium* (blackfly) vector of onchocerciasis or "river blindness". This situation may well continue until such time as an effective substitute to DDT has been found.

In keeping with the dual role of many pesticides — vital controlling agents for injurious pests on one hand, and dangerous contaminants of the environment on the other — has arisen the concept of "target" and "non-target" organisms. In most freshwater habitats where control measures are directed against a particular undesirable organism such as mosquito larvae, intermediate snail hosts, predator fish, etc., the idea of what constitutes a non-target organism is usually understood to mean simply those organisms whose destruction is not intended. In practice, the distinction tends to be less general and to refer specifically to organisms which are considered to play a key role in the ecology of the habitat, particularly with regard to species which form vital links in the food chain or food web which converges eventually in the form of trout or other important food fish. However, the distinction is not rigid, and the same organisms or group of organisms may be "non-target" in general, but come into the category of target species in certain circumstances.

In many rivers and streams the larvae of caddis flies (Trichoptera) and the nymphs or naiads of mayflies (Ephemeroptera) are considered to form important food sources for trout and other valuable freshwater fish. In some areas, however, certain species of mayfly and caddis fly are produced in such enormous numbers as to constitute a nuisance or pest, and their immature stages are then liable to be the direct target of planned control operations with chemical pesticide (Lieux and Mulrennan, 1955; Hoffmann, 1960). Similarly, microcrustacea usually rank high in the list of "non-target" organisms in general, but in parts of the tropics, certain species of copepods (*Cyclops* and its allies) are incriminated as intermediate hosts of the human guinea worm (*Dracunculus*), and their habitat consequently may come under attack by chemicals.

The same flexibility of definition applies to the term "trash fish". Those concerned directly with the management of fishery resources understand clearly that the term applies to fish which are of no commercial or sporting value, and which interfere in any way — by predation or by competition for food — with populations of valuable fish in the same habitat. In most fishery management programmes one species which almost invariably ranks high on the list of undesirable fish is the carp (*Cyprinus carpio*). However, in some instances the carp assumes the role of a desirable species to be protected, in particular as a biological controlling agent for midge larvae (Bay and Anderson, 1965; Lieux and Mulrennan, 1956) or where it is used as an ornamental fish, or as a source of food (Mulla et al., 1967). The well-known mosquito fish (*Gambusia affinis*) would normally be regarded as undesirable or at least of no commercial value from the fishery point of view, but its protection is considered important in many extensive mosquito breeding areas where its feeding activities on mosquito larvae provide a biological method of control supplementary to routine use of chemical larvicides (Mulla, 1966).

However, these rather unusual exceptions should not be allowed to distract the attention from the fact that in any particular type of water the distinction between target and non-target organisms remains clear, and that the ideal of most control operations is to be able to destroy the particular undesirable species at pesticide concentrations which will have the minimal adverse effect on the rest of the freshwater biota.

It must already be clear that the general theme of pesticides and aquatic organisms embraces many disciplines, each of which has been the subject of intense investigation in recent years. In each of these separate disciplines this has produced a remarkable proliferation of published work which even within specialized fields of this general subject, threatens to become increasingly difficult to assimilate and digest because of its sheer bulk and variety. From time to time advances in certain fields are competently reviewed providing a valuable service in assisting workers to keep abreast of developments in their own field. An excellent example of this type of specialized review is provided by "Pesticides and Fishes, a review of select literature" (Johnson, 1968). Even in such specialized reviews, however, the conscientious inclusion of as many references as possible, while increasing the value of the review as a reference source, leaves the reviewer little space or time to attempt any sort of overall assessment of all this work, or to present a critical synopsis or synthesis of its most significant features. These difficulties encountered in specialized fields must inevitably be greatly accentuated when attempting to assess such a multi-discipline subject as pesticides and aquatic organisms in its entirety. It is not surprising that few attempts have been made to do this, and consequently there is an increasing danger that the separation and isolation of the different disciplines involved will continue and intensify.

It is doubtful if a painstaking and comprehensive review of the entire literature on this general subject would on its own stimulate any sort of coordinated interest, as the human brain tends to become numb and insensitive when exposed to a continued bombardment of facts and figures alone. But some attempt must nevertheless be made to draw the attention of the many different fields of interests within this general subject to the fact that many of them are facing fundamentally similar problems of evaluation, whether they are concerned with testing new chemicals for controlling undesirable fish or aquatic snails, or whether they are attempting to measure the impact of toxic chemicals on the freshwater environment. Although they are faced with so many problems in common, workers in these different and often isolated fields, have tended to develop their own techniques and methods of experiment and evaluation, both in the laboratory and the field. Unless these differences in approach, and differences in standards and criteria, are fully taken into account, little of value can emerge by a direct comparison of final figures and data obtained. It seems therefore that the first step towards integrating work and progress in the different fields is to enquire carefully into the methods used to obtain the vital data regarding the reactions of different freshwater organisms to the wide range of pesticides in question. The primary need to emphasize this aspect should become very evident in the course of this review. Not only are these methods and standards of evaluation liable to differ very greatly between different disciplines, but wide differences are also encountered within fields which would appear to be sufficiently specialized as to merit uniformity of approach. An outstanding example of this is provided by the criteria used in different countries, and different laboratories, for measuring fish toxicity, differences which make it quite impossible in some cases to make a direct comparison of data from different sources dealing with the same test species of fish, or with the same chemical compound.

In reviewing the subject of pesticides and aquatic organisms with special reference to basic problems in evaluation, considerable attention will be given to the field of aquatic snail control by means of chemical molluscicides. There are two main reasons for giving full recognition to this subject. Firstly, as most of the work has been done under the general aegis of public health, its rich and varied literature has been published mainly in medical journals and has somehow escaped the attention of pesticide ecologists in general. Secondly, because the subject of snail control and molluscicides has for many years been coordinated by an international organization, the World Health Organization, the methods of evaluation and the criteria adopted have attained a higher degree of uniformity among different workers and in different countries than any other discipline within the general theme. It is hoped that a careful consideration of these first fruits of coordination will act as a stimulus and a model for a much-needed closer coordination among the many different fields concerned with the impact of pesticides on freshwater life.

Within each of these fields, progress has tended to be specially marked in certain directions but less so in others. From this it follows that full awareness of these advances in different fields might help to avoid needless repetition in tackling fundamentally similar problems. A good example of scope for closer liaison on common problems is provided in applied biology by the problem of dispensing pesticide to the flowing water of streams and rivers in order to produce a specified concentration for a definite period of time, and to follow the dispersal, distribution and dilution of that chemical in its course downstream from the point of application. This fundamental problem has been the subject of intensive study by at least four groups of workers, namely those concerned with the control of *Simulium* larvae in streams and rivers, those engaged in the molluscicidal control of aquatic snails in the flowing water of canals and irrigation systems, those studying the effect of chemicals on the streams which form the habitat of sea lamprey larvae, and those controlling mosquito breeding in irrigated pastures by monitoring larvicide to the irrigation water as it is pumped from the well. From a study of the extensive literature produced by those different groups of workers, and from the reference list in each publication, it is evident that the different groups are virtually out of touch with each other regarding methods, ideas and progress, and that there would have been an obvious advantage in close liaison.

At present, significant advances in one field may only make an impact on another purely by chance, and often after a considerable time interval. For example, one of the two main molluscicides at present — Bayluscide (niclosamine) which has been the subject of particularly thorough research — was shown at an early stage to have the disadvantage of being piscicidal at molluscicide dosages, field applications being generally accompanied by fish kills. It was only after a gap of several years that this piscicidal property was re-investigated by workers interested in selective fish poisons rather than molluscicides, and this led to the finding that Bayluscide combined in certain proportions with the sea lamprey larvicide, TFM, is one of the most effective synergistic combinations yet discovered.

The concentrated effort which originally led to the development and successful application of TFM for controlling larvae of the sea

lamprey in the Great Lakes of North America provides what continues to be one of the most outstanding examples of a selective pesticide for controlling a specific aquatic form with minimal effect on
other biota. Yet this work is comparatively unknown or unrecognized
by the majority of workers in the public health field who are equally
occupied with the search — unsuccessful so far — for more selective
chemicals for dealing with such aquatic forms as larvae of mosquitoes and blackflies, and intermediate snail hosts of human parasites.

It is one of the main aims and objects of this present review to try
and bring together, under one cover, the most significant problems
in pesticide impact on fresh water, and the most significant evaluation methods used by different workers to study fundamental similar
problems. While the breadth of ground covered must eventually demand symposial treatment by a cross-section of specialists involved,
it is felt that an overall review by a single author might provide a
useful first step in underlining the common interests of all concerned.

THE EVALUATION OF PESTICIDE IMPACT

Pesticides and toxic chemicals impinge on the environment of
freshwater organisms by diverse means and from a variety of sources.
The methods which have been used to measure this impact show a
wide diversity, ranging from crude observations in the field to extremely refined and precise tests in the laboratory. Many of the
methods developed, and the criteria adopted, have been influenced
by the predominant interest or object of the investigation, whether
for example the object is to evaluate the impact of known applications of pesticide against a particular undesirable freshwater animal
or aquatic plant, or whether the investigation is concerned with the
undesirable effects of pesticide contaminating the habitat of freshwater food fish or other protected aquatic forms.

Although these studies on pesticide impact dealt with such a
diversity of aquatic life inhabiting such an enormous range of freshwater habitats, they have this essential feature in common, namely
that they are all trying to evaluate the reactions of a living organism
in an aquatic environment. Whichever freshwater form happens to
be the main target of study, each investigator is concerned first and
foremost with developing some sort of standard technique for comparing the mortality, or survival rate, of the particular species to
known concentrations of pesticide in the water, for known periods of
exposure. This common objective forms an essential first stage in

all studies on pesticide impact, and forms the vital basis for further refinements in evaluation such as chronic effects on mortality as distinct from acute mortality, effects of prolonged low dosage or sublethal exposure, effects of pesticides on growth, on behaviour, on reproductive capacity and so on.

In developing a sound basis for evaluation the main emphasis has naturally been on controlled laboratory techniques where test animals are exposed under conditions which are exactly reproducible as to temperature, water composition, pesticide concentration, etc. The standard conditions adopted by one group of workers may differ from those developed by others. Sometimes this difference may be sufficiently marked as to make it difficult to compare results obtained by different groups of investigators, even when they are both working on the same test species. There may also be basic differences in technique according to whether temperate or tropical freshwater forms are involved, or whether the test is built round one main organism or a group.

For these reasons it is important to examine at an early stage in this review the wide range of laboratory techniques used, and the different criteria which have been developed to measure the effect of exposure to pesticide chemicals.

When it comes to the measurement of pesticide impact in natural habitats, whether pond, river or lake, the wide range of uncontrollable factors, in particular the wide variation in pesticide concentration from time to time or place to place, all make it extremely difficult to evolve satisfactory standards of measurement. Even the seemingly straightforward estimate of mortality such as "fish kill" may become complicated by the fact that freshwater organisms which become weak or moribund as a result of exposure to pesticide may be destroyed by predators or removed from the observation area by water flow or current in such a way that estimates based on dead organisms recorded by observation or by trapping may be very unreliable.

As all mortality data must be based on estimates of live animals as well as dead ones in the habitat affected by pesticide, it follows that the reliability of various trapping and sampling methods used to estimate populations of different freshwater organisms will play a very important part in determining the accuracy or reliability of the final evaluation. Conscious of these sampling errors and pitfalls in nature, many investigators have adopted the method of releasing known numbers of test animals in cages in the habitat exposed to pesticide, mortality in these cage lots being referrable to control mortalities in similar cages in clean unaffected parts of the habitat.

This method has been applied particularly to large marshes and swamp areas exposed to aircraft application of pesticide, and also to studies on the transport, persistence and effectiveness of pesticide applications in rivers and streams.

Between these more precise laboratory tests in which accuracy of replication is still liable to be offset by the artificial nature of the test animal's environment, and the direct field evaluation which in turn is liable to errors of observation and sampling, many investigators have developed what might be called "semi-natural" or "semi-field" methods of evaluation. These may take the form of large exposed tanks or artificial ponds containing mud and vegetation and designed to create a natural ecosystem. In these large tanks or artificial ponds, various physical factors such as temperature, pH, oxygen content, hardness, etc. can be measured, but not accurately controlled, and they are liable to fluctuate as in a natural environment. Nevertheless, some important factors in evaluation can be accurately controlled, particularly the number, size and age of test animals exposed in the tanks, and the concentration, persistence and exposure period of the pesticide. Again, the actual design of "semi-natural" tests tend to vary according to the main requirements of the investigator, and there is every gradation from the simple to the sophisticated.

Without anticipating a final assessment of all these techniques it might be worth stressing at this stage that all the evidence points to the fact that evaluation based solely on laboratory tests, on semi-field tests, or on direct observation on the habitat alone, can at best provide a very incomplete picture of events. The best hope of unravelling or interpreting the complex situation arising in a natural freshwater body exposed to pesticide would appear to lie in a careful coordination between all phases of testing from the laboratory through "semi-field" to the natural habitat itself.

In the description of laboratory and field techniques in the following pages, it has been considered essential in many cases to enter into some detail in describing what is felt to be significant features of each method. Although this must make for a certain amount or rather dry and tedious text, nevertheless, it is such apparently small details as size of exposure vessel, number and size of test animals, length of holding period, etc., which may have a marked effect on the results obtained, and may account for wide differences and discrepancies when these small features are varied or modified.

It seems fitting that the first subject for critical review and assessment should be freshwater fish and fish toxicity. Fish are so frequently the most obvious, and economically the most important, sufferers from exposure to pesticides and other toxic chemicals in the water, that there is a long history of investigation in many countries. In addition the vigorous development in recent years in the chemical control of undesirable fish populations has necessitated new and more critical standards of evaluation, and has infused a wealth of new material and new concepts into this field.

CHAPTER 2

PESTICIDES AND FRESHWATER FISH

LABORATORY AND OTHER EVALUATION TECHNIQUES IN FISH TOXICITY STUDIES

It is perhaps appropriate that any review of laboratory methods of evaluating pesticide impact on the freshwater environment should start with fish toxicity studies. Long before the pesticide "explosion" of the last twenty-five years, the harmful effects on freshwater fish of various toxic effluents in rivers had been recognized, and methods had been devised to test these reactions more accurately in the laboratory. In the waters of rivers and lakes, inadequate concentration of dissolved oxygen may make it impossible for fish to survive for long; in these freshwater environments, low concentrations of dissolved oxygen are usually caused by respiration of plants and by the oxidation of organic matter. Usually associated with depleted oxygen content is an increased concentration of carbon dioxide. These conditions may occur most severely in rivers polluted with waste waters which contain oxidizable organic matter under a variety of forms from sewage to paper mill effluent. In addition, it has long been known that certain chemicals such as ammonia and heavy metals like copper and zinc have a direct toxic effect on fish, and that these direct toxic effects in turn are further influenced by the oxygen and carbon dioxide content of the water in question (Alabaster *et al.*, 1957).

In many cases the methods which were developed to evaluate the acute toxicity of industrial wastes to fish have been adapted to new requirements and problems created by pesticides. In other cases it has been found necessary to develop new and more critical techniques to deal with new situations created by the increasing use of chemicals for controlling undesirable populations of certain freshwater forms of life. Within the single sphere of fish toxicity studies, evaluation techniques have tended to evolve along different lines, and there is little indication so far about agreement on completely standardized methods which would be acceptable to all investigators and applicable to all conditions.

With regard to the range of laboratory techniques it would be convenient to review these according to whether they are based on static waters in jars and tanks, in water which is periodically replaced, or in continuous flow systems.

1. *Static tests*

The straightforward static test has been widely adopted by public health authorities in the United States (Doudoroff *et al.*, 1951; Henderson and Tarzwell, 1957; Henderson and Pickering, 1958; Henderson *et al.*, 1959; American Public Health Association, 1960). For the purpose of exploratory tests, 1-gal wide-mouthed jars are used as standard. Each jar contains various concentrations in selected dilution water, dilution being made in a logarithmic series, e.g. 10, 5·6, 3·2, 1·8 and 1·0 ppm. Each test jar contains two test fish in 2 l of water of each concentration.

In the full-scale experiment, 5-gal wide-mouth glass jars or bottles are used, each containing five fish in 10 l of the particular pesticide dilution, ten fish being tested at each dilution. As most pesticide chemicals have little or no oxygen demand, artificial aeration was not normally required. With acetone solvent however, slight oxygen depletion was caused, and to compensate this oxygen was bubbled through the solution.

Tests — all at 25°C — were carried out in two dilution waters, "soft" and "hard" as in Table I.

TABLE I

	Dissolved oxygen, ppm	pH	Alkalinity	Hardness, ppm
Soft water	8·0	7·4	18	20
Hard water	8·0	8·2	360	400

Initially, tests involved two "wild" species — fathead minnow and bluegill — and two household species — goldfish (*Carassius*) and guppy (*Lebistes*). The test fish were exposed continuously in the test dilutions, reactions being observed over a 96 h period. From mortalities at 24, 48 and 96 h, the median tolerance limit, or TL_m values (i.e. the concentration sufficient to produce 50% mortality) were obtained by straight line graphical interpolation . The 96 h TL_m was used for making direct comparisons.

These test series were among the first to reveal two very important aspects of fish reaction to pesticides. Firstly, the generally wide differences in reaction to the chlorinated hydrocarbon compounds such as DDT, and to the organophosphorus compounds, and secondly, the very wide potential range in reaction of different fish species to one and the same OP compound. All chlorinated hydrocarbons — except BHC — proved more toxic to fish than the organophosphorus compounds under the same experimental conditions, and there was nearly always an increase in mortality from 24 h to 96 h. In the case of the OP compounds, differences between 24 h and 96 h mortalities were in general minor. Dipterex proved to be an exception as it produced a considerable increase between 26 and 96 h, possibly connected with the fact that this chemical is converted by mild alkali to the water-insoluble and highly toxic DDVP.

As the chlorinated hydrocarbons proved to be generally more toxic to fish, it was found convenient to express the TL_m in parts per billion, ppb (i.e. micrograms per litre or parts per thousand million), rather than in the more conventional parts per million, ppm. One of these compounds, endrin, proved to be the most toxic chemical tested, the 96 h TL_m being 1·0–1·3 ppb.

With regard to reactions of different species, a striking example was provided by the OP compound malathion in which the TL_m for bluegills was found to be 0·095 ppm compared with a figure of 26 ppm for minnows.

Essentially similar laboratory tests in static water are also employed by the Fish Control Laboratories of the United States Bureau of Sports, Fisheries and Wildlife. The noteworthy achievement of these laboratories will be described more fully in Chapter 3 and for the moment it will be sufficient to deal with the evaluation techniques adopted (Lennon and Walker, 1964). The test medium in all the laboratory tests is deionized water (of at least one million ohms resistance) to which the following chemicals have been added per litre of deionized water; 30 mg calcium sulphate, 30 mg magnesium sulphate, 48 mg sodium bicarbonate and 3 mg potassium chloride.

Preliminary screening is carried out in 1 gal glass jars containing 2·5 l of pre-aerated reconstituted water. No artificial aeration is done during the test. In the temperate zone laboratories at La Crosse, Wisconsin, temperatures of water baths are 12°C, while in the subtropical station at Warm Springs, it is 17°C. At least ten fish of each species are used with each concentration of chemical (0·1, 1 and 10 ppm). The weight range of test fish is from ½–2 g each, and the test is arranged so that there is 1 g or less of fish per litre of test medium. Accordingly, there may be but one or two fish per jar, and up to ten jars may be needed for each concentration of chemical. The stock solutions of test compound are prepared, the solvent preferably being water, acetone or ethanol. Where solvents other than water are used, their effect is checked by using the same quantity — which never exceeds four parts per thousand — in the controls. The responses of fish in test jars and in controls are observed after 35 min, $1\frac{1}{2}$, 3, 6, 24 and 48 h.

As these laboratories are concerned with evaluating potential piscicides, the notation used for comparative purposes is EC_{100}, i.e. the effective concentration sufficient to kill all test fish. For purposes of comparison with results obtained in other laboratories, the EC_{50} (sensitivity) of the sample was calculated, which corresponds with the TL_m notation described above.

In the more advanced studies on compounds of particular significance in fish control studies, such as antimycin A — an anti-fungal antibiotic (Walker et al., 1964) — emphasis was placed on the concentrations which delineate the all-or-none survival, i.e. the EC_0 and EC_{100}, after exposure period of 24 or 96 h. More promising chemicals emerging from the preliminary screening are given more advanced static tests in the laboratory in progressively larger containers, from 5-gal jars with 15 l of medium to fibreglass troughs of 4, 8 and 16 ft lengths.

In a more advanced stage of testing, outdoor ponds providing a semi-natural environment are used, but these will more fittingly be described along with similar types of semi-natural tests used by other agencies.

It should be pointed out that while evaluation naturally laid emphasis on acute mortality as the most definite and conclusive evidence of toxic effect and the measurement least likely to be influenced by different interpretation by different observers, full consideration was also given to the various other ways in which fish might show short-term responses to the chemical. These deal with such categories as General Behaviour (whether irritated or quiescent, erratic or convulsive swimming movements, etc.); Changes in Integument (regarding pigmentation reactions of external mucosa, etc.); Respiration (as regards rate and manner); Alimentary Response; Nervous Response; Sensitivity to Stimuli, and Moribundity. Although many of these additional criteria of response are arbitrary and do not lend themselves to exact notation, nevertheless they must form an essential part of any overall evaluation.

2. Periodic replacement tests

No single type of laboratory test designed to evaluate fish toxicity can be expected to provide the ideal technique, satisfying all requirements. Investigators who employ static tests in fish toxicity studies have been fully aware of possible limitations or objections to their techniques. Firstly, there is the possible loss or depletion of pesticide in the exposure jars during the course of the experiment. This loss may be due to adsorption on surfaces, loss by volatility accentuated by artificial aeration, loss by up-take by live test animals or by dead animals not immediately removed. This uptake of chemical by test fish has been clearly demonstrated, and is particularly marked in the case of DDT (Premdas and Anderson, 1963; Holden, 1962). This factor, together with uptake of DDT by surfaces, may cast doubt on the validity of DDT test data based only on static tests (Holden, 1962). In addition, in the course of a test normally lasting up to four days (96 h) continuous exposure, the pesticide might be hydrolysed or otherwise de-activated.

Indirect evidence of this depletion of pesticide is often forthcoming from the fact that with some chemicals the mortality after 96 h in the static test is little greater than that after 24 h. Occasionally the physical or chemical changes on the part of the chemical during the course of the test may intensify the toxic effect. This is the case with Dipterex which is relatively less toxic to fish than other organophosphorus compounds. It is readily hydrolysed, and in a mild alkaline medium is converted to the water-insoluble and highly toxic DDVP. These changes are reflected in the greatly increased mortality after 96 h as compared with 24 h (Henderson et al., 1960).

Many pesticide chemicals do not make any demand on dissolved oxygen, and for many species of test fish oxygen requirements in static tests are satisfied by natural surface aeration. This is confirmed in many laboratories by making routine checks on water quality before and after test runs. However, the inability to control the O_2 concentration, as well as CO_2 and pH in the medium in most static tests has been regarded as a serious drawback in view of the fact that concentrations of these three components at least can play an important part in determining the toxicity levels of certain toxic chemicals (Alabaster et al., 1957). In view of this, many of the laboratories dealing with fish toxicity studies are tending to supplement the basic series of static tests with more advanced tests involving periodic replacement or continuous change in the test medium in which the fish are exposed (Burdick, 1960). Possibly the best example of periodic replacement forming the sole basis of a standard fish toxicity test, under strictly controlled and reproducible environmental conditions, is provided by the methods used by the U.K. Ministry of Agriculture and Fisheries, in their freshwater laboratories (Alabaster and Abram, 1964, 1965). These routine tests are carried out in accordance with an agreement between the Government and the Chemical Industry, in which manufacturers are asked to provide information on fish toxicity when submitting new materials under a "Pesticide Safety Precaution Scheme".

The fish in batches of ten are tested in 500 ml spherical flasks through each of which 100 ml of freshly prepared solution is passed every 10 min. The concentration of dissolved oxygen in the dilution water — before it is mixed with the sample — is close to air saturation level, and the rate of replacement of the test solution is sufficient to supply the respiratory needs of the fish and maintain an adequate concentration of dissolved O_2 in the test vessels containing the fish. This rate of replacement is also sufficient to prevent the fish altering the toxicity of the solution either through a build-up of toxic concentration of excreted ammonia or CO_2, or by lowering the concentration of poison by absorption.

In this standard test the sole test species of fish is the non-indigenous harlequin fish (*Rasbora heteromorpha*), selected because it is conveniently small (1·3–3 cm) and because its degree of sensitivity to toxic chemicals appears to be similar to that of the trout.

A standard dilution water is used in all tests, with a hardness of 20 ppm expressed as calcium carbonate, but supplementary tests with hard tap water (about 270 ppm expressed as $CaCO_3$) can be done. Tests are carried out at 20°C. The recommended number of test vessels is 12, 10 of which contain different dilutions of test material, and two dilution water alone for control purposes.

After preliminary tests, a minimum of four dilutions of test material are chosen in such a way that in the least dilution 50% of the fish are killed after 24 h; in the second, which is not more than twice as dilute as the first, 5% or less of the fish are killed after 24 h. In the third, 50% or more of the fish are killed after 48 h, and in the fourth — which is not more than twice as dilute as the third — 50% or less of the fish are killed after 48 h. The fish, in batches of ten, are poured into the test vessel containing the appropriate test solution. Dead fish are not removed until the end of the 24 or 48 h period when the total mortality is recorded.

A diagram of the apparatus supplying each test vessel is shown in Fig. 2. Without going into too much detail, the dosing apparatus consists of a 105 ml burette, to the lower end of which four tubes are connected. Each of these tubes opens every 10 min while the other three remain closed. The tube connecting the burette with the supply of dilution water opens to allow the required volume of dilution water to enter the burette. Next in the cycle, the tube connected to the air supply opens to aerate the dilution water. Then the tube connecting the burette with the test-material constant head vessel opens to allow the required volume of test material to enter the

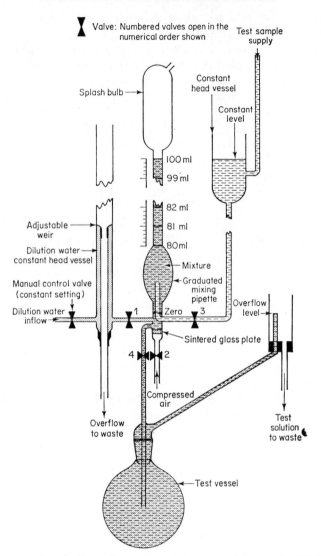

FIG. 2. Diagram of periodic replacement apparatus used in standard fish toxicity tests by U.K. Ministry of Agriculture and Fisheries (after Alabaster and Abram, 1965).

burette and bring the level of the liquid up to the 100 ml mark. Finally, at the end of the cycle, the tube connecting the burette with the test vessel opens to allow the 100 ml of test solution to drain into the test vessel. The design of the apparatus maintains an adequate level of dissolved oxygen, and automatically prevents a rise in the concentration of the respired CO_2 and of excreted ammonia. Results of tests are normally expressed as 24-h median lethal concentrations in parts per million, i.e. the concentration at which 50% of the fish are killed after 24 h.

3. Continuous flow tests

In view of the known limitations and restrictions of static water tests in fish toxicity studies, it would appear desirable to design tests in which the medium is actually flowing or is being replaced continuously. This would represent a much closer approach to what occurs in many natural habitats where fish can move rapidly through the medium, or in the case of the sensitive river-dwelling species, be exposed to a continuous flow of water.

However, there are many obstacles in the way of putting these ideals into practice. Firstly, routine tests based on continuous flow can make heavy demands on supplies of suitable unchlorinated water, which are not readily available in all testing laboratories. In this connection domestic water supplies may not always be relied on as suitable test media if, for example, soft water is distributed through copper plumbing. Secondly, the technical requirements necessary to maintain some degree of control over the composition of the flowing water, with regard to O_2, CO_2, pH, etc., require the establishing of rather sophisticated monitoring systems.

Three examples of the use of continuous flow are provided by tests which have been designed with rather different objectives. The first example was designed to meet the need for a constantly renewed and controllable environment in some studies on the toxic effects of dissolved substances (Merkens, 1957). The second example was designed to provide a continuous monitoring system for detection of contaminants in water supplies (Henderson and Pickering, 1963; Henderson and Tarzwell, 1957); while the third, more recent, example describes methods developed in the United States in accordance with the growing awareness of the value of flowing water versus static tests (Lemke and Mount, 1963; Mount and Warner, 1965; Mount and Stephan, 1967; Burke and Ferguson, 1968; Solon et al., 1968).

In the first example, designed at the Water Pollution Research Laboratory at Stevenage in England, an ideal uncontaminated water supply was available without chlorination or other treatment. Because of hardness due to carbonates and bicarbonates, it was necessary as a preliminary stage in the treatment of the water to remove the carbonates by neutralization with hydrochloric acid and the carbon dioxide by aeration, to produce a water with a final pH of 5.

Oxygen control is achieved by aerating part of the water pumped continuously through the treatment plant, deaerating another part (the O_2 tension being reduced to a low value of about 0·5 ppm by stripping with pure nitrogen from a cylinder) and then blending these streams in suitable proportions. Appropriate amounts of the toxic chemical are then added, the pH adjusted as above, and the water at controlled composition and temperature delivered to the test aquaria.

Each test aquarium, made in perspex, is totally enclosed and completely filled with water so that there is no exposed air/water surface at which transfer of oxygen can occur. Fish are introduced or removed through a hole in a rubber diaphragm normally closed by a bung. Water flows through the test aquaria normally at the rate of 0·7 l/min.

The second example was developed by the U.S. Public Health Service and is based on the use of test fish to detect contaminants or pesticides not readily detectable by odour, colour or chemical assay. A diagram of this continuous monitoring system is shown in Fig. 3,

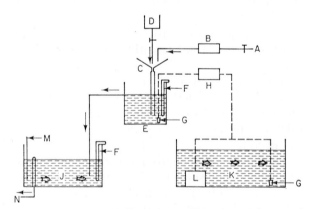

FIG. 3. Diagram of U.S. continuous monitoring system for continuous flow test (after Henderson and Pickering, 1963).

in which most of the features are self-explanatory. In order to ensure that the reactions of the test fish can be attributed to the unknown toxic compound or compounds alone, chlorine must first be removed. As carbon may also remove suspected contaminants and therefore cannot be used for this purpose, sodium thiosulphate has proved satisfactory as it is non-toxic to fish at the concentrations required (7 mg sodium thiosulphate is needed to inactivate 1 mg chlorine, and a 1·0 or 0·1% solution can easily be made up and fed through a constant head siphon or pump).

The test conditions can be adjusted according to whether warm-water fish species are used (20–28°C), or cold-water species (20°C or less). As the levels of dissolved oxygen in water supplies are usually satisfactory for fish, more elaborate control is not normally required. A record of pH measurements is kept during the tests, although in practice the pH range in most domestic water supplied is within a range that does not affect fish adversely.

The test aquaria are usually about 10 gal capacity in which the water level is maintained at the 20-1 mark. The inflow of mains water is adjusted to 10 l/h which allows the water in the aquarium to be replaced completely every 2 h. Ten fish are used at a time in the test aquarium, those being preferably fingerlings less than $2\frac{1}{2}$ in long, weighing less than 2–3 g each. There will be occasions to refer to this test method later in this book when considering bioassay in general, i.e. the use of living organisms to detect unknown types or concentrations of toxic chemicals. It should be noted at this point that while the above is the strict definition of "bioassay", this term is used in a much more general sense in much of the literature from the United States, and includes practically all tests in which living test organisms are exposed to chemicals, including accurate amounts of known pesticides.

It has been found that many species of fish are suitable for use in a continuous monitoring system, and in fact it may be desirable to use more than one species as there may be considerable variations between the sensitivity of different species to different types of toxi-cant. The system can be run continuously; dead fish are removed as soon as detected. The presence of contaminant is usually marked by rapid mortality of a significant number of test fish.

The third example comes from studies in the U.S. on evaluating the effect of surface-active detergents in which a continuous flow test has been developed in preference to the long-established standard tests in static water (Lemke and Mount, 1963). Each test unit con-sists of seven test chambers (one control, and six for different test concentrations), each containing 10 l. Into each exposure chamber a solution of water and detergent is added continuously by gravity from elevated storage tanks. By means of a series of small metering pumps with constant deliveries of the order of 1·2, 2·4 and 4·8 ml/min the concentrated solution of detergent — or other test pesti-cide — is added to the diluting water at a predetermined ratio to yield seven concentrations from 0 to 20 mg/l of active chemical. The test solution flows into a mixing or equalising vessel from which it is siphoned in "slug" dosages of the order of 60 ml volumes of solu-tion at 1 min intervals, into each test chamber. The solution is aerated sufficiently to keep the dissolved O_2 above 5 mg/1. The ten test fish in each chamber are exposed to this continuous through-flow of test solution for 96 h, and the 96 h TL_m value is used as a basis for comparison of different fish.

Although emphasis in most standard fish toxicity tests is on acute mortality within a specified period, incidental observations are frequently made on other evidence of poisoning such as erratic movements, irritability, paralysis, etc. These are usually subjective observations which do not readily lend themselves to clear classification or to exact measurement. However, there is increasing realization that the effect of pesticides on the reactions of fish other than the easily observable mortality effects, must be taken into account in evaluating the complete ecological impact of a contaminating substance. This is particularly important in view of the fact that distinct changes in behaviour pattern may be produced at sub-lethal exposures, that is to say at concentrations of the pesticide which are not sufficient to produce any acute effects on mortality (Anderson, 1968; Anderson and Peterson, 1969).

Acute awareness of the need of this type of laboratory test has led to the development of a constant flow apparatus in which the reactions of test fish to a variety of stimuli can be recorded photographically and measured automatically without any bias on the part of the human observer (Warner et al., 1966). The use of constant flow is considered essential in this respect as static systems with no through-flow of toxicant and water do not adequately simulate natural water systems. The principle of this test is to determine the responses of test fish in a standard exposure cell, in the flowing water system, to a range of stimuli such as light, darkness, mild electric shock and increasing water temperature. When the fish have been conditioned to an exact regimen of changing stimuli, the toxicant or pesticide is added to the continuous flow system — usually running at 300 ml/min — and any alteration in response to these original stimuli can be observed and measured.

In order to measure behaviour responses in an objective manner, each test cell is provided with a translucent PVC floor, marked into counting grids, through which light from substage fluorescent bulbs passes upwards and produces silhouette images of the test fish. The subjects' movements are recorded on film. The sort of tests to which fish are exposed include their reactions to light turned on for short periods (10 sec) followed by 20 sec dark periods; the reactions to a mild electric shock produced in the illuminated half of the cell; the conditioning of the fish to avoid the light and escape to the inactive end before they can be shocked, and the movement pattern of fish exposed to increase in water temperature at a constant rate up to the point of immobilization.

The whole equipment is highly sophisticated and designed for ultimate analysis of data by computer. Tests with different species of fish revealed that despite the rigidly controlled conditions of the test cell and the constant flow environment, distinct behaviour patterns were exhibited for each species in the uncontaminated pre-treatment runs, and that the apparatus did not induce any artificial type of response. The results of this work will be referred to in a later section, but sufficient for the moment to say that it demonstrated that just as different species of fish may show widely different mortality to one and the same toxic chemical, behaviour patterns to standard types of stimuli also revealed wide differences which must be taken into account in trying to form an overall picture of fish reaction.

A useful contrast to the more complex type of behaviour reaction equipment described above, is a very simple type of flowing water apparatus designed to study one particular type of fish reaction, namely, avoidance of toxic chemicals. The equipment was designed with reference to pollution of rivers by heavy metals such as copper and zinc in the northwest Miramichi River, New Brunswick, Canada, but its principles are equally applicable to studies on pesticide chemicals (Sprague, 1964; Sprague et al., 1965). Avoidance of these metals is evidently very strong; records based on counting fences together with information from release and recapture of marked salmon, show that avoidance causes anything from 10–22% of the salmon ascending upstream to turn back downstream, compared to the normal 1–3%.

The design of laboratory equipment to study the exact degree of avoidance to different concentration of chemicals is very simple (Fig. 4). A single fish — young salmon parr — is placed in a transparent plastic trough with water entering at each end and leaving by outlets at the centre. The fish is presented with a choice between ordinary water in one half of the length of the trough, and the chemical solution of known concentration in the other half. Introduction of dye into the water entering one end of the trough demonstrates that a sharp boundary between the two types of water is maintained.

With this apparatus it is possible to establish threshold concentrations for avoidance, and to relate these values to previously established data on lethal and non-lethal concentrations.

4. Semi-natural field tests

In the environment of the strict laboratory tests described so far, careful attention has been given to ensuring that as far as possible the nature of the medium with regard to temperature, pH, O_2 and CO_2

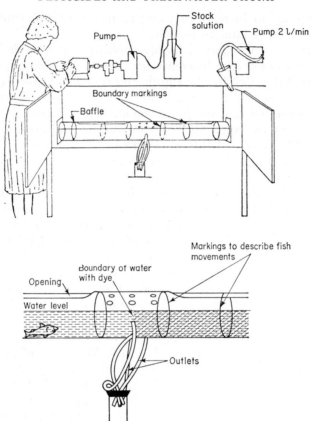

FIG. 4. Apparatus for studying avoidance of chemicals by fish (after Sprague *et al.*, 1965).

duplicates closely optimum conditions which occur in nature. However, in the absence of so many natural features such as vegetation, bottom mud, normal diurnal fluctuations in water composition, and abundant space to move in, the gap between laboratory evaluation and field reality might still be significantly wide. In order to bridge this gap, and expose the test fish under conditions more akin to nature while at the same time maintaining some of the accuracy of the laboratory test with regard to known numbers and known conditions of the test animals exposed, a wide range of what might be called semi-natural or simulated field tests have been designed. In many cases these tests follow on naturally from a preliminary series of screening tests in the laboratory. In other cases they have been designed as the main — or even sole — method for evaluating the reactions of fish to toxic chemicals.

An example of the extensive use of this type of evaluation is provided by the Fish Control Laboratories in U.S.A. described above (p. 20) in which tests in outdoor pools form an essential intermediate step between laboratory testing and eventual field trials with promising compounds. Vinyl wading pools, 9–10 ft in diameter, and 2·5 ft deep, and with a capacity of about 1000 gal, are set up outdoors. Bottom soils of various types, pond or ground water, aquatic plants, invertebrates and fish are established in these as needed during trials with chemicals. The large scale on which this type of evaluation can be organized is well illustrated in Plate 1.

In addition to providing a more natural environment for the fish, this type of evaluation plays an essential part in determining how a particular pesticide or formulation will react in a natural environment where vegetation and bottom mud provide surfaces on which the chemical may be adsorbed or otherwise depleted, and where insolation may accelerate hydrolysis or de-activation of the compound. This type of test also enables long-range observations to be made, for many days or weeks after first exposure of the test fish to pesticide impact.

In practice, some time has first to be allowed for various aquatic plants to become established in these tanks, and for some degree of stability in chemical composition of the water to be attained. This may well take four to eight weeks before fish can be introduced, and a further one to two weeks is then allowed for fish to become thoroughly adapted to the artificial pond (Walker *et al.*, 1964; Lennon and Walker, 1964).

In this type of test pH cannot be controlled as it is in the laboratory. The presence of plants, and the natural insolation contribute to increase in pH and alteration of alkalinity, which in the case of some compounds like Antimycin may cause rapid degradation and detoxification. The effect of degradation can be illustrated by introducing test fish into pools at various periods from 24 to 72 h after the chemical was originally introduced. In addition to the main objective of elucidating the fish toxicity of a particular compound, this type of semi-natural test can also provide first indications of adverse effects on various other pond organisms such as plankton and invertebrates, as well as on vegetation itself.

The use of semi-natural or simulated field tests has also been developed to study the impact of heptachlor on fish. Apart from its use in general insect control, heptachlor is noteworthy because of the vast scale on which it was employed in the fire ant programme

PLATE 1. Vinyl pools used for outdoor bioassay tests at the Fish Control Laboratories at La Crosse, Wisconsin and Warm Springs, Georgia. (Lennon and Walker, 1964. Photos U.S. Bureau of Sports, Fisheries and Wildlife.)

in the United States. Very little of scientific value emerged from that programme regarding the effect of this mass treatment on fish populations, and the only assessment of the likely impact has had to be made in retrospect on the basis of semi-natural tests (Andrews *et al.*, 1966). These tests took two forms. Firstly, exposure of the test fish — bluegills (*Lepomis macrochirus*) — to four levels of heptachlor (0·0125–0·05 ppm) in earth ponds. Each earth pond had a surface area of 0·1 acre, and an average depth of 2·5 ft. The bottom of the ponds was composed of fine sandy loam, and about 500 fish were used per pond. It is worth noting that these fish were not given any special diet as it had been found that all common foods tested in the laboratory contained DDT, DDE and DDD in varying amounts. In the second type of test, the bluegills were held in plastic pools 10 ft in diameter and 30 in deep, at seventy-five test fish per pool. These fish were fed diets containing different amounts of heptachlor. Both tests were designed to study the effect of long-term low-level exposure of fish to heptachlor at levels of exposure ranging from those which produced heavy mortality to the level at which only a minor impact was made.

The development of semi-natural laboratory tests or simulated field tests as an essential step towards the interpretation of events in the field has also played an important part in situations involving streams and running water. Such tests are essential to allow observations to be carried out, and replicated, at different controlled rates of water flow. They also enable the pesticide under trial to be monitored into experimental channels in such a way that the test fish are exposed to strictly controlled concentrations of the chemical for any required period. In addition, such controlled tests provide the first clue to the reactions of a particular chemical or formulation in running water versus static water.

The development of such experimental channels, raceways or simulated streams has been particularly marked in the extensive programme aimed at finding suitable selective piscicides for controlling larvae of the sea lamprey (*Petromyzon marinus*) in the Great Lakes (Applegate *et al.*, 1961; Howell *et al.*, 1964). In that programme, which is concerned not only with the stream-dwelling larvae of the target species, the lamprey, but also with the effect of the chemicals on the trout in the same habitat, the experimental raceways take the form of concrete troughs 65 ft long, 6 ft wide and 30 in deep. Lake water is delivered to the head of the raceway through a surge tank which stabilizes the flow. The volume of water discharged into the experimental "stream" is measured through a "V" weir. An artificial stream bed is constructed on the floor of the raceway for each test with materials taken from the beds of local rivers. The "stream" is arranged in such a way as to provide a small mixing pool at the head of the race, followed by a shallow gravel riffle, and then a pool about 18 in deep. A second shallow water area, usually of sandy materials, is located about midway along the race, and beyond this is another silt-bottom pool. At the foot of the latter pool is a final shallow riffle of sandy or silt materials.

Test fish are introduced into the artificial stream well in advance of treatment so as to allow an adequate period of adjustment. Large test fish of various kinds are allowed to move unrestricted throughout the 65-ft long test area. Smaller fish are placed in cylindrical screened cages at various points throughout the "stream". Larval lampreys were kept in similar screened cages set deeply enough into the bottom to permit the larvae to establish themselves in burrows. Restriction of smaller fish and larval lampreys to such cages allowed more rapid and accurate determination to be made of mortalities. About fifteen species of fish were employed in each of these tests.

Each experimental treatment was conducted for 24 h, the chemical in question being metered into the water by an electric motor-driven pump which delivered the concentrate — diluted with lake water — into the mixing pool at the head of the raceway. During the test, observations were made on all test animals hourly. Water flow through the raceway was maintained at 0·336 cusec in this particular series of tests, but could naturally be increased or decreased for other requirements.

At this point it is worth noting that the use of artificial streams or channels plays a vital part in the complete evaluation of pesticides required in a very different context, namely, larvicides for the control of blackfly (*Simulium*) larvae which live in fast flowing water in streams and rivers.

REVIEW AND ASSESSMENT OF FISH TOXICITY TESTS AND CRITERIA

The test methods and standards which have been described in the previous sections are selected examples, and can only provide a very incomplete picture of methods currently practised in all countries. However incomplete the record may be it is abundantly clear from the available data that not only is a wide variety of test methods and procedures being brought to bear on this common problem of fish reaction to toxic chemicals, but also that the criteria for measuring these reactions are still far from uniform, and may even vary considerably within the same country, e.g. the U.S.A.

One feature which is common to several of the routine laboratory tests on fish toxicity is the use of continuous exposure of test fish until the point of death or the end of the test period, whichever occurs first (usually 96 h, i.e. four days). The number of dead fish after standard periods of exposure (24, 48, 72 and 96 h) is recorded as a measure of acute toxicity, and the most widely adopted measure of this toxicity is the TL_m, or concentration of toxicant sufficient to kill 50% of the test animals within the specified period. The TL_m is obtained by plotting the log concentration against the mortality at each concentration, and finding at what point the straight line obtained crosses the 50% mortality level. In order to avoid the trouble of converting the range of concentrations tested into logarithms, a widespread practice is to arrange the concentrations selected for the test in logarithmic series.

The use of the 50% mortality level as the basis for comparison is based on the fact that at this point results are more consistent and less variable than at high or low mortality levels, particularly those approaching zero mortality and 100% mortality. Exactly the same notation as the TL_m has been expressed by some workers as the EC_{50} (Cope, 1966; Sanders and Cope, 1966) or the more generally familiar expression used in work on larvicides and molluscicides, the LC_{50} (Marking and Hogan, 1967). For purposes of comparison between different species of test fish, some laboratories prefer the 96 h TL_m (Henderson et al., 1960) while others prefer the 48 h limit (Cope, 1966) or even 24 h as used by the U.K. Ministry of Agriculture and Fisheries.

In laboratories more concerned with the immediate practical needs of finding the minimum concentration sufficient to kill 100% of the test fish, the notation EC_{100} is usually selected. This figure, together with the EC_0, or highest concentration compatible with zero mortality or 100% survival, provides the vital information about the sometimes very narrow range of concentrations in which the toxicant may produce an all-or-none effect. Laboratories evaluating piscicides also base their EC data on a wider range of exposure periods, comparison being made at 24 h as well as at 96 h.

In some investigations, additional observations are made at frequent intervals within the first 24 h exposure period. In one example observations were carried out at 0·75, 1·5, 3, 6, 24 and 48 h (Lennon and Walker, 1964), while in another mortality was recorded at 15 min intervals for the first hour, after which 30 min and/or hourly checks were continued until all fish died (Ferguson et al., 1966). This additional data from the same basic type of test enables toxic effects to be measured by rather a different yardstick, namely, the time taken to kill fish exposed to different concentrations. By analogy with the LC_{50}, this is conveniently expressed as the LT_{50} or exposure period in hours required to kill 50% of the test fish. This can be supplemented by additional values such as the LT_{25}, LT_{95}, etc.

With regard to the composition of the dilution water used in these fish toxicity studies, different laboratories tend to show a rather different approach to the need for standardizing test conditions in order to ensure that at least their own results are strictly comparable. Some laboratories use a standard dilution water prepared with special reference to hardness, alkalinity and pH. Others carry out tests at two hardness levels, "hard" water and "soft" water. In some laboratories elaborate methods are adopted to ensure that adequately controlled levels of O_2 and CO_2 are maintained throughout the test, while in other laboratories it is considered that in most cases the needs of test fish are normally met by natural surface aeration.

Temperature conditions in these tests are standardized in most laboratories, but the actual levels selected vary from country to country and are largely determined by the conditions most suitable for the particular test species used. Where duplicate tests are carried out on both cold climate and subtropical species, conditions may be standardized to 12°C in the former case and 17°C in the latter (Lennon and Walker, 1964). In the case of the harlequin fish (*Rasbora*) used in standard tests in the U.K., 20°C is the selected temperature for this non-indigenous species. In other laboratories, all tests are carried out at 25°C (Henderson *et al.*, 1959). In still other laboratories, tests are replicated at a wide range of temperature, say 13°C, 18°C and 24°C (Cope, 1966) or 12°C, 17°C and 22°C (Walker *et al.*, 1964). In special investigations the temperature may range from 7°C to 29°C (Cope, 1966).

With regard to choice of test fish, this naturally varies very widely according to the objectives of the tests and the resources of the laboratories concerned. For routine studies on evaluating the effects of contaminating chemicals, whether pesticides, herbicides or toxic chemicals in general, there is a marked contrast between the common practices in the U.S.A. and those in the U.K. In the United States, fish toxicity is judged on the basis of the reactions of a wide spectrum of test species, while in Britain the current practice is to use a single indicator species — *Rasbora* — whose reactions are considered to be indicative of those of the river trout.

In laboratories concerned with evaluating piscicides, while the main emphasis is naturally on the particular injurious, predatory or otherwise undesirable fish, tests generally cover a wide range of species, and are aimed at evaluating the impact of a particular piscicide on the complete range of fish fauna in the habitats likely to be treated.

As all fish toxicity studies endeavour to arrive at a figure or index which will be reasonably representative of that fish population as a whole, it follows that tests should ideally be based on large numbers of animals to allow for the fact that response to the pesticide may vary from individual to individual. Test results based on only one or two specimens of test fish would clearly be inconclusive, while on the other hand the problems raised by the maintenance, bulk, transport and cost of large batches of fish for every test would be equally impracticable. The relationship between numbers of test fish and results obtained is well illustrated in Fig. 5 which refers to rainbow

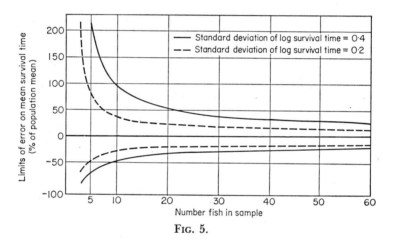

FIG. 5.

trout (Alabaster and Abram, 1964). This shows that while the error on the estimate of the median time of survival of fish kept at a constant concentration of poison, reduces rapidly with increase in sample size, the reduction is considerably less after a sample size of ten has been reached. Most laboratories do in fact base their data on samples of at least ten fish at each concentration, although these numbers are not necessarily tested in one and the same exposure.

Most laboratories try to ensure some standardization or uniformity with regard to size of test fish, as reaction may on occasions vary considerably according to size, age and physical condition. Absolute uniformity with regard to size is not usually practicable or essential, but uniformity with regard to maintaining size within a certain range is usually achieved. For example, the test species, *Rasbora*, is selected within a range of 1·3–3 cm, and this general size range also applies to the much wider range of test species used in fish toxicity studies in the United States, where size is recorded in weight — normally between 0·5 and 2·5 g. In more advanced laboratory evaluation and in semi-natural tests, fish covering a much wider range of sizes are used, and records are kept of the exact size of all fishes exposed.

Relative sizes of fish has also been a major consideration in the choice of a single non-indigenous indicator species, the Harlequin fish (*Rasbora heteromorpha*) in the British Standard Test (Alabaster and Abram, 1964).

Initially, the rainbow trout (*Salmo gairdnerii*) was chosen because it is sensitive to poison and readily available. Studies on the O_2 consumption of trout and on the ammonia production, indicated that in static water tests these factors could be controlled by aeration. However, aeration itself would have introduced a variable factor due to possible loss of dissolved test material to the atmosphere. All these test requirements could best be met by constant replacement of test solution with dilution water of controlled O_2 content. Experiment and calculation indicated that the average weight — 20 g — of trout, and their respiration rate, were such that an inconveniently large size of test chamber and excessive quantities of replacement solution would be necessary. As no British species of freshwater fish are sufficiently small all the year round, the non-indigenous Harlequin was selected. This species has an average weight of 0·14 g, and a respiration rate only about one fiftieth that of adult trout. Its respiratory requirements could be dealt with adequately by a flow of 10 ml/min — equivalent to about 10 l/g of Harlequin per day.

The U.S. practice referred to above of using a wide range of fish species in routine fish toxicity studies has provided a wealth of information on the widely different reactions which different fish may show to one and the same chemical, under test conditions which are as uniform as it is possible to achieve. For example, the 96-h TL_m for the organophosphorus insecticide malathion to bluegills was found to be 0·095 ppm compared to a value of 26 ppm for fathead minnows, a difference of over 270 times (Henderson *et al.*, 1959). There are innumerable less extreme examples of differences in specific reaction among fish, but rather than quote further examples, the situation can best be appreciated by referring to Fig. 6 showing reactions of twenty-four species of fish to Antimycin (Walker *et al.*, 1964).

The extreme example in that series of tests is illustrated by the sensitivity of the gizzard shad (*Darosoma cepedianum*) which were all killed within 24 h at 0·04 ppb of Antimycin at 22°C, and black bullhead (*Ictalurus melas*) which required a concentration of at least 120 ppb. The most sensitive group of fishes — which included

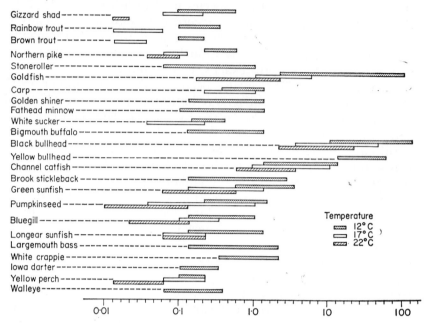

Fig. 6. Twenty-four hour response of twenty-four species of fish to Antimycin
(after Walker *et al.*, 1964).

gizzard shad, rainbow trout and brown trout — were more than
100 times as sensitive as the more resistant group represented by
goldfish, black bullhead, yellow bullhead and channel catfish. It
should be noted that these results from the Fish Control Laboratory
are based on comparing the all-or-none responses of each species, i.e.
the EC_0 and the EC_{100}, whereas in the example quoted above for
bluegills and fathead minnow, the comparison is between the TL_m,
i.e. the concentration sufficient to produce 50% kill.

Reference is frequently made to the range of fish *species* tested in
different laboratories. In many cases this really underestimates the
range, as the test fish usually cover a wide range of *genera* as well.
Some test series do actually include groups of closely related species
of the same genus, such as rainbow trout (*Salmo gairdnerii*) and
brown trout (*Salmo trutta*). Different species of bullhead and catfish
belong to the genus *Ictalurus*, while bluegills and sunfish belong to
the genus *Lepomis*. While the reactions of different species of the
same genus often follow a similar pattern, distinct differences in
sensitivity do emerge. A particularly striking example is provided
by the reactions of the tropical food fish, *Tilapia* to the molluscicide,
Tritylmorpholine (Shiff *et al.*, 1967). In flowing water treated at

0·04 ppm, *Tilapia mossambica* survived seven days, while under the same conditions 63% of *T. melanopleura* died. Specific differences between closely related species of *Tilapia* were also revealed in studies on their reactions to dieldrin treatment, one species *T. pangani* being very much more tolerant than the other two species tested, *T. melanopleura* and *T. macrochir* (Webbe, 1957).

The differences in sensitivity between closely related species of fish also emerges from studies on detergents (Thatcher, 1966) where such closely related species as the bluntnose and fathead minnows (*Pimephales notatus* and *P. promelas*) may differ distinctly in reaction, the TL_m values being 7·7 and 11·3 ppm respectively to ABS. With four species of shiners (*Nototropis*) tested, the TL_m values ranged from 7·4 for the emerald shiner to 17·0 pm for the common shiner.

The use of a wide spectrum of test species of fish has also thrown a great deal of light on general problems in evaluating fish toxicity, and the interpretation of laboratory data. Particularly illuminating have been the critical studies on reactions of a wide range of species to *p,p* DDT (Marking, 1966). The main purpose of that investigation was to find a standard reference chemical which would be used as a basis for comparing the results of fish toxicity tests carried out in different laboratories or by different techniques. The standard reference chemical required was one that produced a rapid, non-selective and consistent toxicity to fish, and also one which had a known mode of action against fish. The reactions of most fish to DDT with regard to irritability and excitement, erratic swimming movements, and loss of equilibrium follow a generally similar pattern; the final toxicity however showed the wide differences one had come to expect. Of particular interest in the present context was the finding that toxicity tended to vary among different lots of the same species, and that results were influenced by the fact that some species did not stand up so well to the two to four days' starvation imposed during the test period, or did not thrive best at the particular temperature selected for the test.

These variables were particularly marked in the case of goldfish, to such an extent that LC_{50} values for lots ranged from 21 to 180 ppb. In addition, this species showed that increase of concentration within the survival and mortality range, produced relatively little effect within the 94-h exposure period. When concentration is plotted against percent mortality, the regression curve produced is flat rather than steep, and contrasts strikingly with that for rainbow trout in which the steep curve reveals a narrow margin between survival and mortality (Fig. 7). In the case of fathead minnows, the finding that toxicity did not increase uniformly with increased concentration up to 1000 ppb within 96-h, presented unique problems making it impossible to obtain a reliable LC_{50} in repeated trials.

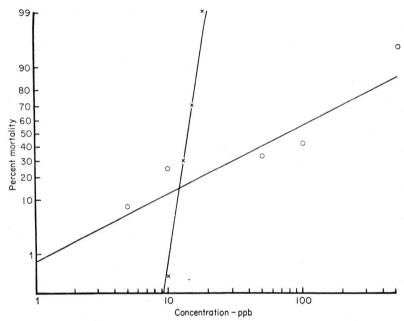

FIG. 7. Variations in regression curves of different species of fish to DDT (after Marking, 1966). X—rainbow trout; O—goldfish.

1. *Resistance*

In studies on fish toxicity a slight degree of variability is normally encountered between different individuals of the same batch or the same species. Usually, there is the odd specimen that succumbs to the effect of the toxicant before the main batch, or the odd individual that manages to survive a little time longer when all the others are dead. This natural variability is allowed for in routine tests by basing results on not less than ten test fish exposed at each concentration, although ideally if cost and space were no object, much larger samples would be more effective in minimizing possible errors due to the extreme susceptibility or tolerance on the part of the occasional individual.

The experience with goldfish and fathead minnows reported above shows that the reactions of different batches or lots may on occasion differ markedly, making it extremely difficult to obtain consistent values for the population as a whole. Some of these differences might be attributed to differences in robustness according to the source habitat; some batches or samples which have developed under optimum conditions presumably being more "vigour tolerant" than others. The existence of different strains within one and the same species of fish might have to be taken into account in comparing test data from different parts of the country, or in attempting to correlate results obtained by different laboratories on the same species of test fish.

A further development of this phenomenon is the appearance of actual physiological resistance to particular chemicals on the part of the fish population. This has now been clearly demonstrated in some areas which have been under particularly heavy treatment with pesticide for a number of years (Vinson *et al.*, 1963; Ferguson *et al.*, 1964; Vinson, 1969). In the Mississippi cotton growing areas, the mosquito fish (*Gambusia affinis*) has developed broad-spectrum resistance to many compounds such as DDT, BHC, dieldrin and endrin. In some cases the level of resistance developed may be very high, e.g. over 300-fold in the case of Strobane (related to Toxaphene) (Boyd and Ferguson, 1964). Similar investigations on bullheads (*Ictalurus natalis*) in cotton sprayed areas with regard to endrin showed that the 36 h TL_m values indicated a sixty-fold increase in resistance as compared to batches from uncontaminated sources (Ferguson and Bingham, 1966a).

These represent extreme examples from areas which are known to be under continuous and heavy insecticide pressure. However, there may be other areas where pesticide pressure or contamination is less obvious and where the steady increase in tolerance, or actual development of resistance, on the part of the test species of fish may introduce an unforeseen or unsuspected variable into toxicity tests.

The development of resistant strains has an important bearing on another aspect of the evaluation of pesticide impact, namely, in correctly interpreting data on the uptake of toxic chemicals by fish, and on the residues of DDT and other persistent insecticides detected in the bodies of live and dead fish. This will be considered more fully later.

The majority of routine tests on fish toxicity are based on mortalities observed under conditions of continuous exposure up to a period of four days. This general approach is in striking contrast to laboratory methods for evaluating molluscicides and larvicides in which the test specimens are normally exposed for a standard period — 24 h — and then transferred to clean water for a holding period. The practice of testing fish toxicity by this latter method, and possibly allowing them to recover from the effects of particular pesticides or particular concentrations, has only been carried out on a very limited scale, although the need for this additional type of evaluation has been stressed from time to time (Alabaster and Abram, 1964).

The use of short exposures — 15–30 min — followed by a 24 h holding period has been used in some studies on toxicity of various herbicidal materials to fish (Bond *et al.*, 1960). The value of this approach has also been endorsed by other studies on herbicides which revealed, for example, that in batches of fish kept in Reglone (diquat) for only 30 min, some took up to a week to die (Alabaster and Abram, 1964).

Short 2 h exposures of fish followed by a prolonged period of observation has been practised in studies on the reproduction of guppies (*Lebistes reticulatus*) after a single exposure to dieldrin (Hubble and Rieff, 1967). They established a 2 h ML_o (equivalent to the TL_m or the LC_{50}) of 0·05 ppm dieldrin for guppies and 0·01 ppm for harlequin fish (*Rasbora*) and trout (*Salmo sp.*).

A 2 h exposure period, in addition to 24 h tests, was also employed in laboratory tests on tropical fish in evaluating the effects of DDT applied to West African rivers for control of *Simulium* (Post and Garms, 1966). In this case the selection of short as well as long exposure periods was influenced by the fact that in practical *Simulium* control in the field, the DDT is applied to the rivers for a brief period of 30 min, and that fish at varying distances below the dosage point were liable to widely different degrees of exposure to the insecticide.

2. *Prolonged exposure and long-term effects*

The majority of routine tests for evaluating fish toxicity are short-term ones designed to provide reproducible figures regarding *acute* toxicity of the chemical in question. However, it has long been recognized that this practice measures only one aspect of toxicity and that ideally this should be supplemented by some standard method for measuring *chronic* toxicity, i.e. the long-term or delayed effects of exposure to pesticide concentrations which are not immediately lethal (Wurtz, 1965; Alabaster and Abram, 1965). Despite the acknowledged need for more precise data on chronic effects of chemicals, comparatively few laboratory studies have been made on this aspect. This may be partly due to the fact that long-term evaluation of this kind — perhaps extending over many months — is too time-consuming to be added to an already heavy burden of routine toxicity tests, and partly due to the firm belief that chronic effects of sub-lethal dosages can only be assessed in the natural habitat rather than in the prolonged artificial environment of the laboratory.

The question of evaluation in the field will be dealt with in the next section. With regard to the possibility of assessment of chronic effects of exposure to toxic chemicals being complicated by the unnatural conditions of life and confinement in the laboratory, while this uncertainty must undoubtedly be constantly in mind, there are still many factors of the environment which can be more readily controlled and measured in the laboratory than in the natural habitat in the field. For this reason, there are some aspects of chronic toxicity which will continue to remain obscure until the variable factors can be controlled, or eliminated one by one, in a manner which is only possible by means of carefully designed laboratory techniques.

Two examples of long-term evaluation in the laboratory are illuminating. The first of these was concerned with the effect on the pumpkinseed sunfish (*Lepomis gibbosus*) of chronic exposure to lethal and sub-lethal concentrations of dieldrin (Cairns and Scheier, 1964). In soft water at 20°C it was found that the TL_m values were as follows:

24 h	0·0155 ppm
48 h	0·0120 ppm
72 h	0·0075 ppm
96 h	0·0067 ppm

With a prolonged exposure of twelve weeks to a concentration of 0·00168 ppm it was observed that although the fish survived, their swimming ability and their oxygen consumption were both affected.

In the second example, the approach was rather different in that the test fish were exposed for a 2 h period to the concentration — 0·055 ppm — of dieldrin which kills 50% of the sample, and the surviving fish were then maintained in clean water for a twelve-month observation period (Hubble and Reiff, 1967). This particular study was concerned with the long-term effects of a single exposure to dieldrin on the reproductive capacity of the test fish. The viviparous guppy (*Lebistes reticulatus*) was well suited for this type of evaluation, its reproductive capacity being expressed as "fish months", i.e. the number of female fish multiplied by the number of months during which they were fecund. Surprisingly enough, it appeared that none of the surviving females had suffered from the short exposure; in fact they showed a better reproductive rate than unexposed fish, due to the fact that the initial exposure eliminated the weaker fish and left the more robust ones alive.

These two examples illustrate that the question of chronic toxicity can be appraised in rather different ways, and that in this type of long-term evaluation, initially small differences between the physiological condition or vigour of different individual fish, or different batches of fish, may have a cumulative effect which ultimately determines whether they survive or die. Allied to this is the possibility that some test fish, or some batches, may have had prior prolonged exposure to substances which — although producing no obvious lethal or harmful effect — nevertheless have increased their susceptibility to toxic chemicals. The most likely predisposing causes of this kind are detergents and herbicides which are playing an increasing role in contamination of rivers and streams.

The influence of chronic exposure to substances other than pesticides is illustrated by the finding that Goldfish with a prior history of exposure to "hard" detergents, ABS, were more susceptible to the toxic effects of dieldrin and DDT than were fish with no previous history of exposure (Dugan, 1967).

The question of physiological and behavioural effect of sub-lethal exposures to pesticides has recently been closely examined in the case of DDT as part of an extensive fishery research programme in Canada. Fish treated with sub-lethal dosages of DDT exhibit a violent avoidance reaction when they encounter — when swimming in a horizontal temperature gradient — water of about 5°C or colder. This "cold response" is totally absent in untreated fish, and from the rapidity with which the response occurs it is concluded that it is initiated by sensory nerves (Ogilvie and Anderson, 1965). Allied to this is the finding that exposure of trout for 24 h to DDT concentrations ranging from 0·1 to 0·3 ppm renders the lateral line nerves hypersensitive to mechanical or other experimental stimuli, this effect being more pronounced at lower temperatures (Anderson, 1968; Anderson and Peterson, 1969). This avoidance of lower temperatures may possibly be related to the finding that DDT is more toxic to fish at lower than at higher temperatures.

There is evidence from other sources that the behaviour of fish in response to pollutants may be an important factor in determining the toxicity of such chemicals in nature (Summerfeld and Lewis, 1967). In general, avoidance reactions to toxic chemicals are not well marked at concentrations below lethal level, but there are substances like tear gas, chloroacetophenone or ACP, which produce such a marked repellent effect — on green sunfish at least — at concentrations as low as 0·5 ppm, and avoidance reactions at concentrations as low as 0·05 ppm, both of which are below the lethal level of 0·7 ppm.

From these examples it appears that in order to interpret the complexities of fish reaction to sub-lethal exposures it is necessary to take into account not only the direct behavioural response of the fish to the toxicant itself, but also the indirect response to other factors of the environment — of which temperature is the most easily measured — caused by the physiological effects of the pesticide in question.

Up till recently fish toxicity studies have been almost entirely concerned with the reaction of the fish themselves. Increasing interest is now being shown in the reactions of fish eggs, particularly in connection with the increasing exposure to surface active detergents (Tarring, 1965). At this point it is worth noting that there have recently been similar trends in the study of insects and insecticides where there is renewed interest in the possibilities of some new compounds being effective — at normal field dosages — against the eggs of mosquitoes (Jakob, 1968) and those of blackflies (*Simulium* (Muirhead-Thomson and Merryweather, 1970) long regarded as the particular immature aquatic stage most resistant to the effect of pesticides.

In fish egg studies, the basic technique of evaluation is the same as with adult fish and aims at establishing a TL_m as a measure of acute toxicity. However, as the effect on eggs cannot be assessed directly, but only on subsequent hatching, the TL_m values for different times of exposure were calculated from one day up to a maximum of nine days, by which time all surviving eggs had hatched (Pickering, 1966). In comparing the effects of the older "hard" detergents — alkyl benzene sulphonate or ABS — and the newer "soft" detergents — linear alkylated sulphonate or LAS, the nine-day TL_m figures for eggs of the fathead minnow (*Pimephales promelas*) showed that the acute toxicity of LAS is more than twice that of ABS.

The question of studying the reactions of fishes' eggs leads naturally to a very specialized problem where the main target of investigation is the larva of a fish rather than the adult. The fish in question is the sea lamprey which has done so much damage to the fishery industry in the Great Lakes of North America. For the five years of its life the larval lamprey is confined to streams running into the lakes, and in these streams it is much more amenable to chemical control than the wide-ranging adult. Accordingly the greater part of the extensive screening and evaluation programme has been concerned with finding chemicals which show a differential toxicity with regard to the larval lampreys which have to be controlled and rainbow trout which have to be protected. The lamprey larvae range in size from 3·5 to 5 in and the rainbow trout (fingerlings) from 4·5 to 5.5 in. Fuller details of this programme will be described in a later section.

EVALUATION OF PESTICIDE IMPACT ON FISH IN THE FIELD

Over the last twenty-five years there has been a rapid build-up in information about the impact of pesticides and toxic chemicals on freshwater organisms. This information has ranged from casual, isolated or disconnected observations to scientifically planned field tests and experiments. Some of these investigations have been confined to freshwater fish either by design or simply due to the fact that fish appeared to be the most obvious and visible indicators of contamination. In other cases observations have extended to a wide range of freshwater organisms.

The sum total of these observations — made in many countries, and often recorded in local or little-known journals dealing with fish and wild life — is impressive, but at the same time rather bewildering because of its sheer bulk and variety. While it would undoubtedly be extremely useful to have a complete up-to-date summary of all these scattered records for reference purposes, it is felt that an equally useful purpose would be served at this stage by trying to sort out and select from the material available and attempt to arrange it into groups or categories. As all this material has been collected from observations and investigations which differ widely in objective and in evaluation standards adopted, it seems that the most useful and practical grouping must take into account both the reliability of the evaluation methods employed and the accuracy of information about the timing, the nature and the degree of exposure to pesticide or toxic chemical. Although any classification or grouping on this basis must be an arbitrary one, it is an essential first step towards a more critical and constructive approach to the evaluation of pesticide impact in the field. A second essential step is to apply this arbitrary classification to different groups of freshwater organisms in turn, before attempting any sort of overall assessment of the total impact of chemical on the ecosystem. It would be convenient therefore to concentrate first of all on what is known about the impact of pesticides on freshwater fish in nature, as distinct from the evidence already reviewed about the impact under laboratory or controlled semi-field tests.

The arbitrary grouping of information is as follows:

I. Information based on evaluation of general contamination of water by pesticides of uncertain nature and origin.
II. Evaluation of pesticide impact due to known area-application of insecticide for control of agricultural or forest pests.
III. Evaluation based on known application of specific chemicals directly to water bodies.

Before discussing available knowledge under these headings, it is important to remind ourselves that different investigators tend to attach different weight to the relative value of field observations versus controlled laboratory testing. While few people will question the fact that the ultimate criterion of pesticide impact is the effect on exposed populations in their natural habitats with regard to growth, mortality, behaviour, etc. there is perhaps more diversity of opinion as to how these effects can be accurately assessed in the complex environment of a stream or lake. Natural variations and fluctuations in the physical environment of freshwater organisms may extend to unmeasurable or unpredictable variations in the degree of exposure to toxic chemicals, making it difficult in extreme cases to attribute all observed effects directly to pesticide contamination, or to a specific type or concentration of toxic chemical.

It is hoped that the following assessment made under different headings may assist in seeing the situation in clearer perspective, and help us to decide which particular approach to the problem of evaluation in the field has proved the most appropriate or reliable.

I. The development of DDT and other organochlorine insecticides in the 1940s opened up enormous new possibilities for control of insects of agricultural and public health importance. The scale of application of DDT and later groups of synthetic insecticides increased prodigeously, particularly in crop protection and the control of forest pests. Characteristically, it is in the United States that these new pest control methods were followed up with a maximum degree of vigour and enthusiasm, and on a vaster scale than in any other region. Perhaps not unconnected with this is the fact that in the United States, after the initial upsurge of enthusiasm, the first healthy doubts began to be expressed about the possibility that large-scale insecticide application might have a harmful effect on wildlife and on natural environments.

From about 1950 onwards increasing attention was paid to the undesirable aspects of pesticide application, particular attention being given to the freshwater organisms of streams and rivers which formed not only a collecting ground for insecticide applied over wide areas by aircraft, but also a means of transporting persistent insecticides such as DDT over long distances to the permanent water of lakes. Despite the increasing interest it was some time before this subject was examined critically or experimentally, and many of the early dramatic reports about harmful effect and "fish kills" could be attributed to obvious misuse of insecticide — such as cleaning spray equipment in ponds and streams — or to careless disposal of insecticide containers. In fact, by the middle 1950s some ecologists had reached the conclusion that pesticides were less harmful to fish and wildlife than were changes brought about by land and water development and use.

A milestone in a new and critical approach was provided by the second seminar held in 1959 at Cincinnati, Ohio, on the subject of Biological Problems in Water Pollution. A large part of this seminar was devoted to the effects of pesticide on aquatic life, and brought together for joint consideration a wide range of experience reported from many parts of the United States and Canada. Much of this information concerning insecticide impact on streams and rivers could be related to known area-application of specific insecticides, and as such will be discussed under the second category in this chapter. Even where observations on harmful effects on fish and other aquatic forms can be associated with well-defined episodes of pesticide application or contamination, the correct interpretation of data is still exposed to many errors and pitfalls. In the absence of well-defined episodes, and where even the identity of the contaminating agent is in doubt, such errors are magnified making it extremely difficult on occasions to attribute fish kills or fish mortality directly to the effect of a suspected pesticide.

This conclusion is endorsed by subsequent developments in the United States. In 1960 the U.S. Department of Health, Education and Welfare started an annual census of reports received from all over the country concerning fish kills with regard to number of fish, conditions at the time and probable cause (U.S. Department of Health, Education and Welfare, 1964). In 1964 the fish kills reported amounted to 18,387,000 based on 485 official reports from cooperating state fish and game agencies, from leading conservative agencies, and from the U.S. Fish and Wildlife Service. Of the total number of reports, 193 incidents — accounting for the largest number of fish kills, 12,715,000 — were attributed to industrial pollution. Municipal wastes accounted for 4,100,000 fish kills, while toxic substances from agricultural operations took third place with 1,522,000 kills.

There are naturally considerable errors involved in nearly all these observations. In some cases the fish kills reported amount to impressive numbers, but it is very rarely that these numbers can be related to the total fish population exposed. Little is known about the natural mortalities of fish in unpolluted habitats, and dead or dying fish are rarely seen even though the natural mortality must be high at certain seasons or following natural phenomena such as flood and drought. Fish mortalities occurring during the fishing season are also much more likely to be observed and reported than if they occur in the autumn when the fishing season is over (Graham, 1960).

Many of these possible errors in interpreting observed fish kills must still be allowed for even when dealing with definite episodes of pesticide application, as will be discussed in the next section. But the possibility of error is naturally much more real when there is uncertainty about both the identity of contaminating pesticide and about the existence or otherwise of other sources of chemical and biological pollution. This uncertainty is a feature which is tending to intensify rather than decrease. The appearance of a wide spectrum of synthetic pesticides in recent years contrasts striking with the situation twenty years ago when the scene was dominated by DDT and a comparatively small number of allied organochlorine insecticides. At the present time streams, rivers and lakes in many regions are liable to be exposed to a dozen or more different kinds of pesticide in the environment, as well as to a whole new range of industrial and domestic pollution associated with such chemicals as detergents, plastics, etc. Where unduly high fish mortality is now observed in such an environment, the unravelling of the tangled complex in the hope of establishing a clear cause and effect, becomes a formidable task.

In countries where there is heavy application of pesticide and where fish kills are frequently reported, the emphasis has naturally been on the acute toxic effects produced on the fish. However, the long-term effects of sub-lethal exposures cannot be underestimated, and this may prove to be the most important aspect of contamination of water bodies in the countries of Western Europe such as Britain (Holden, 1964, 1965). In those countries low but persistent concentrations of organochlorine insecticides such as DDT and dieldrin may contaminate streams and rivers from agricultural land treated with pesticide. BHC and dieldrin may also reach streams when used as sheep dips (Hynes, 1961). As the effects of chronic exposure are difficult to assess by observations on fish in their natural habitats, attention has been concentrated on the detection of pesticide residues in various organs of the fishes' body, and in body fat in particular, and in attempting to assess the levels of pesticide in organs and tissues at which lethal or sub-lethal effects may be expected. As the chlorinated hydrocarbon insecticides combine a very low solubility in water with a high solubility in oils and fats, there can be a high build-up of DDT in the bodies of fish exposed to very low concentrations of insecticide. At the time of death this concentration in the gills may be as much as three hundred-fold (Holden, 1962). In one particular Scottish trout loch, dieldrin residues detected in trout have revealed levels which might be sufficiently high to account in whole or in part for the observed poor condition and decline in growth rate in recent years (Holden, 1965).

In England, summer mortalities of coarse fish are fairly common, and on occasions mortality may reach a very high figure. An enquiry into such an occurrence was made in the Bude Canal in Cornwall in June 1967 when over 20,000 roach and rudd, and a few dace, were found dead or dying (Cross, 1968). Such an explosive mortality occurring within the space of two weeks would in many cases be attributed either to presence of pesticide, heavy metal or some other toxic chemical, or possibly to bacterial infection. However, associated with the heavy mortality was a prior sharp reduction in the volume of the habitat which had been reduced to one half for bank clearing. The consequent overcrowding of an already dense population produced abnormal behaviour in the fish attributed to population pressure and "stress", and it is this factor which was considered the primary cause of the mortality. Under such conditions of stress various sub-lethal factors which the normal fish could tolerate, tend to have a cumulative effect so that the fish suddenly reach a critical phase of susceptibility either to the toxic chemicals or to pathogenic infection. The need to give full consideration to all other factors which might predispose fish to sudden heavy mortality is also emphasized by the finding that goldfish with a prior history of exposure to alkyl benzene sulphonate detergent (ABS) are more susceptible to the toxic effects of dieldrin and DDT than are fish which have no previous exposure to ABS (Dugan, 1967).

II. By far the greater bulk of information about the impact of pesticides on fish and other freshwater organisms has emerged from studies associated with known wide scale application of insecticide, DDT in particular. The bulk of this work was originally stimulated by reports of fish kills following aerial application of DDT, and most of these investigations were concentrated on special areas where freshwater fisheries were directly affected. Despite the increasing scale of DDT for the control of agricultural and forestry pests from as far back as 1954 onwards, surprisingly little in the way of collateral study on the environment effects of DDT spraying was done in the earlier days, although many far-seeing ecologists and conservationists were fully aware from the start of the ecological hazards and implications of mass application of insecticide. One of the few examples of anticipation of events comes from Canada where the first large scale application of DDT for control of injurious forest insects was *preceded* by laboratory and field tests of toxicity to other forms of wild life (Webb, 1960). These investigations included fish and aquatic life, and although somewhat limited in scope, were sufficient to establish — what has since been fully supported — that aquatic organisms are particularly susceptible to the effects of aerial application by DDT.

In contrast to that anticipatory exploration, much of the evidence on impact of DDT on fresh water is based on unplanned observations made after the episode, often after periods of many weeks or months.

One of the first critical investigations into the possible hazards of the new insecticides to fish and freshwater organisms originated in the widespread application of DDT by aircraft for control of defoliating forest insects in the U.S.A. and in Canada (Hoffmann, 1960; Hoffman and Droor, 1953). In the forest areas of Montana and the Yellowstone National Park for example there was heavy DDT spraying against the spruce budworm from 1952 to 1956 over an area of more than two million acres. Four months after spraying there were reports of dead and dying fish in the Yellowstone River along a ninety mile stretch within and below the sprayed area. The fish most affected were whitefish (*Prosopium williamsoni*) and brown trout (*Salmo trutta*); densities of dead fish of the order of 600 fish in less than 300 yds of stream were noted (Graham, 1960; Cope, 1961).

In view of the conflicting evidence about the relation of fish kill to DDT spraying in at least eleven States, and also in Canada, a systematic trial was planned to determine if aerial application of DDT at 1 lb/acre had a deleterious effect. The general plan was to sample stream bottom organisms and fish populations prior to and following spraying. The fish populations were sampled with an electrical shocking device, sampling being done in sections 300 ft long. Only fish at least 3 in long were used in population index numbers since smaller fish could not be efficiently collected. In addition, 158 trout were held in live cages in two streams during spraying. None of these died on the spraying day or during the following three days. Interpretation of results was rendered difficult because high water prevented efficient pre-spraying sampling making it difficult to compare populations before and after spraying. However, no fish losses were revealed within nine months after spraying. The stream was studied again in the following year to observe delayed effects, but results were inconclusive (Graham, 1960).

In view of the variable results, a single experiment on one stream was designed in 1957 based on: (i) chemical analysis of the water vegetation, sediments and fish tissues to determine presence of DDT;

and (ii) patrolling the stream to observe fish mortality. Three miles of the stream area was sprayed at the rate of 1 lb DDT/acre. Dead suckers (*Catostomus sp.*) began to appear within a few days after spraying, and were found throughout the summer and fall, but in smaller numbers.

In Canada, where the extensive forest areas provide one of the country's most valuable natural resources, control of the spruce bed-worm was a matter of serious concern, and wide scale application of DDT began as early as 1945–6, reaching a peak between 1952–8. The greater part of this aerial spraying took place in New Brunswick and adjacent areas of Quebec, a region which includes watersheds of some of the finest Atlantic salmon streams in the world. In sprayed areas of New Brunswick, as well as in British Columbia on the Pacific Coast, drastic reduction in the smallest age classes of salmon were reported (Kerswill and Elson, 1955; Keenleyside (1959); Elson, 1966; Webb, 1960). In one part of these investigations numbers of young salmon in the northwest Miramichi River were estimated yearly at ten stations by repeated electrofishing combined with marking and recapture of fish (Elson, 1967). The results show that the numbers of young salmon increased from 1950 to 1953, apparently because predatory birds were controlled. In 1954 spraying virtually eliminated salmon fry and killed most parr. Larger numbers of fry in 1956 were attributed to reduced competition, good spawning conditions and absence of spraying. In 1956–7 the numbers of fish were again reduced in forest areas.

By 1957 recovery of the young salmon in the north-west Miramichi River was almost complete, and conditions were back to normal in 1960.

In the very earliest phases of DDT aerial spraying, the accepted rate was 1 lb/acre. This was subsequently reduced, and the bulk of the aerial spraying in New Brunswick for example was at the rate of 0·5 lb/acre. In order to minimize the harmful effects on salmon streams in the treated areas, there has been increasing use of DDT at the rate of 0·25 lb/acre—sometimes taking the form of two applications about ten days apart. Since 1962 increasing attention has been given to finding a replacement for DDT in spruce budworm control, especially in the neighbourhood of such important salmon-rearing streams. Preliminary experiments with such compounds as the carbamate Zectran, and the organophosphorus compounds Sumithion, malathion and phosphamidon showed that these compounds were all relatively much less toxic to fish than DDT, and also had the advantage of being relatively short-lived. From these tests phosphamidon has emerged as the most suitable compound, with least toxicity to fish.

The toxicity of phosphamidon to juvenile Atlantic salmon (*Salmo salar L*) was tested in the laboratory. The lethal threshold for a 1 h exposure, after which fish were removed to clean water, was about 220 mg/l. This is much higher than the concentrations of about 0·1 mg/l which might be expected in streams following aerial spraying operations. This insecticide accordingly is regarded as relatively "safe" from the point of view of danger to young salmon (Elson and Kerswill, 1966).

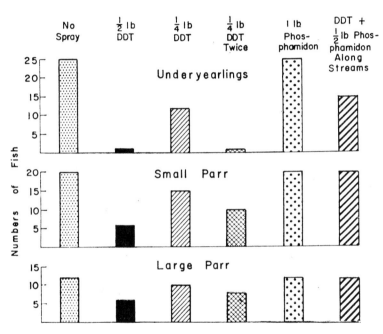

FIG. 8. Average abundance of wild young salmon per 100 yd² (84 m²) of a stream bottom after various aerial forest spraying treatments (1 lb per acre) (after Elson and Kerswill, 1966).

A comparison of the effects on salmon of the different DDT treatments and of phosphamidon is shown in Fig. 8. Estimates of the number of fish were based on electroseining in sample areas of about 50–100 sq yd in the streams in which the data were obtained by fishing over the area several times on one day.

The results show clearly the sharp improvement — especially with young salmon — following the use of a single application of DDT at 0·25 lb/acre as compared with 0·5 lb/acre. Two treatments at the reduced rate are however as harmful as the single treatment at 0·5 lb/acre. Phosphamidon alone at 0·5 lb/acre appears to make the least impact on young fish.

The New Brunswick investigations are recognized as a classic contribution to the problem of pesticide impact. Certain aspects of the life history of the Atlantic salmon render them particularly vulnerable to such impact; the young, hatching in the gravel, emerge at a time when the forest spraying is in progress. They depend on food organisms which are also susceptible to the changed environment, and they remain potentially exposed to the river environment for the two or three years of their freshwater existence. Reports from other areas in North America in which forest spraying with DDT has also been carried out, suggests a rather less drastic impact on stream fish (Bartsch, 1966). As few of these cases have been followed as thoroughly or as continuously as the New Brunswick investigations, it is difficult to say whether the reported differences in effect are due to specific differences in the fish concerned, or to slight differences in methods or timing of DDT applications.

Before leaving the New Brunswick studies it is worth noting that the long history of DDT spraying in that region introduced difficulties in interpreting the effects of a completely different kind of contamination of part of the river system by toxic chemicals, namely, intermittent contamination with copper and zinc from a base metal mine and mill operated in 1957–8, and then from 1960 onwards (Sprague et al., 1965).

In contrast to the many investigations on the possible hazards to freshwater fish produced by aerial spraying with DDT — particularly in the extensive treatment of forest areas for the control of spruce budworm — is the almost complete absence on collateral observations on another mass aerial application of insecticide, namely, the one aimed at the eradication of the imported fire ant by dieldrin and heptachlor. This vast eradication programme was organized in 1959 so rapidly that little time and few staff were devoted to collateral studies, but the ensuing effect of these two insecticides — generally considered ten to twenty times more toxic than DDT, and often applied at rates as high as 2 lb/acre — was evidently disastrous in many areas. Quite apart from wildlife, fish kills were reported in many southern States including States such as Alabama where a very high value is attached to fish resources. Despite all this, nothing of real value emerged about the effect of this catastrophe on the fish population, or on recovery and repopulation after the ill-advised eradication programme was finally terminated. From studies carried out in various laboratories unconnected with this campaign, it is evident that dieldrin and heptachlor have a high toxicity to a wide range of freshwater fish, to say nothing of a wide range of invertebrates and other aquatic fauna (Andrews *et al.*, 1966).

Some of this laboratory work has provided a good example of how standard fish toxicity tests may be used to forecast the likely impact of a particular field dosage in terms of lb per acre (Henderson *et al.*, 1959). The method consists of working out the 96 h TL_m values of the insecticides to test fish, and then computing the rates of field application necessary to achieve this concentration in water 3 ft deep. The 3 ft value is an arbitrary one but is selected on the basis that it approximates to the average depth of many farm ponds and smaller streams in the test area. An acre of water 3 ft deep also measures approximately 1,000,000 gal.

Applying this method to a particular test fish (bluegills) it was calculated that the field application sufficient to produce a 50% mortality over 96 h (i.e. the 96 h TL_m) for dieldrin, DDT and heptachlor were 0·07, 0·13 and 0·16 lb/acre respectively. Even allowing for errors involved in applying laboratory findings directly to field conditions, the figures give strong support to the fact that dieldrin applied at 2 lb/acre must inevitably have had a drastic effect on fish population.

It seems that this method of appraisal based on a wide range of laboratory TL_m values and a wider range of test fish might be applied in other cases where aerial application of pesticide is being planned on a large scale and is likely to have a harmful effect on non-target freshwater fish and other aquatic organisms. Simultaneous field observations would help to define more clearly the accuracy or otherwise of this method of forecasting, especially in view of the fact that in the field certain unpredictable factors such as, for example, the degree of adsorption of DDT on mud and plant surfaces, might widen the gap between theoretical expectations and practical realities.

III. Many of the difficulties in evaluating impact of pesticides on fish are removed when the exact identity of the pesticide is known as well as the exact timing and duration of application to the freshwater body, together with information on persistence and dispersal of the pesticide after application.

This is precisely the range of information which is known, or should be known, in all cases where pesticides are deliberately applied for the control or destruction of undesirable aquatic forms such as larvae of mosquitoes and blackflies, aquatic snail intermediate hosts of human parasites, and undesirable fish or fish larvae. In many cases the interpretation of field events has been further facilitated by the fact that in the course of laboratory screening and evaluating such pesticides, preliminary tests on fish toxicity are also carried out. This applies particularly to such pesticides as molluscicides which are destined to be applied on a very large scale to irrigation systems or to static water bodies where fish are being cultured.

In the case of pesticides destined for control of trash fish or injurious species such as the larvae of the sea lamprey, periodic application in the field is usually preceded by a series of laboratory and semi-field investigations sufficiently thorough to enable a high degree of accuracy to be brought to bear on the final evaluation of field events.

If we leave for the moment the question of evaluating the effect on fish of piscicides themselves, we find that there is a vast amount of scattered and often uncoordinated information about the harmful or undesirable effects of applied pesticides on "non-target" species of fish, including valuable food fish. The possibility of such harmful effects is very much in mind at present, and the majority of large-scale operations involving direct application of pesticides to swamps, marshes, ponds, rivers and irrigation systems include essential observations on toxicity to fish at least, and often to other representative aquatic fauna as well. Much of the earlier awareness of the possible harmful effects on fish of large-scale applications of DDT, for example for control of mosquito larvae, originated in the United States where insecticides have been applied on such a vast scale. As DDT and organochlorines have been replaced since about 1964 by more recent mosquito larvicides, particularly organophosphorus compounds such as malathion, Baytex, Dursban and Abate, and by carbamates such as Sevin, parallel field observations on fish toxicity have almost become an established routine (Mulla, 1966a; Mulla *et al.*, 1964, 1966).

A useful indication of the fish toxicity rating — based on field hazard — of a wide range of compounds currently used for control of mosquito larvae is provided by a rough classification according to whether the harmful effects are low to moderate or high to very high (Travis *et al.*, 1968) as in Table II.

In view of the fact that several of these new mosquito larvicides are so toxic to fish, it has been suggested that advantage might be taken of this in deliberate control of undesirable fish populations. Tests have been carried out in large fibreglass tanks using carp (*Cyprinus carpio*) as a good test example of undesirable or trash fish (Mulla *et al.*, 1967). The results showed that the organochlorine compound, endosulphan, was highly toxic to carp, but would not be

TABLE II

Low to moderately toxic to fish	Toxicity high to very high	
Paris green	Parathion	Lindane
Carbaryl	Pyrethrin	Malathion
Abate	Naled	Heptachlor
Methyl parathion	EPN	Methoxychlor
Carbophenothion	Chlordane	DDT
Vapona	Dursban	Dieldrin
Fenthion		

of practical value because of persistence and accumulations in the habitat. Several organophosphorus compounds such as ethyl guthion were also effective, while others such as Parathion, Fenthion and Abate were only toxic at much higher levels than normally used in field mosquito control. As the OP compounds are unstable in water and have no tendency to accumulate in non-target components of the biota, the more toxic compounds might have some value in deliberate fish control.

Of particular concern in many mosquito control campaigns has been the non-target species *Gambusia affinis* which feeds on mosquito larvae and plays an important part in natural regulation of numbers. The "mosquito fish", more than any other, has long been used as a supplementary method of reducing mosquito larval populations both in the Old World and in the Americas, and has been introduced into many countries outside its normal range. In the choice of insecticide, dosage and formulation for large-scale aerial application as mosquito larvicide, the preservation of the *Gambusia* fish population is now an important consideration. As part of this concern, the question of development of resistance to insecticide such as DDT and other organochlorines on the part of the *Gambusia* population under continued insecticide pressure, receives constant attention. While the ideal would be to use completely selective mosquito larvicides in such a way as to kill all larvae while leaving the *Gambusia* population unaffected, in practice the same result might be achieved if short-term toxic larvicides were used in such a way that treatment could be followed quickly and safely by restocking the breeding grounds.

In the California Mosquito Abatement Program, OP compounds — including parathion — have been widely used, but the search continues for less hazardous insecticides. In that region the average number of treatments per mosquito season is four, but in some areas up to ten treatments are necessary. In such circumstances fish like *Gambusia* — as well as other freshwater fauna — are under very heavy insecticide pressure.

In evaluating the toxic effect of field treatments with mosquito larvicides, the method most frequently adopted is to expose fish in screen cages in experimental ponds which can be treated with known concentrations of various insecticides and their formulations. A common design of fish cage is 1 ft square by 15 in long in which twenty-five test fish are exposed. Fish are exposed in the water immediately after treatment, and mortality is recorded after 24 h, or at longer periods. The addition of fresh cages of test fish to the mosquito breeding area at intervals after treatment provides information about the persistence of the larvicide at fish-toxic levels. Observations on free-swimming fish, such as *Gambusia*, indicate that they duplicate the high mortality recorded in cages.

Such screened cages or "live boxes" have also been used to study the ecological effects of aerial treatment of salt-marsh mosquito habitats with the organophosphorus compound Dursban (Ludwig *et al.*, 1968). Using mullet and several small native fish for the test, it was demonstrated that there was no significant fish mortality at dosages of Dursban which achieved control of the salt-marsh Aedes mosquitoes.

In the control of salt-marsh mosquitoes, aerial application of larvicide is liable to produce patchy distribution of chemical, with overdosing in some places and insufficient dosage for larvae control in others. Although the use of ground equipment involves additional time and labour, it does have the advantage that applications can be made at more accurate concentrations. One of the most useful formulations for this purpose are slow-release granules which have been used in connection with the New Jersey Mosquito Control Program (Shinkle, 1968). Improved accuracy of dosing enables more precise limits to be defined regarding treatments which are adequate for larval control but which do not destroy fish populations. For example, methoxychlor granules (5%) and EPN granules (5%) applied at the rate of 30 lb/acre — 1·5 lb/acre actual toxicant — were both found to be highly effective for larval control. Unfortunately they were also lethal to zebra killie (*Fundulus heteroclitus*) and to the sheepshead minnow (*Cyprinodon variegatus*), the EPN being particularly toxic. At this dosage between twenty-five and thirty-five dead killie fish per square foot of salt-marsh meadow were recorded after treatment. When the treatment was reduced to 0·5 lb/acre actual toxicant, excellent mosquito larval mortalities were still obtained but the effect on fish was now negligible.

Some of the most varied and illuminating examples of field studies on fish mortality following direct application of pesticide to water bodies come from Africa. These have been made mainly in connection with two public health programmes, namely the application of chemical molluscicides for the control or elimination of the aquatic snail species which form the intermediate hosts of the parasite of human bilharziasis (*schistosomiasis*), and the application of larvicide for controlling breeding of *Simulium*, the insect vector of onchocerciasis or "river blindness". Both activities have now been going on for a number of years in different countries, and in both cases the scale of operations is likely to extend and intensify over the next few years.

In *Simulium* control, involving treatment of rivers and river systems, the various countries of West Africa such as Guinea, Upper Volta, Ghana and Nigeria are particularly involved. Of particular interest is the fact that control programmes in those countries have been based almost entirely on the use of DDT, and that this insecticide, or the allied chlorinated hydrocarbon — methoxychlor — may continue to be the larvicide of choice for several years, until such time as a more selective, less persistent and less generally biocidal chemical can be developed.

In the case of molluscicides for control of aquatic snails, many more countries are involved, from Egypt in the north to the Union in the south, and a much wider range of water bodies receive treatment. The snail habitats include many static bodies such as ponds, storage dams, lakes and reservoirs whose importance depends on the particular species of snail incriminated, and the particular area. But in general the most important targets of molluscicide application are irrigation and drainage systems, ranging from the long-established patterns of the Sudan and the Nile delta to the rapidly extending systems of irrigation characteristic of so many developing African countries.

The increasing range of molluscicide application is likely to be intensified by the construction and completion of man-made lakes in many of these countries. Parallel with these developments in recent years has been an increasing interest in fish culture, in the construction of fish ponds and in the stocking of impounded waters with fish (Lockhart *et al.*, 1969). Particular attention has been given to the several species of *Tilapia* which are well suited for impounded water as well as open water, and whose culture on a large scale is planned in connection with several of the new man-made lakes (Lagler, 1969; White, 1965). Species of *Tilapia* also inhabit the larger rivers of Africa, including several in areas affected by *Simulium* control programmes.

Despite the fact that several of these long-established control programmes must obviously have had some effect on the non-target food fish, it is only comparatively recently that the question has been examined critically and scientifically. In fact one of the first systematic approaches to this problem was not associated with either of these major programmes but in connection with evaluating the impact of mosquito larvicides on experimental fish ponds in Tanzania (Webbe, 1957; Webbe and Shute, 1959). The larvicides tested were different formulations of DDT, gamma BHC and dieldrin. The experimental ponds measured 48 sq yd in area, with a depth of 3 ft at one end shelving to 1 ft at the other. Thirty fingerlings of each of three species of *Tilapia* were used for each trial. The selected formulations were then applied at calculated dosages; in most cases insecticide was applied weekly, but in some cases a single treatment was followed by three weeks' observation period. Field assessment of mortality was made by removing all the fish from the treated and from the control ponds, and by counting the number of survivors. In order to determine whether a treatment which proved fatal to fish continued to exert a toxic effect after treatment was stopped, a further series of trials were made. Surviving fish were carefully washed in clean water, placed in an untreated pond and observed for a further given period.

These trials revealed differences in reaction between the three species of *Tilapia* studied which have already been referred to, and confirmed evidence already available from experiments in the United States about the toxicity to fish of oil solutions of DDT, and that it is in fact the DDT and not the oil vehicle which kills the fish. In contrast to the toxic effects of DDT, gamma BHC in oil solution produced no deaths among fish either at 2 quarts or at 4 quarts/acre applied weekly for three weeks, and also did not appear to have any harmful effect on breeding or growth of the fish. Formulation evidently played a vital part in determining fish toxicity. Dust forms of DDT, dieldrin and aldrin as well as granular formulations of dieldrin, produced unexpectedly low kills of fish at a dosage of 1 lb/acre for twenty weeks.

While the use of DDT, dieldrin and other organochlorine insecticides is no longer practised in mosquito control either in Africa or elsewhere, DDT — after over twenty years of use — continues to be the main larvicide for controlling *Simulium* larvae and streams and rivers. Moreover, the formulation preferred, the emulsifiable concentrate, is one which allows DDT to exercise its maximum toxic effect on other freshwater stream organisms. The first successful applications of DDT to rivers in east and central Africa were made with the single objective of controlling the *Simulium* vector of onchocerciasis, regardless of the consequences. Drastic fish kills were observed, but preoccupation with the main objective left little time or interest to study such harmful ecological side effects. It was not until DDT had been in use for several years that this question was investigated more critically. For example, observations carried out on the Victoria Nile at Jinja in Uganda before and after March 1956, when the river was treated with DDT, are particularly illuminating as they were able to demonstrate differential effects on fish populations. These differences appeared to be brought about not by specific differences in acute mortality but indirectly through the effects of the DDT treatment on the food supply. The DDT treatment eliminated not only *Simulium* larvae but probably all lithophilous insect fauna which formed the main diet of several species of fish. One of these — *Mastacombelus* — was revealed as a specialized feeder which proved to be unadaptable and which either suffered starvation as a result or was compelled to move away (Corbet, 1956, 1958). In contrast, an unspecialized feeder such as *Clariallabes*, which had previously fed on 90% lithophilous insects, was able to survive by feeding on plants, molluscs, etc., unaffected by the DDT treatment. It was suggested that treatment of highland streams would have had a more drastic effect, as many fish in that situation rely mainly on lithophilous insects. Further details about these investigations insofar as they concern the effect of DDT treatment on stream invertebrates are discussed later.

The observations at Jinja have a wider significance in that they indicate that the actual disappearance of a particular non-target fish from rivers under pesticide pressure cannot always be attributed to the direct toxic effect of the chemical. The same effect may be produced if the fish die as an indirect result of destruction or removal of their main food organisms. Migration of fish away from a treated area because of this food shortage could also account in whole or in part for observed depletion in fish populations. Most investigators have also been fully aware of the possibility that one of the indirect causes of fish mortality might be the ingestion of aquatic insects which have been killed by treatment. Although this appears to be a real possibility, it is difficult to obtain proof of at least any immediate or short-term effects. Quite early in the history of DDT application it was found that carp remained healthy after feeding for four days on *Aedes aegypti* larvae killed at concentrations of 0·05 to 0·1 ppm. In the River Colne in England it was observed that 80% of the gudgeon (*Gobio gobio*) diet was composed of chironomid larvae. Gudgeon were fed chironomid larvae dying as a result of treatment with TDE used for midge control, about ninety larvae per fish being ingested over four days. No fish deaths were recorded over a seven-day post-ingestion period of observation (Edwards *et al.*, 1964).

In addition to the indirect effects of pesticides on fish outlined above, there is a great deal of evidence of immediate or direct effect on fish following DDT-treatment of rivers. For example, DDT emulsion applied at the rate of 0·1 ppm for 30 min to the River Niger at Kouroussa in Guinea produced high fish mortality within 20 min of application, and up to 10 km below the application point. Laboratory tests on tropical fish carried out firstly in Guinea and later in Hamburg using 2 h exposures and 24 h exposures showed that irreversible damage could be produced after some hours exposure to such low concentrations as 0·05 ppm to 0·01 ppm DDT. In contrast, the organophosphorus compound Baytex, which was also being tested in the field as a possible alternative to DDT, could be tolerated by fish at concentrations up to 3 ppm for many hours (Post and Garms, 1966). Several species of fish were involved in these field and laboratory observations, including *Tilapia, Puntius, Barbus* and *Chelaethiops.*

More information about the effects on fish of DDT applied to African rivers has been provided in a different context, quite unconnected with *Simulium* control. This was the attempt made in 1957 to control the nuisance caused by chironomid midges (*Tanytarsus*) at Khartoum by direct application of DDT as a larvicide to the Blue Nile (Brown *et al.*, 1961). DDT was applied by aircraft at a calculated concentration of 0·11 ppm over about 1 h, 50 min of flow. Numbers of fishes were killed, and examination of dead specimens showed DDT concentrations of 2·5 ppm in *Labeo sp.*, and 79 ppm in *Synodontis schall.* Laboratory investigations showed that *Tilapia nilotica* could survive exposures to 0·02 DDT for 3 h, although — in view of the investigations on the Niger described above — this does not rule out the possibility that irreversible damage may have been caused by this exposure. In view of the fish kills produced, this particular midge nuisance was dealt with more effectively by using DDD rather than DDT, and applying the larvicide to the Sennar Reservoir.

In contrast to these experiences with DDT in African waters it is worth noting that in one of the early classic examples of *Simulium* control in large rivers, namely DDT-treatment of the Saskatchewan river in Canada (Arnason *et al.*, 1949), no adverse effect on fish life could be detected following aerial treatment at conventional rates, viz 0·1 ppm DDT for 30 min approximately. This was confirmed by tests at higher concentrations in which it was found that DDT as high as 25 ppm had no noticeable effect on such common river fish as the goldeye (*Amphiodon alosoides*), pickerel (*Stizostedion vitreum*), river chub (*Platygobio gracilis*) and ling (*Lota maculosa*).

Effect of molluscicides

In the control of the aquatic snails which act as intermediate hosts of the parasites causing human bilharziasis, the situation over the last ten to fifteen years has been marked by a succession of molluscicides which have dominated the scene for a short time until replaced by progressively more effective chemicals. Originally, the water-soluble copper sulphate was the chemical of choice — and it is still preferred in the irrigation systems of the Sudan. This gave way to another water-soluble compound — sodium pentachlorophenate (NaPCP) — which in turn was almost completely superseded by the low-solubility compound Bayluscide. Bayluscide (Bayer 73) has been the mollusicicide of choice for a wide range of habitats for several years, and for a time its only serious competitor was the I.C.I. compound Molucid until the production of that compound was suspended. The most recent and effective molluscicide is the Shell compound Frescon (N-tritylmorpholine).

Bayluscide in the form of a wettable powder formulation is usually applied to the water of ponds, lakes and irrigation systems at the rate of 4–8 ppm. At a comparatively early stage in its development it was found that Bayluscide was about equally toxic to fish (*Lebistes*) as it was to snails, in the range of 0·3 to 1·5 ppm for 24 h. Reports from the field have all tended to confirm that normal snail control treatments are harmful to a wide range of fish species, including *Tilapia*. In Brazil for example it was found that a local food fish *Poecilia januarensis* were all killed at 1·6 ppm within 2 h, while at 0·4 ppm, 96% survived after 48 h (Paulini *et al.*, 1961).

In Africa one of the most critical investigations on the ecological effects of Bayluscide treatment was particularly concerned with the influence of soft and of hard water (Harrison, 1966). The object was to study the effect of a single treatment with Bayluscide on streams and impounded waters. The streams chosen were about 1 m wide and 5–10 cm deep, one with moderately hard water, the other with low carbonate and bicarbonate content. In the soft water stream the effect of Bayluscide treatment on fish (the soft-water minnow, *Barbus trimaculatus*), was very marked. The fish began to jump out of the water within minutes of spraying, and most fish were dying within 5–10 min even at 0·10 ppm Bayluscide. In hard water on the other hand, the fish kill was much slower, even though most water samples contained over 0·2 ppm, and no fish mortality occurred until after 2 h.

3*

Despite its established fish toxicity, Bayluscide is still the molluscicide of choice in many countries, particularly where the problem of bilharziasis control is the overriding consideration and where there is no serious conflict with fish culture or fish industry. In those areas where the extent of snail breeding in fish ponds necessitates some form of snail control which is inimical to fish, alternative molluscicides are available (see below).

One of the most interesting repercussions of Bayluscide's high toxicity to fish is the adoption and development of this compound in the U.S.A. as a piscicide for the control of undesirable fish populations (Marking and Hogan, 1967). This aspect will be discussed more fully under the section on piscicides, but for the moment it is worth noting that investigations have shown that Bayluscide is highly toxic to eighteen species of freshwater fish, including such as the catfish which are resistant to other chemicals. This study revealed a range in sensitivity from the most sensitive species such as flathead catfish and rainbow trout to the most tolerant species, goldfish and carp. It was also shown that Bayluscide is toxic to fish in very brief exposures and does not become proportionately more toxic with increased exposure.

A generally high toxicity to fish also characterizes the most recent major molluscicide, Frescon (N-tritylmorpholine). Application of the emulsifiable concentrate at 0·25 ppm to storage dams in Rhodesia killed large numbers of fish, mainly *Barbus sp.* and *Clarias sp.*, and fish were also killed by treatment of irrigation canals (Shiff, 1966). In other areas *Barbus* and *Tilapia* were killed in canals treated for 6 h at the rate of 0·1 ppm (Boyce *et al.*, 1966). Further field investigations on the fish toxicity of Frescon have revealed features of wide significance in fish toxicity studies in general. It was shown for example that different closely related species of *Tilapia* may differ markedly in their reactions to tritylmorpholine. *Tilapia mossambica* survived seven days' exposure in flowing water treated at 0·04 ppm, while under the same conditions 63% of *T. melanopleura* died (Shiff *et al.*, 1967). This forms an interesting comparison to the specific differences shown by *Tilapia* species to DDT and other mosquito larvicides.

The time/concentration factor was also shown to be an important consideration in evaluating fish toxicity. In the experiments described above it was noted that *Barbus* and *Tilapia* were killed in canals treated for 6 h at 0·1 ppm tritylmorpholine. However, when an equally effective method of snail control was devised in which a much lower concentration of molluscicide — 0·025 ppm — was applied continuously for thirty days, these fish survived the treatment, suggesting the real possibility of an exploitable degree of selectivity between snails and fish (Boyce *et al.*, 1966).

Most workers involved in the development and evaluation of molluscicides in the last ten years have been acutely aware of the fact that the most effective and economical compounds for snail control are toxic to fish at field dosages. It is true that in most cases the fish population, despite the immediate drastic effects, is not eliminated and that repopulation usually follows cessation of treatment. In some cases the irritant effect of the molluscicides may steer the fish away from the zones of high chemical concentration, and allow them to escape the full effect of chemical treatment. For example, in treatment of canals in the Nile Delta with acrolein as a combined herbicide/molluscicide, in many instances the downstream travel of the chemical could be followed by observing the reactions — jumping and swimming — of the fish trying to escape ahead of the chemical. Despite the piscicidal properties of this compound, fish became reestablished in the canals within a few weeks after treatment (Unrau *et al.*, 1965).

There are, however, circumstances in which the piscicidal properties of most current molluscicides or formulations rule out their use in water bodies used for fish culture, and where it is imperative to use more selective compounds. With this in mind considerable attention has been given to various copper compounds. Copper, in the form of the water soluble sulphate was one of the earliest molluscicides to be used on a large scale in the field. In this form it is less toxic to fish than to snails, but the difference is not sufficiently great — 3 ppm versus 1 ppm — for safe use in fish ponds. In fact, copper sulphate was one of the first chemicals to be used in the United States for control of undesirable fish populations.

However, in the case of low-solubility copper compounds such as cuprous oxide, cuprous chloride and a complex cuprosulphite (sel de Chevreul) formed by the interaction of potassium sulphite and copper sulphate, much wider differences between snail toxicity levels and fish toxicity levels were disclosed (Deschiens *et al.*, 1965; Floch *et al.*, 1963, 1964). In the case of copper cuprosulphite, the molluscicide dosage on a 24 h treatment is 1–2 ppm. By comparison, the fish tested (*Carassius*, *Gasterosteus* and *Lebistes*) require a concentration of 90 ppm to achieve the same mortality. Toxicity to both snails and fish is greater at low pH levels than high (Hopf *et al.*, 1963).

In field practice in fish ponds, molluscicide applications of cuprous oxide at 5 ppm and cuprous chloride at 2 ppm have been shown to have no harmful effect on either full grown or young fish (Deschiens and Floch, 1964).

The difference between snail toxicity levels and fish toxicity levels is even wider in the case of micronized metallic copper which kills snails at concentrations of 50 ppm (24 h exposure), but which leaves fish unaffected by concentrations as high as 20,000 to 30,000 ppm. Unfortunately manufacturing costs and difficulties rule out the use of this form of copper in practical field control.

Another possibility which has been investigated in the continuing search for a more selective molluscicide or molluscicide formulation has been the use of bait formulations, with particular reference to the most recent major molluscicide, Frescon, or tritylmorpholine. Laboratory experiments showed that it was possible to develop a wheat grain-based bait formulation sufficiently attractive to aquatic snails to act as an "arrestant", i.e. one on which snails will continue to feed once they have located the bait, while at the same time having no adverse effect on fish living in the same tank. Unfortunately, in the field, baits tend to disintegrate rapidly, as well as being attacked by fungus or covered with silt and detritus to such an extent as to render them ineffective.

An illuminating example of the successful use of a molluscicide being applied in a selective manner, with minimal impact on fish, is provided by recent work with Frescon (N-tritylmorpholine) in England (Crossland, 1970). This molluscicide was used to deal with an unusual snail control problem, namely the control of *Limnaea peregra* in its role as intermediate host to the trematode parasite, *Diplostomum spathaceum*. At one phase of its cycle this parasite is found in the intestines of several species of gull in Europe, where heavy infection may cause high mortality. In another phase of its cycle, the parasite develops in this particular aquatic snail, from which motile forms — *cercariae* — are released into the water and infect a variety of freshwater fish. Stages of the parasite encysting in the eyes or the brain of the fish can cause blindness.

An outbreak of blindness in trout in Lodge Reservoir, Chelmsford, England, was drawn to the attention of the Essex River Authority and led to a careful investigation of the possibility of controlling this fish parasite by means of chemical attack on the intermediate snail host, *Limnaea*. In order to minimize the effect such molluscicidal treatment might have on fish, preliminary laboratory experiments were carried out in order to establish the toxicity thresholds for fish and snails. It was found that a concentration of 0·05 ppm Frescon produced 100% mortality in snails but only 10% mortality in fish, and it was therefore decided that the appropriate selective dosage for field use would be 0·025. The molluscicide — in the form of a diluted suspension — was applied at this concentration from a boat in such a way as to distribute the active ingredient as evenly as possible throughout the reservoir, whose surface area was 17 acres with depth varying from 11–16 ft. Two weeks after the first spraying of the whole reservoir, the perimeter was given a second treatment with Frescon applied at 0·1 ppm to a 5 m swathe offshore.

The first treatment produced a very high mortality of *L. peregra*. Rainbow trout were not affected but some stickleback (*Gasterosteus aculeatus*) were killed. After the second perimeter treatment no living *Limnaea* could be found, and again there was no apparent effect on fish other than sticklebacks. This perimeter treatment had the effect of reinforcing the selective action of the molluscicide as the treatment was concentrated on the shallow margins of the reservoir where the snails congregated, and avoided the deeper water where fish were more abundant. The selectivity of the treatment evidently included aquatic molluscs themselves as most other aquatic snails, in particular *Hydrobia jenkinsii*, were unaffected by the treatment which proved lethal to *Limnaea*.

This example provided a model of what can be achieved by close collaboration between all parties concerned in the practical and ecological aspects of such problems. In this case the four bodies involved were the Shell Research Laboratory, the Nature Conservancy, the Salmon and Freshwater Fishery laboratory of the Ministry of Agriculture, and the Essex River Authority, and staff of all these organizations participated in the project.

Effect of aquatic herbicides on fish

Associated with the explosive advance in the development of insecticides and synthetic pesticides in general, there has been a great development in recent years in the use of herbicides for control of undesirable aquatic vegetation. As a wide range of plant species, growing under a wide variety of conditions, are involved, a correspondingly wide range of chemicals and chemical formulations have been developed to meet each particular requirement. This range of conditions and plant species is well illustrated by those in the irrigated part of the Nile Delta (Dawood *et al.*, 1965), in which a simple classification of aquatic plants applies to many other parts of the world as well, viz.:

Floating weeds	e.g. *Eichornia* (water hyacinth)
	Salvinia (water fern)
Submerged weeds	with fine roots, e.g. *Potamogeton crispus*
	with no roots, e.g. *Caratophyllum demersum*
Emergent weeds	*Panicum, Scirpus, Typha*

The increasing scale of herbicide use drew attention at an early stage to the possibility of harmful effects on fish, and led to a series of laboratory investigations based on techniques described earlier in this section (Bond *et al.*, 1960; Surber and Pickering, 1962).

Those tests showed that many of the compounds were only toxic to fish at levels higher or much higher than field herbicide dosage, and thus allowed an adequate safety margin. However, there were wide differences between the different test species of fish to one and the same herbicide, and their reactions in turn were affected in some cases according to whether the water was hard or soft.

Two of the most widely used herbicides are the allied compounds diquat and paraquat which are of particular interest in the present context in that their effect on fish has been carefully studied at both laboratory and field levels. Diquat has been found to be effective in weed control at 1–3 ppm, which is found to be very much lower than the levels at which fish become affected. In laboratory tests the 48 h TL_m for largemouth bass was 11 ppm, for fatheads 23–26 ppm, for Chinook salmon 29 ppm, and for bluegills 80–210 ppm, the range in the last case being determined by whether the test medium was soft or hard.

In the field, treatment of ponds with diquat at the rate of 1·0 ppm had no adverse effect on fish although the nuisance weeds in question (*Elodea canadensis*) were all dead and decomposed within a week after treatment (Hilsenhoff, 1966).

In the case of paraquat, laboratory tests also indicated low toxicity to fish (trout), but when field trials were carried out, unforeseen events occurred which are of considerable ecological interest (Water Pollution Research, 1966, 1967). A lake, 17,850 m² in area, containing trout, roach and perch was treated with paraquat at 0·5 ppm. Within five days the minimum daily oxygen content of the water had fallen from about 110% saturation to 4%. By that time aquatic weeds had begun to disintegrate and all captive trout were dead. Captive perch still survived. The interpretation of these events was that the lethal effect on trout was caused entirely by the indirect effect of the herbicide destroying the plants and inhibiting photosynthesis; respiration continued, and the oxidation of the organic matter produced by the disintegrating plant material led to severe oxygen depletion.

In interpreting the effects of herbicides on fish populations or other biota in treated habitats, it is clear that a distinction must be made between the direct lethal effect of the herbicide — which may well be minimal and can be checked by laboratory tests — and the indirect effect on the environment which may be drastic enough to have serious repercussions on some freshwater organisms.

There is another sphere in which herbicides may exert a dual effect, this is in the control of aquatic snails which are intermediate hosts of bilharzia. Many of these snail species are associated with profuse growth of marginal or submerged aquatic weeds, and the removal of such vegetation is considered by itself to be an important snail control measure (Dawood *et al.*, 1965). As a further development of this is the finding that several of the herbicides suitable for this purpose are also molluscicidal, this applies particularly to acrolein (aqualin), diquat and paraquat. Acrolein in molluscicidal dosage was found to be piscicidal in trials in Egypt (Unrau *et al.*, 1965) and in the Sudan (Ferguson *et al.*, 1965), in many cases the downstream travel of the chemical being marked by intense activity and irritability on the part of the fish trying to escape ahead of the molluscicid wave.

The rapid appearance and proliferation of aquatic weeds marks certain phases in the evolution of man-made lakes. The control of this vegetation is important not only from the point of view of obstruction of waterways and impeding flow (Lagler, 1969) but is also of public health importance in that it can provide suitable foci for establishing foci of intermediate snail hosts. Volta Lake for example was formed in 1964, and already by 1966 some sections of the lake shore had been invaded by aquatic weeds. These were mainly *Ceratophyllum*, but to a less extent *Pistia* and *Scirpus*, which were soon supporting large populations of the snail host *Bulinus truncatus rohlfsi* (Paperna, 1969). The establishment of snails was followed by a heavy epidemic of bilharziasis as previously vector snails had never been found in the Volta River, but only in small lakes in the lower reaches (Onori *et al.*, 1963; McCullough, 1962).

In Lake Kariba, a similar weed problem has been caused by *Salvinia*, which also provides ideal conditions for proliferation of snail (Hira, 1969). It remains to be seen to what extent the weed problem can be dealt with by chemical means without impairing the proposed Lake Kariba fishery development schemes.

One of the molluscicides which was prominent for several years was sodium pentachlorophenate (NaPCP). From the snail control point of view this substance had the additional advantage of burning up the vegetation along the margins of water courses, but the disadvantage of killing fish at molluscicide dosage. In 1957, at the peak of its period of usefulness, sodium pentachlorophenate was introduced as a herbicide in rice fields in Japan, and since that time it has been suspected as a frequent cause of mass deaths of fish and shell

fish (Hashimoto, 1969). Lake, river and inshore fishing are important industries in Japan and the Ministry of Agriculture — acutely
aware of accidental fish kills caused by drift of other pesticides such
as gamma BHC and carbaryl — has drawn up a classification of pesticides according to their fish toxicities.

One of the most widely used aquatic herbicides is the phenoxy
compound 2,4-D, and on occasion very large quantities may be applied to water, for example 87 tons during a one-month period in
two Tennessee Valley Authority reservoirs (Smith, 1963). While most
reports indicate low toxicity to fish, there is considerable variation in
toxicity levels recorded, and this has been attributed to the fact that
not only are several 2,4-D compounds used as herbicides (acid, ester,
etc.), but there is also a wide range of solvents and emulsifiers. It
seems likely that the latter two components may account in the main
for the toxicity attributed to the herbicide.

The butoxyethanol ester of 2,4-D has been the subject of an unusual study on the effect of long-term exposure, the test fish — fathead minnow (*Pimephales promelas*) — being exposed for ten
months under flow-through conditions (Mount and Stephan, 1967).
This work has already been referred to more appropriately under
laboratory evaluation, and it will be sufficient for the present that
during such continued exposure a concentration of the 2,4-D ester
of 1/19 of the 96-h median tolerance limit (TL_m) will not harm
growth or reproduction of the test fish.

CHAPTER 3

PISCICIDES: THE CHEMICAL CONTROL OF UNDESIRABLE FISH

The use of chemicals — insecticides — for controlling harmful or undesirable insects has long become a familiar and accepted fact of life in most countries of the world. Rather less well known is the use of chemicals — piscicides — for the control of undesirable fish.

Emphasis on the possible adverse effects on fish of modern pesticides used in forestry and agriculture has perhaps created the impression that all fish species and populations must be protected. Certainly, in Great Britain for example, the concept that certain species of freshwater fish might be undesirable because they compete with game fish or food fish is not a familiar one, and the deliberate use of chemicals to control such populations has not been practised in this country (Holden, 1964, 1965).

However, the situation is very different in some other countries. In the United States for example there is a long list — compiled from at least thirty states — of freshwater fish which are labelled as undesirable "trash" species, quite apart from the predacious species which actually feed on food fish, particularly on trout and salmon. As in many other fields of applied biology there has been a great intensification in the development and practical use of piscicides in the last ten years, particularly in the U.S.A. and the U.S.S.R. Much of this rapid development is associated with the development and manufacture of an increasingly wide range of new synthetic pesticides, some of which possess unique and highly desirable selective properties.

In the development and application of piscicides it would be useful to make a distinction between two objectives which determine the choice of piscicide and the mode of application.

Firstly, there is the development of selective piscicides which kill particular species of undesirable fish at concentrations which do not have an adverse effect on the desirable food fish. The outstanding example of this is the successful development of selective chemicals for controlling the sea lamprey (*Petromyzon marinus*) in the Great Lakes of North America by destroying the larval stages which inhabit the streams and rivers flowing into the lakes.

Secondly, there is the use of piscicides to eliminate entire populations of trash fish from lakes which, after a suitable interval, can then be re-stocked with trout. As this aspect of fish control has rather a longer history, it would be instructive to deal with it first.

One of the first compounds to be used in fish control was copper sulphate which proved useful in certain soft-water areas. At this point it is worth noting that copper sulphate was also the first chemical to be used on a large scale for control of the aquatic snail intermediate hosts of human bilharziasis.

The first piscicide to be used extensively in fishery management was rotenone which has been used in the United States since 1934. In some instances as much as 105 tons of rotenone have been used in a single fish eradication experiment (Hooper, 1960). Rotenone has not been used as a selective toxicant, and in addition to its relatively high cost it has the drawback that it is subject to rapid breakdown in most lakes and ponds, to the extent that toxicity may be lost before the chemical has had time to become thoroughly dispersed throughout the waters of the lake.

TOXAPHENE: THE ELIMINATION OF ENTIRE FISH POPULATIONS

The development of new synthetic insecticides disclosed valuable piscicidal properties on the part of Toxaphene — chlorinated camphene. Toxaphene is three times as toxic as rotenone and has the greatest toxicity to fish of any chlorinated hydrocarbon except endrin (Fukano and Hooper, 1958; Hooper, 1960; Hooper and Grzenda, 1957). It also has a lower acute toxicity to humans than either endrin, dieldrin, aldrin or rotenone. It is now accepted as a general replacement for rotenone, and, in the state of Wisconsin for example, over thirty lakes have been treated with this piscicide in the ten years from 1955–65 (Johnson et al., 1966).

The effective application rate varies according to conditions and to fish species involved, and usually ranges from 0·02 to 0·1 ppm. Increased experience with the use of Toxaphene has disclosed one undesirable feature, namely its persistence and slow rate of detoxification in some lakes. Normally, lakes treated with Toxaphene for complete kill require two to twelve months before detoxification reduces the concentration of chemical to a level suitable for re-stocking. However, some lakes have remained toxic for periods up to four years.

Although different species of fish vary in their response to Toxaphene, these differences are not sufficiently marked to make this chemical of value as a selective piscicide. There are occasions where one particular species of trash fish is the main object of attack, such as in Big Bear Lake, San Bernardino in California where goldfish are the most serious competitors with trout for food. Application of Toxaphene at various concentrations showed that this chemical was too lethal to other fish, and not completely lethal to goldfish. It was not therefore recommended for goldfish control (Johnson, 1966).

However, one unusual instance of fish control with Toxaphene does provide a striking example of how such a chemical can be applied in such a manner as to prove completely selective, eliminating the undesirable species while leaving the valuable food fish completely unharmed. In Alaska, the coastrange sculpin (*Cottus aleuticus*) is a significant predator on pink salmon fry (*Onchorhynchus*) in Big Kitoi Creek. This stream was treated with Toxaphene in July at a time when salmon fry had migrated to sea, and returning adults had not yet entered the creek. Treatment was carried out for $18\frac{1}{2}$ h at an average concentration of 1·5 ppm. This treatment eliminated all sculpins and some other fish in a 1000 ft section of the stream, and sculpins were not observed again up till one year later (Meehan and Sheridan, 1966).

The wide use of Toxaphene, and the investigations into the most suitable field rates of application, has also led to a type of field trial which has possibly much wider application in general problems of fish toxicity levels in natural habitats. In North Dakota, sixteen lakes of various sizes were treated with concentrations ranging from 0·005 ppm to 0·035 ppm in order to determine the minimum lethal concentration of Toxaphene to fish (Henegar, 1966). In five of the seven lakes in which mortality was complete, it was possible to re-stock successfully after seven months. The implication from this is that one of the factors determining the long persistence of Toxaphene in certain lakes may be the use of dosages unnecessarily high for that particular lake.

A compound very similar, but not identical, to Toxaphene, called Polychlorpynene, or PCLP for short, has been used extensively for fish control in U.S.S.R. in recent years (Burmakin, 1968). In that country, particularly in the temperate zone, many of the smaller lakes have long been dominated by such species as perch (*Perca fluviatilis*), roach (*Rutilus rutilus*), ruff (*Acerina cernua*) and others, none of which have any commercial value. Attempts to change the composition of the fish by re-stocking alone have been unsuccessful, and in only a few cases did introduced fish survive. Since 1957 however research on piscicides, or "ichthyocides", has been conducted vigorously, and by the end of 1964 over 200 lakes with a total area of about 16,000 ha. had been treated. In fishery practice the concentrations of PCLP used vary from 0·05 ppm to 0·15 ppm according to species, depth of water and temperature, and as with Toxaphene, PCLP has been found in some cases to persist for a year or more.

ANTIMYCIN: THE SELECTIVE CONTROL OF TRASH FISH

Reference was made earlier in chapter 2 to the establishing of Fish Control Laboratories by the U.S. Bureau of Sports, Fisheries and Wildlife at La Crosse, Wisconsin in 1959 and at Warm Spring, Georgia, in 1963. The purpose of these laboratories was to develop efficient and scientific methods for controlling fish populations, with special reference to finding selective chemicals to deal with a wide range of undesirable fish. In addition to having no value as food fish, these species compete with valuable food fish and may provide a serious obstacle to establishing commercial fisheries. The importance of these "trash" fish varies in different regions and according to conditions, but at least a dozen species have been labelled as major target species, such as longnose and shortnose gars, gizzard shad, goldfish, carp, squaw fishes, white sucker, black bullhead, rock bass, green sunfish, pumpkinseed, yellow perch and freshwater drum.

The search for selective pesticides in those laboratories has been stimulated by the striking progress made under the Great Lakes Commission in controlling the sea lamprey by means of chemical methods against the larval stages. Intensive work in these laboratories has produced within the last few years an equally striking example of the development, and final successful commercial application, of a selective piscicide in the form of Antimycin A, formulated as Fintrol-5 (Walker *et al.*, 1964; Lennon and Walker, 1964; Berger *et al.*, 1969).

Antimycin is an antibiotic produced by microscopic plants in much the same way as penicillin is produced by a mould. It was discovered in 1945 by scientists in the Department of Plant Pathology at the University of Wisconsin, and was named Antimycin (antifungus) because of its powerful fungicidal properties.

In 1963 Antimycin was reported to be very toxic to fish, and from that point onwards its full investigation was taken in hand by the laboratory at La Crosse. Laboratory tests involving more than thirty species of fish revealed a wide range of reaction (Figs. 6 and 9). Among the most susceptible species were carp, pumpkinseeds and green sunfish, which succumbed to such extremely small quantities as 1 to 5 ppb in water. The indication from these results were that this compound could be used for selective control of certain undesirable species at dosages which would be harmless to food fish such as trout, bream and catfish.

Tests in a Nebraska pond showed that it was possible to eradicate completely large populations of carp and green sunfish with an amount of Antimycin which allowed Large Northern pike and large-mouth bass to survive.

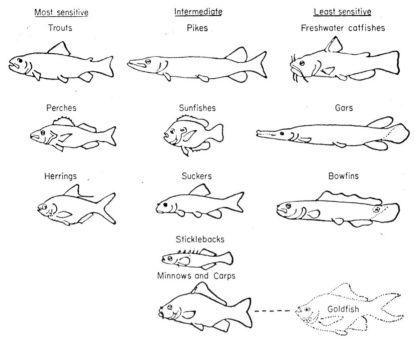

FIG. 9. The order of sensitivity of eleven families of fish to Antimycin A in the laboratory and the field (after Walker *et al.*, 1964).

In the last few years there has been a great increase in commercial production of channel catfish in the United States to meet increasing demands (Burress and Luhning, 1969). In many cases plans to establish, or to extend fish production in ponds has been frustrated by fish populations dominated by various undesirable trash species. Tests were carried out in a Mississippi fish farm in a series of ponds ranging from 0·9 to 1·4 acres in area, with an average depth of 5–7 ft. The experiments were carried out in the following stages: (a) sampling fish populations in six ponds prior to any treatment, by seining (usually a 30-ft 1-in mesh seine); (b) applying Antimycin in the Fintrol-5 formulation to three ponds; and (c) recovering scalefish from the treated ponds. After an interval of two to three months, a final evaluation was made by draining all ponds and analysing fish populations. In the year prior to the experiment, each pond had been stocked with about 2000 fingerling channel catfish (*Ictalurus punctatus*), and in addition all the ponds contained the scalefish golden shiners (*Notemigonus crysoleucas*) and green sunfish (*Lepomis cyanellus*).

The piscicide was applied at the recommended dosage of 5 ppb of Antimycin. Three days later, as a few scalefish had evidently survived the treatment, a supplementary treatment of 10 ppb was applied. The combined application of Antimycin was very successful as it removed scalefish populations regardless of composition. Some idea of the heavy populations involved may be gained from the fact that from one of the ponds, just under an acre in extent, more than 31,000 golden shiners were recovered after this treatment, this figure representing a 99·99% mortality. In another pond, an acre and a quarter in area, over 60,000 green sunfish were recovered, representing a mortality of 98·3%. The exact proportions surviving tended to differ from pond to pond. In all of the three ponds there were hundreds of scalefish large enough to consume food pellets and to compete directly with the catfish for food.

In contrast to the drastic effect of Antimycin on the populations of these scalefish, the three treated ponds produced a rich harvest of over 5000 channel catfish representing nearly 5000 lb in weight for a combined area of $3\frac{1}{2}$ acres.

This field trial showed quite clearly that Antimycin can be used to control scalefish in softwater ponds without killing catfish, even fingerling catfish not being killed by recommended levels of treatment.

Further tests in a wide variety of ponds showed that with regard to undesirable sunfish populations in particular, selective removal could be achieved by applications of Antimycin from 1·0 ppb down to 0·4 ppb, i.e. at concentrations very much lower than used in trials just described (Burress and Luhning, 1969). This selective treatment could be carried out at all seasons of the year, at temperatures ranging from 46°F to 75°F, and under a variety of weather conditions. There were indications that concentrations less than 0·4 ppb might be adequate when water temperatures were 75°F or more, and the pH above normal.

Field trials with Antimycin have also been carried out in a wider range of waters, differing ecologically, in east, mid-west and western parts of the United States. These trials were carried out in twenty ponds and lakes — ranging in area from $\frac{1}{4}$ acre to 63 acres — and in five streams and were designed to evaluate the efficiency of Antimycin in several formulations against as many species of fish as possible in cold and warm waters, acid and alkaline waters and clear and turbid waters. Included in the fifty-four species of freshwater fish represented in these trials were such prime target fish as carp, suckers and green sunfish (Gildenhaus *et al.*, 1969).

Trials carried out over a wide range of water quality showed that these prime target species can be eliminated by concentrations of 3–10 ppb of Antimycin, depending on water quality and temperature. Goldfish, bowfish and gar are more resistant and may require considerably more than 10 ppb for control. Bullheads and catfish were relatively unharmed by concentrations used in the trials. It is interesting to note that of the very large number of fish species now known to be killed by Antimycin are the African food fish *Tilapia mossambica*, introduced into the United States in 1961, and larvae of the sea lamprey (*Petromyzon marinus*).

Antimycin has also provided the solution to a rather unusual problem involving an undesirable predatory fish, namely the large-mouth bass (*Micropterus salmoides*) which preys on the chicks of the rare giant pied-billed grebe (*Podilymbus gigas*). The world's population of this rare bird is now confined to Lake Atitlan which lies at over 5000 ft in the mainland of Guatemala, the refuge itself taking the form of a small bay enclosed as a sanctuary (Powers and Bowes, 1967).

In 1956 the largemouth bass was introduced into the lake for its sport and angling value, where it thrived to such an extent that it became a vicious predator not only of native freshwater crabs, but also on the grebe chicks. While the lake itself is 12 miles long and 10 miles wide, the actual refuge is a shallow bay only 460 ft long and 150 ft wide, and it was in this restricted area that Antimycin (in its Fintrol-5 formulation) was applied. Prior to application a large canvas was placed across the opening of the grebe sanctuary in order to prevent, as far as possible, loss of toxicant into the lake itself and to reduce water exchange. A mesh screen gate was also constructed to prevent re-invasion of the sanctuary waters by largemouth bass.

Application of Antimycin at the rate of 9·3 ppb successfully eliminated the bass population within a few hours of application. Within ten days the Antimycin had degraded to a sufficiently low level to allow re-stocking of the refuge with fingerlings of small fish — *Poeciliopsis gracilis* and *Poecilia phenops* — which provide ideal food for the giant grebes.

The particular formulation of Antimycin used in the field trials in ponds and lakes, Fintrol-5, is a sand formulation consisting of Antimycin incorporated in Carbowax and coated on sand in such a way that the toxicant is released into the water within certain depths as the sand grains sink towards the bottom. According to whether the toxicant is to be released evenly within the first 5, 15 and 30 ft of depth, the formulations are designated as Fintrol-5, Fintrol-15 and Fintrol-30.

The trials with Fintrol-5, the only formulation registered and on the market at that time, provided some general conclusions of wide significance in all piscicide evaluation. For example, in waters less than 3 ft deep and where the bottom is very soft, the sand grains may sink into the mud before releasing all the Antimycin. Antimycin appears to have very little adverse effect on a range of non-target aquatic organisms including frogs, salamanders and also waterfowl. Degradation appears to be complete by 48 h after application, thus eliminating possibilities of persistence and build-up. Although Antimycin degrades rapidly in water there are occasions when it may be desirable to de-toxify treated water, and it appears that potassium permanganate may prove valuable for this purpose.

Fish do not appear to show any avoidance reaction to Antimycin; even with the liquid formulation in ethanol used for streams, there is no indication of fish fleeing ahead of the wedge or "slug" of toxicant moving downstream (compare the reactions to molluscicides). Antimycin is most effective in soft water and at lower pH values. Laboratory tests showed that with fingerling goldfish for example a complete kill — in 96 h at 12°C — was obtained at 0·20 ppb at pH 5. At pH 8, the concentration required increased to 1·10 ppb, while at pH 10, it had arisen to 60 ppb (Berger *et al.*, 1969). In view of the fact that the pH in many such ponds rapidly increases during the day, it has been suggested that a more advantageous exposure time would be achieved if application of Fintrol-5 was made at daybreak. The effects of Antimycin are slow and unspectacular but appear to be irreversible; once fish exhibit symptoms of distress, they die even if placed in fresh water.

Intensive laboratory investigations on Antimycin have revealed unusual qualities of high purity and ease of formulation. The crystals are readily soluble in quantities of acetone or ethanol which themselves are not harmful to fish. Because of this property, Antimycin is now being used as a reference compound in routine bio-assays of unknown chemicals. Reference was made earlier to the need for such a stable compound to check whether fish of any species may vary from lot to lot and from season to season in their sensitivity to a chemical. In addition, fish within a lot may increase or decrease in sensitivity according to individual robustness or to stresses induced during holding and acclimation in the laboratory.

The original suggestion that DDT might be adopted as such a reference compound had to be abandoned in the light of intensive laboratory tests which revealed great variation in its action and performance. The recognition of Antimycin as a standard stable reference compound would clearly be a significant advance towards establishing universally acceptable standards of testing and evaluation.

The field trials with Antimycin have also drawn attention to many general problems in evaluation not only of piscicides but also of any control chemical applied to water bodies. There are still many physical difficulties in making exact measurements of area, depth and water volume of large ponds or lakes used in field trials or in control operations. Many current methods provide estimates rather than measurements, and this uncertainty also applies to estimates of flow and velocity in streams (Gildenhaus *et al.*, 1969). In large ponds and lakes it is also increasingly important to know more about the performance of the toxicant at depth. For example, trials in which fish were held in live boxes in water below the 5-ft level showed that mortality usually occurred more slowly, and was sometimes reduced in the deeper waters (Burress and Luhning, 1969). If a thermocline exists whereby lower levels of the water are stratified, or uncirculated by wind or other factors, it may be advisable to calculate concentration of Antimycin on a basis of pond volume above the thermocline rather than on total pond volume. Otherwise the concentration might be higher than intended, with a corresponding greater reduction in the fish population. There are many circumstances in the application of pesticide where the question of occasional overdosing has no more serious repercussions than that of being uneconomical. But where chemicals are being applied in a strictly selective manner, the need for accuracy is imperative. The work on Antimycin has highlighted the urgent need for greater accuracy not only in measuring the extent and volume of the water body involved, but also the need for more accurate information about the particular proportions of that total volume in which the toxicant will actually disperse evenly at the calculated concentration required.

The evaluation of selective piscicides also demands more critical approaches to the methods of measuring pre- and post-treatment populations of fish. Some methods of sampling by seine-net work well in comparatively shallow fish ponds, but have to be augmented by other methods in deeper ponds. In some cases the ponds may be too deep for effective seining, while at the same time gill netting is contra-indicated because it would kill too many fish (Burress and Luhning, 1969). Periodic draining of some ponds is feasible, but is not possible with lakes. Results may be obscured by fish being carried in by overflow from adjacent untreated ponds, and evaluation has also to take into account such questions as variations in time of stocking and degree of competition from scalefish populations. Many of these variables make it difficult to compare treated and untreated ponds simply on a basis of differences in total weight of food fish harvested, and there appear to be advantages in assessing results by a direct comparison of weight gains in untreated controls and in treated ponds, following treatment. It is true that the need for accurate assessments of results of treating fish ponds with selective toxicants is in many cases stimulated or motivated by the commercial interests of the fish farmers themselves. But rather than allow these practical considerations to prejudice ourselves in any way, full advantage should be taken of these needs as they all serve to emphasize the wide range of ecological factors which must be taken into consideration before we can arrive at anything approaching a complete scientific evaluation of the effect of chemicals on fish populations.

CHEMICAL CONTROL OF THE SEA LAMPREY

One of the most striking examples in recent years of the development and practical application of a selective chemical for the control of harmful fish populations is provided by the campaign against the sea lamprey (*Petromyzon marinus*) of the Great Lakes in North America.

The sea lamprey has long been a resident of the St Lawrence River and Lake Ontario, but its path to the other Great Lakes was blocked until the Welland Canal by-passed this obstacle in 1829. However, it was not until 1921 that the first lamprey eels were reported in Lake Erie, and they evidently had difficulty in establishing themselves there. But by the 1930s the lamprey had found its way into Lake Huron and Lake Michigan with disastrous results to the lake trout (*Salvelinus namaycush*) and the fishing industry over the following twenty years (Eschmeyer, 1957). By the end of the 1950s the lake trout population in the last stronghold — Lake Superior — appeared to be on the verge of extinction (Applegate, 1950; Applegate and Moffett, 1955).

The sea lamprey spends only a small portion of its life in the Great Lakes. The fully grown and sexually mature adults migrate into streams to spawn and thereafter die. On hatching, the larvae remain in the stream bottom for five years or longer before metamorphosis into the adult form. Following this transformation, the young lampreys migrate downstream to the lakes to begin their parasitic existence (Howell, 1966; Moffett, 1966).

Control of adult lampreys distributed throughout a body of water as large as one of the Great Lakes is simply not feasible by any known and available technique, and it is accordingly the larval forms, in their more restricted habitat, that have become the obvious target for attack and control by chemicals. As this problem was a joint concern of the United States and of Canada, vital cooperation was early established, and was formalized by the establishing of the Great Lakes Fishery Commission under whose direction a major programme was initiated whose object was to search for or isolate chemicals which would be acutely toxic to larval sea lampreys at extremely low concentrations while at the same time being non-toxic to other fishes inhabiting the same natural environment, in particular the lake trout.

In the course of an intensive screening programme involving nearly 6000 chemicals, a compound of great promise was discovered in the form of a halogenated nitrophenol, and this led in due course to finally establishing the unique properties of tri-fluoro methyl nitrophenol, TFM for short, and to its successful formulation as a 30% concentrate in the form of "Dowlap" (Applegate et al., 1957, 1961; Moffett, 1958; Baldwin, 1963, 1969).

Laboratory toxicity tests on larvae of the sea lamprey (*Petromyzon marinus*) and fingerling rainbow trout (*Salmo gairdnerii*) established the clear-cut selective action of this compound (Fig. 10). The minimum lethal dose for larval lampreys (i.e. the concentration killing 100% of the test larvae within 24 h) was found to be 2·0 ppm at three selected temperatures, 35°, 45° and 55°F. In contrast to this, the rainbow trout were unaffected by concentrations up to 8·0 ppm, allowing a very wide safety margin. In practice, emphasis was given to an arbitrary measure — the "maximum allowable dosage" — representing the concentration which would kill approximately 25% of rainbow trout within 24 h, giving a figure of 8·9 ppm at 55°F and 9·7 ppm at 35°F.

TFM is most effective in soft acid waters. With increasing pH, conductivity and alkalinity there is a sharp increase in the dosage level necessary to produce 100% kill of larval lampreys, which may be as much as 8·0 ppm in the hardest and most alkaline waters tested. However, the reactions of rainbow trout also show corresponding changes so that the end result — the differential toxic action of TFM — is retained regardless of the level of activity in any given water.

Until this phase, all the information about the performance and selective action of TFM had been obtained from an exhaustive series

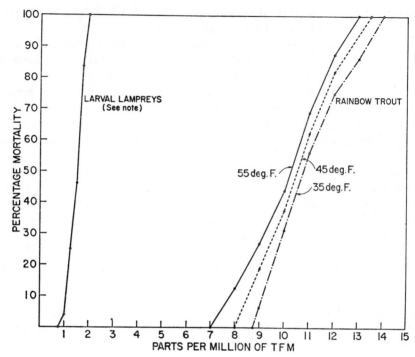

Fɪɢ. 10. Chart showing selective action of lamprey larvicide, TFM (after Applegate *et al.*, 1961).

of tests in static water. The next stage of testing was carried
out in running water raceways, 65 ft long, 6 ft wide and 30 in
deep, under conditions which would approach more closely to those
of natural streams. These simulated stream tests involved about fifteen species of fish, of which the smaller fish were placed in cylindrical screen cages at various points throughout the "stream", while
the larger fish, including mature sea lampreys, were allowed to move
unrestrictedly through the length of the test area. The larval lampreys were placed in screened cages set deep enough into the bottom
to permit the larvae to establish themselves in burrows.

These tests showed that under simulated stream conditions the
differential toxic effects of TFM between lampreys and rainbow
trout were essentially the same as those established in the bioassay
tests. The mortality of larval lampreys was 100% at concentrations
as low as 3·0 ppm, while rainbow trout were not affected by a 24-h
exposure to concentrations as high as 11·0 ppm. Of particular interest was the finding that mature adult sea lampreys (upstream
migrants of the spawning run) and recently transformed lampreys

(downstream migrants) were also killed by concentrations as low as 3·0 ppm.

Brook and brown trout tolerated TFM as well as rainbow trout. At the other extreme, among the so-called "rough" fish, bullheads died in significant numbers when the concentrations exceeded 3·0 ppm, and they thus appear to be almost as susceptible to TFM as lampreys. Between these two extremes, it was found that Yellow perch were affected at concentrations above 7·0 ppm, and that accordingly if survival of this species was desired, maximum concentrations of the chemical in the stream could be reduced without altering the effectiveness of the larvicide treatment.

Finally, TFM in a formulation known as Lamprecid 2770 was tested out in 1958 in three tributaries of Lake Superior infested with sea lamprey larvae. As the successful application of selective piscicides demands a high degree of accuracy in dosage and concentration of chemical in the stream, a transportable pumping system was used in which the pumps were arranged to feed a concentrated stock solution of TFM into a pipe containing a stream of water drawn from the river by a centrifugal pump. The initial dilution of the TFM in this circulating system results in a more efficient distribution of the chemical in the river than does the direct introduction of undiluted formulation. In addition, the introduction of the diluted TFM into the river through a perforated pipe under considerable pressure aids in mixing the chemical with the water.

The experience gained in the technique evolved for field application of TFM forms a striking contrast to methods currently used for application of *Simulium* larvicides to rivers, and molluscicides to irrigation systems. In both these cases undiluted formulation is dripped or fed directly to the flowing water. These differences in dosage technique again underline the much high standards of accuracy required with selective pesticides.

In those streams flowing into Lake Superior, pre-treatment studies were made in order to determine the distribution of larval lampreys and to form some estimate of their numbers, as well as surveying the range and abundance of other fish species. Prior to stream treatment, larval lampreys were placed in forty to fifty cages containing a total of 1000 larvae or more, distributed among three to five stations in the rivers. The test cages allowed the effects of treatment to be followed hour by hour with great accuracy. In addition, quantitative estimates of the effect of treatment on resident sea lamprey larvae were made by intensive sampling using an electric shocker. The Lamprecid formulation was applied for a period of 9 h in one river and $13\frac{1}{2}$ h in another at rates designed to produce concentrations of 3 ppm at the point of application.

The results in all cases showed that all larval lampreys confined to cages were dead within 8 h of exposure to the chemical, 99% being killed within $5\frac{1}{2}$ h. Dead and dying larvae were seen in the treated areas of the streams after about 2 h of exposure to the larvicide. Sampling of the resident population revealed complete eradication. Some idea of the huge natural populations involved may be gained from the estimate, in one of the streams tested, that the number of dead lamprey larvae ranged from $\frac{1}{2}$ to $\frac{3}{4}$ million.

In contrast, only occasional fish of other species were affected, and in general they remained as abundant as they were prior to treatment. Only the log perch appeared to be affected to any significant degree by the larvicide. All these applications of TFM appeared to have a minimal effect on most groups of non-target invertebrates.

Following those successful trials, TFM has been widely used in the Lake Superior and Lake Michigan basins for treatment of streams containing larval lampreys. The effect of this intensified control programme became evident within two to three years. In 1961 there was

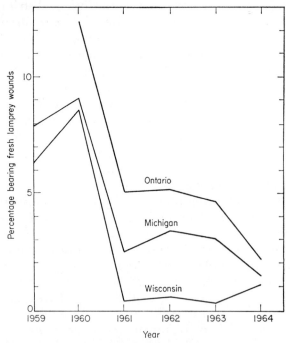

Fig. 11. Percentage of legal-size lake trout bearing fresh lamprey wounds in Lake Superior during September, 1959–64 (after Baldwin, 1963).

a sharp decline in the percentage of lake trout bearing fresh lamprey wounds, and by 1964 the incidence of wounds had dropped to the lowest level yet recorded (Fig. 11). Prior to 1961 the rate of wounding of lake trout followed a distinct pattern each year, highest in the fall, winter and spring, and low in the summer after mature lampreys had entered the streams to spawn and die.

Treatment of lamprey streams was extended to Lake Huron and Lake Michigan in 1960, but was later restricted to Lake Michigan because increased costs precluded extended operations. In 1960 however, when it became evident that the cost of maintaining control in Lake Superior and Lake Michigan would be significantly less than expected, the programme on Lake Huron was re-activated. More than half its lamprey streams have now been treated and it was planned to dispose of the remaining streams by the summer of 1970 (Baldwin, 1969). Prior to the actual initiation of control measures, a considerable amount of survey work has to be carried out in order to locate the lamprey-producing streams of which there are nearly 100 in the Lake Michigan area alone. Re-establishment of larval lampreys has occurred in two thirds of the streams treated, and it is evident that re-treatment will have to be carried out to allow for the fact that young lamprey may transform and emigrate four years after hatching.

Although the discovery of the remarkable selective properties of TFM has opened up new possibilities and new horizons in scientific control of undesirable fish populations, this is by no means regarded as a complete and final solution to this problem. Increasing field experience with TFM has shown that large amounts of material are required, and the consequent high cost has prompted a search for materials which might supplement it or replace it in a control programme. The screening programme therefore continues. In one direction studies have been directed to a wider investigation of the group of chemicals to which TFM belongs (mononitrophenols containing halogens) and to an attempt to find how the structure of these compounds is related to their biological activity, particularly in relation to selective toxic action on larvae of the sea lamprey.

In another direction, the extended screening programme has revealed a new class of selective toxic piscicides in the form of substituted nitro salicylanilides, a group which contains one of the most widely used molluscicides, namely Bayluscide or niclosamine (Bayer 73). Bayluscide has been extensively used in tropical and subtropical countries for a number of years for controlling the aquatic snails which form the intermediate hosts of the parasites of human bilharziasis. It had long been recognized that fish in treated ponds, canals and irrigation systems were liable to be killed at molluscicidal dosage, but this was not regarded as of too great consequence because of the overriding public health needs for bilharziasis control. Scientific knowledge about the actual piscicidal properties of Bayluscide remained at a low or superficial level for several years, until investigations in the United States — made quite independently of molluscicide studies — revealed the true potential of this compound and others related to it (Marking and Hogan, 1967; Howell *et al.*, 1964; Starkey and Howell, 1966).

Bayluscide has been shown to be toxic to at least eighteen species of freshwater fish, including catfish which are resistant to many other chemicals such as Antimycin. Although some of these fish species are more susceptible than others, its selectivity does not appear to be of a sufficiently high order for practical purposes. Bayluscide itself is more than forty-three times as toxic to larval lampreys as TFM, but its toxicity to rainbow trout is also so great that it is practically non-selective between the two.

However, the real potential of Bayluscide in the sea lamprey problem came to light when screening tests revealed that small amounts of this compound improved the toxicity of TFM without affecting significantly the latter's selectivity towards larval lampreys (Howell *et al.*, 1964). This is well brought out in Table III which shows the effect on sea lamprey larvae and rainbow trout of Bayluscide and TFM alone, and the effect of combinations of these two

TABLE III

Actual amounts of TFM and Bayluscide in the minimum lethal and maximum allowable concentrations of various percentage mixtures (after Howell *et al.*, 1964).

Percentage composition of test material		Minimum lethal concentration for larval lamprey (ppm)	Amount in minimum lethal concentration (ppm)		Maximum allowable concentration for rainbow trout (ppm)	Amount in maximum allowable concentration (ppm)	
TFM	Bayluscide		TFM	Bayluscide		TFM	Bayluscide
100	0	3·50	3·50	—	8·00	8·00	—
99	1	2·25	2·23	0·02	6·00	5·94	0·06
98	2	2·00	1·96	0·04	4·00	3·92	0·08
97	3	1·50	1·46	0·05	3·00	2·91	0·09
96	4	1·50	1·44	0·06	2·50	2·40	0·10
95	5	1·13	1·07	0·06	2·00	1·90	0·10
0	100	0·08	—	0·08	0·09	—	0·09

chemicals containing 1, 2, 3, 4 and 5% Bayluscide. The tests were designed to ascertain two levels of concentration, namely the Minimum Lethal Concentration (MLC$_{100}$) which is the lowest concentration in a series which will produce 100% mortality among larval lampreys, and the Maximum Allowable Concentration (MAC$_{25}$) which is the highest concentration which does not kill more than 25% of the rainbow trout.

Proof of synergistic action is provided by the fact that the amount of each compound present at the MLC$_{100}$ levels for the mixtures is considerably below the concentration required to produce the same mortality with the compounds separately. The same synergy is evident in the responses of rainbow trout to mixtures containing 1 and 2% of Bayluscide. Mixtures containing 3, 4 and 5% of Bayluscide are not synergistic since the amount of Bayluscide is equal to or greater than that required to produce a MAC$_{25}$.

The mixture containing 98% TFM and 2% Bayluscide was selected as one of special significance. The MLC$_{100}$ for this combination is 2·0 ppm, and the amount of each component is 1·96 ppm for TFM and 0·04 ppm for Bayluscide. These concentrations individually are non-toxic to larval lampreys; the minimum lethal concentrations for TFM alone is 3·5 ppm and for Bayluscide alone 0·08 ppm — but they coact to produce 100% mortality.

The same synergism applies to the Maximum Allowable Concentration for rainbow trout which is 4·0 ppm for the mixture containing 2% Bayluscide. This mixture contains 3·9 ppm of TFM and 0·08 ppm Bayluscide; neither of these concentrations is toxic to rainbow trout, but on combination they produce 25% mortality.

Further research with this particular combination, designated TFM.2B were carried out in order to study the effect of chemical conditions of the natural waters on the toxicity, selectivity and relative degree of improvement over TFM alone. Finally, treatment of six streams on the eastern shores of Lake Michigan showed that effective treatment with this combination could be carried out at less than half the cost estimated for treating the streams with TFM alone. The effect of the control campaign on sea lamprey catch in sixteen streams tributary to Lake Superior is shown in Fig. 12.

With regard to the overall beneficial effects of the lamprey larvicide programme, rainbow trout (*Salmo gairdnerii*), lake trout (*Selvelinus namaycush*) and whitefish (*Coregonus clupeaformis*) populations have all responded favourably to the reduction of lamprey. Spawning of lake trout has resumed in Lake Superior and it is estimated that if the lamprey control can continue to be held down to 5% of pre-control level, the potential harvest of lake trout by the

4+

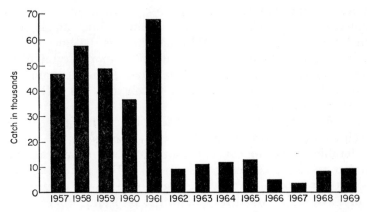

FIG. 12. Sea lamprey catch for sixteen streams tributary to Lake Superior, 1957–69 (after Baldwin, 1969).

sport and commercial fisheries will be four million pounds by 1976, roughly 85% of "normal" production (Baldwin, 1969). Even greater benefits may be realized in Lake Michigan and Lake Huron with a major expansion of sport fishing for Coho salmon (*Oncorhynchus kitsutch*). It is expected that lamprey control will be well established in all of the upper Great Lakes, i.e. Superior, Erie and Ontario, by 1970.

IMPACT OF PISCICIDES

Toxaphene has been used at different dosages for controlling undesirable fish populations in a wide variety of lakes under a wide range of conditions. Reports of the impact of these treatments on the fish populations themselves tend to vary considerably, and it might be expected therefore that the effect on non-target insect larvae and other invertebrates and bottom fauna would also be subject to wide variations. Most treatments with Toxaphene appear to have a marked effect on one section or other of the lake invertebrates, particularly against insect larvae (Meehan and Sheridan, 1966). Bottom samples collected every two weeks with an Ekman dredge have shown that Chironomid larvae may be severely affected, large numbers of these "blood worms" sometimes being washed up on the lake shore after treatment (Cushing and Olive, 1957). *Chaoborus* larvae have also been eliminated by treatment in some areas, while in others the immediate effect is less drastic, and an actual increase in population has been recorded after treatment.

Microcrustacea in general appear to be less affected than insect larvae. Quite early in the development of Toxaphene it was noted that treated lakes can support large numbers of *Daphnia* while they are toxic to fish (Tanner and Hayes, 1955), and laboratory tests have confirmed that *Daphnia* has a 24 h TL_m value seventy-five times greater than that of the common target species of fish, the bluenose minnow which competes with trout for food (Hooper and Grzenda, 1957). Sensitivity among invertebrates appears to vary widely. *Gammarus* for example has been recorded as much more sensitive than *Asellus* or *Ephemerid* nymphs, although all these invertebrates in turn have much higher TL_m values than the minnow.

However severe the effect of Toxaphene on different sections of the non-target fauna, re-population usually occurs sooner or later, and conditions are reported as normal within a year of treatment.

The Russian workers, using the analogue of Toxaphene called polychlorpynene (PCPL), have defined four ecological phases through which lakes pass following treatment (Burmakin, 1968). In the first stage — introduction of piscicide — indigenous fish are killed and the number of invertebrates decreases. The toxicant usually completely eradicates insect larvae as well as microcrustacea such as *Diaptomus*.

In the second stage, the toxic effect of PCLP becomes weaker, and conditions favourable for mass development of invertebrates arise due to lack of predation by fish. This increase in standing crop may take the form of a real explosion, up to 500 times in the case of some microcrustacea. This growth is accelerated by the addition at this stage of mineral fertilizer.

In the third stage, the water is no longer toxic; there are no fish predators and no competition, and sometimes no parasites. At this stage fish are re-introduced and this is followed by a reduction in the standing crop of food organisms. In the fourth stage eutrophication of water takes place under the influence of fertilizer accumulation, and the standing crop of food invertebrates increases once more.

With regard to the lamprey larvicide TFM, initial investigations on the reactions of a wide range of non-target stream invertebrates to this compound have been carried out under laboratory conditions (Smith, 1967). The question of impact under natural conditions has been studied in a series of streams in the Lake Superior watershed and in the Lake Michigan basin (Torblaa, 1968). A very comprehensive list of all stream invertebrates was obtained from bottom samples, and a comparison was made between these samples on the day prior to treatment and one week after treatment. Although the total number of organisms after one week was reduced to 40% of the pre-treatment figure, there was no major adverse effect either with TFM itself or with TFM/Bayluscide. Further sampling in some streams at six weeks and one year after treatment showed that reduced populations were usually back to pre-treatment levels by six weeks, and that conditions after one year showed a complete return to normal.

CHAPTER 4

THE CHEMICAL CONTROL OF FRESHWATER SNAILS IN PUBLIC HEALTH

MOLLUSCICIDES IN THE CONTROL OF BILHARZIASIS

Bilharziasis or schistosomiasis is a widespread human disease in tropical and subtropical countries. It is particularly prevalent in parts of Africa, in several countries of the Middle East, in the Philippines and Japan and in countries of Central and South America. The human disease is caused mainly by three species of parasitic worms (*Schistosoma*) which become established in certain parts of the human body. Eggs produced by these worms pass out of the body via the urine or the faeces, and if deposited or washed into the water of ponds or streams, hatch into free-living larval forms which penetrate certain species of aquatic snail (or amphibious snails in the Philippines and Japan) and undergo a cycle of development there. Finally, motile stages of the parasite are released from the snail's body; these are infective forms which complete the cycle by penetrating the skin of humans who are washing, bathing or in some other way exposed to contact with the water. Allied parasitic worms of domestic stock undergo a similar type of cycle involving other species of aquatic snails, which often share the same habitat as those involved in the human disease.

Of the various possible methods of controlling the disease by attacking the parasite in the human body, by preventing contact between humans and water bodies likely to contain snails producing infective forms of the parasite, or interrupting the cycle of transmission at some point or other, the most practical and reliable method is the control or destruction of the snail intermediate hosts which form a vital link in the cycle. By far the most effective way of reducing or eliminating these snail populations is by the use of chemical molluscicides applied to the streams, ponds, irrigation ditches and canals and other water collections which form the habitats of the different snail species (Webbe, 1969).

The development and practical application of molluscicides has been carried out with increasing intensity over the last twenty-five years. In addition to establishing a strong foundation of fact about snail control over a wide range of climatic and environmental conditions, the experience gained over that period, particularly in the last ten years, has provided a wealth of new information regarding the more general problem of pesticide impact on aquatic organisms. A great deal of this information is published in medical journals, which are not normally considered as a possible source of ecological material by freshwater biologists and conservationists. For example, there was no mention of molluscicides and no contribution on the subject of molluscicide evaluation in the otherwise very comprehensive international Seminar on Pesticides in the Environment held at Monkswood Experimental Station of the Nature Conservancy in England, 1965 (*J. appl. Ecol.*, 1966, Vol. 3 Suppl.). For this reason it is considered important in the present overall review to bring as much of this material as possible to the attention of all those engaged in similar problems of pesticides and their effect on freshwater organisms.

The main target of these snail control operations have been certain species of Planorbid snails belonging to the genus *Bulinus* and *Biomphalaria* which usually occur in shallow water of ponds, streams, irrigation ditches and canals, or near the shores of lakes. In South America, the main intermediate hosts are *Australorbis* (recently reclassified as *Biomphalaria*) and *Tropicorbis*, while in the Philippines and Japan the intermediate hosts are amphibious snails, *Oncomelania* spp in which newly hatched snails pass through an aquatic stage which lasts two to three weeks, but in which a large portion of the older snails' active life is spent out of water, on wet surfaces. In general the same chemical methods have been applied and found effective against both aquatic and amphibious snails. However, different species of aquatic snail tend to differ in susceptibility to different molluscicides. In addition, different intermediate host snails prefer different habitats, and this also may determine the extent to which they respond to chemical treatment.

Over the years, a very impressive body of fact has accumulated about the role of different species of snail as intermediate hosts of one or other of the three main types of parasite worm, *Schistosoma*, which are responsible for bilharziasis. As bilharziasis is one of the most important public health problems in many parts of the tropics and subtropics, with the number of infected individuals estimated at 150 million, the stimulation and coordination of measures against this disease has become a major concern of the World Health Organization (W.H.O., 1965). W.H.O.'s role in coordinating research and control work has resulted in an unusually high degree of concerted effort and approach. Since W.H.O. convened the first group of international specialists in 1952, all those engaged have had unusual opportunities for meeting at intervals, exchanging information, and being kept constantly in touch with relevant developments in all countries. One of the latest fruits of this cooperation took the form of a manual on "Snail control in the Prevention of Bilharziasis", a joint effort based on the contributions of twenty-six international specialists (W.H.O., 1965).

In addition to the benefits of regular interchange of information resulting from this high degree of coordination, equally important is the closer approach achieved to the ideal of establishing standards and techniques of evaluation acceptable to all workers. Considering the wide range of experience of workers in different countries and their different opinions and conclusions, an unusually high degree of unanimity has been achieved. On the particular question of snail control this agreement has taken the form of two successive reports on molluscicides in 1961 and 1966 produced by international groups of specialists meeting in Geneva (W.H.O., 1961, 1966). The techniques and standards recommended by these groups have provided the material dealt with later in this chapter. It should be pointed out that even the most representative international meeting cannot allow for complete coverage of all opinions, or represent the opinions of all concerned. In addition, the study of bilharziasis moves rapidly, and the development and field trials with new molluscicides in particular in the last five years has rendered even the snail control manual issued in 1965 out of date in parts. Both of these factors have to be taken into account in attempting to make an up-to-date assessment of the contribution which molluscicide evaluation can make to the general problem of pesticide impact on aquatic life.

In the development of molluscicides over the last twenty to twenty-five years attention has been concentrated on a succession of different chemical compounds in turn, each of which has shown progressive improvements in snail control. Initially copper sulphate was the mainstay of snail control. In most countries this was superseded about 1960 by another water-soluble compound, Sodium pentachlorophenate or Santobrite, which was much more lethal to snails. This in turn gave way to Bayer 73 or Bayluscide — now renamed niclosamine — a low solubility compound which had to be formulated as a wettable powder for field application. More recently, the molluscicide field has become increasingly dominated by N-tritylmorpholine or Frescon — originally designated WL.8008, which is also a low solubility compound which has to be formulated as an emulsifiable concentrate. In addition, there are a number of other compounds which have been tested or used from time to time to deal with specific problems or particular habitats. In general Bayluscide is the molluscicide most generally used in all countries where snail control is practised, but its position as the major molluscicide is being steadily challenged by Frescon.

Copper sulphate. This is the longest established molluscicide which is still in regular use in certain bilharziasis areas such as the Sudan. While toxic to snails it has negligible toxicity to man and domestic animals. Copper sulphate is much affected by the chemical composition of the water, pH in particular, and the highly soluble sulphate is in certain conditions rapidly precipitated to insoluble compounds which deposit on the canal or stream bed. This precipitation is accelerated by organic matter such as that produced by abundant vegetation. For those reasons, the effective field dosage may have to be as high as 30 ppm, a much higher level than suggested by laboratory tests.

In some countries copper sulphate has been applied continuously to canal systems at much lower concentrations — under 1 ppm — after the initial snail infestation has been removed (Sharif el Din and Nagar, 1955; Teesdale *et al.*, 1961). Although the effectiveness of this particular method of control is not fully established, it is worth special attention in view of the fact that the technique of low continuous dosage has been found to be particularly effective with the latest molluscicide — Frescon.

Sodium pentachlorophenate (NaPCP) and *pentachlorophenol* (PCP) are much more toxic to snails than copper sulphate, effective control with NaPCP for example being achieved at applications of the order of 10 ppm for 8 h. In addition NaPCP is more toxic to snail eggs, as well as to *cercariae, i.e.* the free-swimming infective forms of the parasite itself, *Schistosoma*. Sodium pentachlorophenate also possesses herbicidal properties which are useful in helping to eliminate the dense aquatic vegetation much favoured by aquatic snails. Unlike copper sulphate, sodium pentachlorophenate was found to be particularly effective against the amphibious intermediate snail hosts of bilharziasis in Japan and the Philippines. Under the trade name of Santobrite this compound has been widely used for agricultural pests, and has recently attracted public attention in England where its misuse has been responsible for contamination of streams and reported fish kills.

Bayluscide (Bayer 73 or niclosamine) is the molluscicide which has been the most extensively investigated over the last ten years, and a great deal is known about its performance under a wide variety of conditions, and against all the known species of snail host. It has very low solubility in water. Formulation difficulties have made it impossible to produce an effective emulsifiable concentrate — usually the ideal form for application to water bodies — and it is produced as a wettable powder for field use. It has low toxicity to man and mammals, but is very toxic to snails, the effective field dosage ranging from 4–8 ppm. This concentration is also effective against snail eggs. Bayluscide is toxic to most fish at molluscicide dosage, an aspect which is dealt with in more detail in Chapter 2.

N-tritylmorpholine (WL 8oo8, Frescon). This compound is the latest in the armament against the intermediate snail hosts, and is by far the most lethal of any of its precursors. Molluscicidal concentrations range from 0·1 to 0·5 ppm for 1 h exposure, and from 0·01 to 0·05 ppm for 24 h applications. Eggs, however, remain unaffected by normal field dosages. This compound has a very rapid action and has been used effectively in snail control at very short exposures such as 4 ppm for 15 min. Of particular interest is the use of Frescon at low continuous dosage, e.g. 0·025 ppm for thirty days, which has been found particularly effective for treatment of canals and irrigation systems (Crossland, 1967). All treatments appear to have remarkably little effect on other forms of aquatic life, and there is minimal toxic hazard to man and animals (Boyce *et al.*, 1966, 1967). This compound also has a very low solubility in water, and is usually formulated as an emulsifiable concentrate.

Among other molluscicides which have shown promise in one direction or another, but have not been used as extensively in field control as Bayluscide, brief mention must be made of the insoluble copper compounds and their possible value in tropical fish ponds and other snail habitats where fish kill is undesirable (Hopf *et al.*, 1963; Floch *et al.*, 1963, 1964). The aquatic herbicides aqualin (acrolein), gramoxone (paraquat) and reglone (diquat) are of particular interest in that they have bivalent properties. They are not only toxic to snails directly, but they also further reduce snail populations by eliminating aquatic vegetation which forms the natural harbourage of several snail species. Organotin and organolead compounds have been found to be very toxic to both aquatic snails and their eggs, but appear to be highly biocidal to other forms of aquatic life as well (Hopf *et al.*, 1967).

Despite the great increase in snail control activities in nearly all countries where bilharziasis is endemic, and despite the progressive development of more effective molluscicides, the problem of bilharziasis will tend to increase rather than decrease. This is due to the fact that increasing development in water conservation in developing countries, especially in arid zones, tends to increase the extent of potential snail habitats. Of particular importance are irrigation systems because several of the intermediate snail host species find

4*

ideal conditions for proliferation in the variety of canals, irrigation channels and drainage ditches provided. The long established irrigation system of the Nile Delta provides a model of a recurring problem in control of intermediate snail hosts, and similar ideal situations for snail proliferation are likely to be produced in many of the actual or projected expansion of irrigation areas in Africa and the Middle East. For example, there is the Aswan High Dam in Egypt, the Awash Valley scheme in Ethiopia, the Tana River scheme in Kenya, the Hippo Valley Triangle area in Rhodesia and the Limpopo River scheme in Mozambique.

The range of problems encountered in the control of aquatic snails on a large scale is well exemplified by progress in two parts of Africa which have been the centres of particularly intensive ecological studies, namely the Nile Delta and Rhodesia.

The bilharziasis control programme in Egypt is the oldest and most extensive in the world (Farooq, 1967; Dawood *et al.*, 1966). Until the last century a system of basin irrigation was used to exploit the annual overflow of the Nile. In 1821 a system of perennial irrigation was introduced which now extends over the whole of the delta. These innumerable watercourses provide standing water throughout most of the year, and form ideal snail habitats. As most of the canals and drains pass within a short distance of villages, ideal conditions are created for the cycle of transmission between man and intermediate snail host and back to man again. In view of the difficulty of interrupting bilharziasis transmission under such conditions, a special project called Egypt 49 was started in 1961 as a combined operation by the U.A.R. Government, W.H.O. and U.N.I.C.E.F. The main object of this project, which was carried out in an area selected because there was no previous history of molluscicides or organized control measures, was to develop effective and economic methods for the control of bilharziasis. In this area both species of parasitic worms responsible for urinary and intestinal forms of bilharziasis respectively, were present as well as the two species of aquatic snail host, *Bulinus truncatus* and *Biomphalaria alexandrina*.

The two main species of snails show marked differences in ecology. *Bulinus* is more abundant in canals while *Biomphalaria* reaches maximum density in drains (Dazo *et al.*, 1966). Both species are generally more abundant in parts of the habitat with abundant aquatic vegetation. Since its inception a great deal of intensive research has been carried out in this area, not only by the international team members, but also by visiting scientists from many countries. Among the activities which have a special bearing on the general theme of pesticide impact on aquatic organisms, critical studies on snail populations and sampling techniques have been noteworthy (Dazo *et al.*, 1966; Hairston, 1961; Farooq, 1967). By studying data on growth, mortality, egg-laying and population changes, a real attempt has been made to evaluate molluscicide treatment not just in terms of estimated mortality but in terms of the population as a whole, its reproductive rate and its survival at different seasons of the year. Extensive trials were carried out in the Egypt 49 project on evaluating the effect of large scale treatment with such molluscicides as Sodium pentachlorophenate, Bayluscide, the molluscicide/herbicide Aqualin (acrolein) and, more recently, tritylmorpholine (Frescon). Information from these studies is described in more detail in appropriate sections of this book.

The problem of controlling bilharziasis in Rhodesia is closely linked to the great development in water conservation in the last twenty-five years. Before that programme was instituted, rivers and streams had been subject to heavy flushing and flooding during the relatively short season of heavy rain. Following this, because of the quick run-off, rivers and streams soon dried up. After the Second World War a country-wide programme was encouraged to build reservoirs and to construct retaining weirs on rivers on streams. This campaign increased the number of water bodies which were potential snail habitats, and created perennial bodies of surface water in which snails could survive the long dry season from May to September. By 1955 most of the farms in the country had one or more water reservoirs, dams constructed in valleys or weirs across streams (Clarke *et al.*, 1961).

The proliferation of snail populations took place not only among the intermediate host species of human bilharziasis but also in other species of aquatic snail such as *Limnaea natalensis* which is the main intermediate host of bovine fascioliasis in Rhodesia. As far as the farmer was concerned, the latter was probably of even greater and more direct economic importance than the human disease. In 1959 for example, over 50% of livers from cattle slaughtered in central abbatoirs where qualified meat inspection is the rule, were condemned as unfit for human consumption.

The snail control programme in Rhodesia has consequently been a bivalent one, and molluscicide application has been aimed at controlling the intermediate snail hosts of both human bilharziasis and bovine fascioliasis which commonly share the same type of habitat.

In addition to this widely dispersed water conservation on the farmlands, water impoundment and storage has been developed on a vast scale in certain localities. For example, the construction of the Kyle Dam and catchment area led to the development of a lake extending to 24,000 acres. When the lake began to fill in 1960, both snail intermediate hosts of bilharzia — *Biomphalaria pfeifferi* and *Bulinus (Physopsis) globosus* — became established almost immediately in the inundated valleys. The problem of the extension of snail habitats has been further intensified in recent years by the rapid expansion of irrigation systems.

Intensive snail control measures in Rhodesia over the last twenty years have been based on a succession of molluscicides. The original programmes used copper sulphate, then proceeded to sodium pentachlorophenate, Molucid (ICI 24223) and subsequently to Bayluscide and Frescon. As the same group of workers has been closely involved in these successive changes, a very imposing record has been established concerning the problems of molluscicide evaluation under a wide variety of field conditions. (In addition, the ecological work associated with these programmes has contributed greatly to our knowledge about molluscicide impact on freshwater fauna in general, and has thrown considerable light on many general problems — discussed in other parts of the book — concerning evaluation of pesticide impact in general.

At present, control measures are based on snail surveillance and the application of molluscicide in a carefully selected manner, rather than by indiscriminate complete coverage (Shiff and Clarke, 1967). Following an initial blanket treatment of water bodies in the surveillance area in order to reduce the overall population of intermediate snail hosts, the detection and treatment of snail foci is then put into operation. Surveillance entails a detailed examination of water bodies over an area of over 4000 square miles, and is done by means of a scoop designed for snail sampling. Molluscicidal treatment is restricted to focal points where snails are actually recovered. The rationale of snail control by surveillance is based on several considerations which have been studied both in the laboratory and the field. Infected snails for example are more susceptible to molluscicide than healthy ones. If a population of snails reaches dangerous proportions it will easily be discovered by the ranger teams in their normal round. Uninfected snails surviving a surveillance cycle will, if exposed to miracidia, take an average of six weeks prepatent period prior to producing numbers of the infective cercariae. With regard to general ecological effect, as molluscicides are applied to restricted parts of water bodies, and seldom if ever to complete river systems, the interference with non-target freshwater biota is considered to be minimal.

Introduction

In the last ten to fifteen years the development of molluscicides and their evaluation under a wide range of field conditions in tropical and subtropical countries has become increasingly a co-ordinated effort in which the W.H.O. has played a vital role. An essential part of this coordinated effort was the constant search for new and more effective molluscicides. The cooperation of the chemical industry was necessary in order to assist in the preliminary work of screening large numbers of compounds for molluscicidal properties. Research institutes in many countries also cooperated in carrying out further evaluation of candidate molluscicides on local species of vector snail, and under local conditions, in order to establish tolerance limits at different time/concentrations and with different formulations. On the basis of laboratory findings, small field trials in natural habitats were carried out to determine the effect of different treatments under natural conditions. At this stage unfavourable properties of certain molluscicides or certain formulations might be revealed, such as rapid deactivation under intense sunlight or as a result of organic matter, silt, hardness, pH, etc. Finally, the most promising molluscicides were applied in large-scale field trial in which the effect on snail populations over a wide area could be assessed.

In the case of outstanding molluscicides developed in the laboratories of large chemical firms such as Bayer (Bayluscide) and Shell (Frescon) the scientific staff of those firms were able to play an active part in all stages of evaluation from laboratory screening to final field trials, thus ensuring a valuable continuity of techniques and standards, and also ensuring that formulation problems first encountered at the field trial stage of evaluation could be referred back to laboratory investigation with minimum delay. In other cases, however, promising molluscicides revealed by routine screening in the laboratories of chemical companies were dependent for further evaluation on outside institutes and outside research workers, and possibly on entirely different groups of workers for final field assessment.

In view of the coordinated programme, in which so many scientists participated, it was early realized that acceptable standards of testing should be established, so that results obtained by investigators in different countries were strictly comparable, at least as far as the laboratory phase of evaluation was concerned. Suggested standards of testing and criteria were first proposed at an international meeting held in Geneva in 1960 (W.H.O., 1961), and these were completely revised and brought up to date in a similar type of meeting in 1964 (W.H.O., 1966). The interval between these two meetings had been marked by a great intensification in screening and testing new molluscicides, and consequently the participants in the second meeting were able to bring together an impressive mass of experience provided by their own work and that of co-workers in many countries.

It must be emphasized that while fairly strict standardization is desirable, and can be achieved, in the early stages of screening and testing molluscicides in the laboratory, allowance is still made for flexibility at a later stage in laboratory evaluation in order to deal with features peculiar to local species of snails or local conditions. The need for a certain degree of standardization is not so rigid as to discourage or suppress originality on the part of individual workers.

In view of the wide range of habitats used by the different species of aquatic snail, the range of species involved, variations in the composition of the water in different areas, etc., the degree of accord reached on vital criteria of evaluation by all investigators is a noteworthy example of what can be achieved when there is a clearly defined common goal. It is hoped that investigators in less coordinated fields of pesticide evaluation will view their own specialized interests, not as isolated studies, but as a vital part of a much vaster programme urgently in need of a more concerted approach.

Laboratory evaluation

In molluscicide evaluation it has been found convenient to divide laboratory screening into three stages. Firstly, there is preliminary screening, the very first process by which routine screening of new chemicals may provide evidence of molluscicidal activity. The second phase is definitive screening, and it is at this stage that definite standards of testing are laid down explicitly (W.H.O., 1966), both for aquatic snails and amphibious snails. It is essential for example to state the specific identity of the test species, and whether it is from a standard laboratory strain — the usual practice at this stage — or from local field collections. The great majority of tests at this stage are carried out with laboratory colonies of *Biomphalaria glabrata*, which is the main intermediate snail host in the Americas and one specially adaptable to laboratory conditions. The important African species of *Bulinus* and *Biomphalaria* do not readily lend themselves to mass culture. Other particulars deal with the size and nature of the test container, number of test snails, snail age, and preparation of standard dilutions of the molluscicide to be tested. At this stage a standard exposure period of 24 h is adopted, followed by thorough washing and a recovery period in clean water which varies according to the speed of action of specific chemicals.

At each concentration, two containers each with ten snails is considered a test minimum, and a complete test might be expected to require at least eighty snails. On the basis of mortality data after a 24-h exposure LC_{50} and LC_{90} values are computed, and these figures form the basis of comparison between different chemicals or between different species of snail exposed to the same molluscicide. For example, standard tests carried out on *Biomphalaria glabrata* by different investigators regarding N-tritylmorpholine (Boyce *et al.*, 1966; Paulini, 1965) showed that the LC_{50} ranged from 0·025 to 0·05 ppm while the LC_{90} varied from 0·04 to 0·08 ppm. Compared to this the LC_{90} with Bayluscide varied from 0·20 to 0·33 ppm, while with Sodium pentachlorophenate (NaPCP) the range is 0·8 to 3·3 ppm.

Following the definitive screening, the third phase is comprehensive laboratory evaluation which aims at building up a more complete picture of the impact of the molluscicide on aquatic snails. Two important features of this stage are the establishment of time/concentration relationships at a range of exposure periods additional to the standard 24 h, and a comparison of the reactions of different age groups or "stage size arrays" of the test snails. In studying the time/concentration relationships it is recommended that LC_{50} and LC_{90} data should be obtained for exposure periods of 6 h and 1 h in addition to the standard 24 h. In practice many investigators extend this range in order to be able to produce a more accurate regression line relating increased mortality to increased exposure.

In the study of stage-size relationships, four groups of snails are tested separately, that is newly hatched (1 to 24 h old), juveniles (3–5 mm diameter), adolescents (8–10 mm diameter), and mature (13–15 mm diameter). In addition, the reactions of snail eggs are tested at two different stages in development, that is newly laid, and those with incubation nearly complete.

Among the other standard tests at this stage is the chemical stability of the candidate molluscicide in which dilutions of the molluscicide equivalent to the LC_{90} value are set up and allowed to stand. Test snails are added to these solutions for an exposure period of 24 h after intervals of 6 h and one, two, four and eight days. A further point for note at this phase is the behaviour reactions of the snails when exposed to chemical. Most aquatic snails have a protective mechanism by which they withdraw into the shell and secreting a mucous plug over the opening. This provides some protection from low concentrations of chemicals or from very brief contact with higher concentrations. Some chemical molluscicides are also irritant, and the snails may escape from the test dish if not prevented by a or screen. Reactions of this kind have important implications under natural conditions in the field where the air-breathing Pulmonate snails can survive long periods out of water.

The nature of the comprehensive laboratory evaluation phase of molluscicide testing permits a more flexible approach to the question of the effect of length of exposure on the responses of the test snails. Consequently, there is a tendency at this stage for different workers or different research centres to adopt their own convenient standards, particularly with tests involving local snail host species. In Rhodesia, for example, comparison between different species was based mainly on a 5 h exposure followed by a 48 h recovery in clean water (Shiff and Ward, 1966). This was supplemented by tests with shorter exposures of 1 h and of 15 min, and by longer exposures of 24 h, each being followed by a 48 h recovery period. Workers in the neighbouring Union of South Africa adopt a standard exposure of either 1000 min or 24 h (de Villiers, 1965; de Villiers and Grant-Mackenzie, 1963). In laboratory studies on N-tritylmorpholine, a 4 h exposure followed by a 48 h recovery period in clean water is adopted for comparing the reactions of different stage-sizes of snails (Boyce et al., 1967) and these tests are carried out at three temperature ranges (Boyce and Williams, 1967).

In more critical studies on the influence of exposure time, the same group of workers have ranged the exposure period through 1, 2, 4, 8, 17 and 32 h at concentrations of N-tritylmorpholine from 10 ppm down to 0·0075 ppm (Boyce and Williams, 1967). These experiments are of wide interest in that they provide two different sets of data, *viz.* the LC_{50} and LT_{90} values for different exposure periods, and the LT_{50} and LT_{90} values as well, that is the time of exposure in hours sufficient to produce a mortality of 50% and 90% for each concentration respectively. In Puerto Rico the American workers have adhered to an exposure period range of 1, 3, 6 and 24 h (Ritchie et al., 1963, 1964; Ritchie and Fox, 1968).

Out of the mass of information which has emerged from all this work about the precise effect of molluscicides on snails under laboratory conditions there are two aspects of evaluation which have considerable significance in the much wider field of aquatic organisms. Firstly, is the critical study on aquatic snail response according to "stage-size arrays", i.e. according to age and size, and secondly is the penetrating investigation into time/concentration relationships. As part of intensive studies on N-tritylmorpholine (Frescon) the susceptibility of snails was determined as a function of their shell diameter, using snails ranging from the newly hatched — 1 mm diameter — to old specimens 20 mm diameter using *Biomphalaria glabrata* as test species (Boyce *et al.*, 1967b). Snails were exposed for 4 h to a range of five concentrations of molluscicide, and then transferred to clean water. After 24 h the survivors were again transferred to clean water and the total mortalities recorded 48 h after treatment. The relationship of LC_{50} values to shell size is shown in Fig. 13.

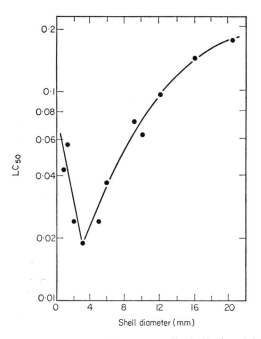

FIG. 13. Relationship of LC_{50} values to snail shell size (after Boyce *et al.*, 1967).

From this figure it is seen that there are two distinct phases in the relationship. As snails grow to a diameter of 3 mm they become more susceptible, but further growth results in a reversal of the correlation, snails becoming less susceptible. In these experiments the weights of snails of each size-group were determined after removal of extraneous water followed by a period of drying on filter paper. When the LC_{50} is corrected to unit body weight, susceptibility is now found to increase continuously as snails grow (Fig. 18), but the tendency for the relationship to change slope at the shell diameter stage of 2–m mm remains.

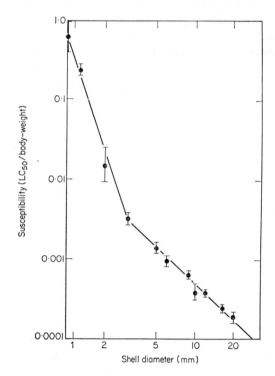

FIG. 14. Relationship of LC_{50} values to snail weight (after Boyce *et al.*, 1967).

This change in slope in the relationship between shell diameter and susceptibility to N-tritylmorpholine may possibly be due to metabolic and physiological changes which take place during a phase of "pre-juvenile growth" extending — in this series of experiments — from hatching up to a period of between fourteen and twenty-one days. These experiments also revealed that although this molluscicide is much less toxic to snail eggs at these short exposure periods used, extension of the exposure period to 24 h inhibits hatching in young embryos, while older embryos develop normally but die after hatching.

The peculiar relationship between size and snail susceptibility shown by N-tritylmorpholine does not necessarily hold for other molluscicides. For example, in the case of Bayluscide (niclosamine) and a related nitrosalicylanilide (PSA) there is a progressive increase in LC$_{90}$ values as snails grow larger. For example, with PSA, the LC$_{90}$ for newly hatched snails is 0·04 ppm as compared to a figure of 0·066 ppm for the 13–15 mm snail group (Ritchie and Fox, 1968).

The question of time/concentration relationships is one that has received considerable attention in the evaluation and field application of molluscicides. It is particularly important in the many cases where the molluscicide has to be applied to the flowing water of canals, irrigation channels and streams where it is essential to know the lethal time of exposure for a given concentration of molluscicide. With many molluscicides, as well as with other pesticides, there is — within a limited range of concentration — a constant relation between the concentration and the time of exposure. In order to produce the same mortality effect on the snails, say 50% and 90%, there is a range of concentrations over which any reduction in exposure time requires an exactly proportional increase in molluscicide concentration. Over this range, lethal concentration × lethal time exposure produces a constant factor for each molluscicide. For this reason most tables summarizing the properties of

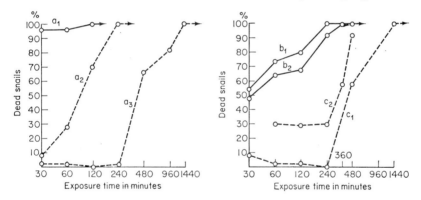

FIG. 15. Relationship between snail mortality and time exposure to copper sulphate, NaPCP and Bayluscide (after Gonnert, 1962). Results obtained by different workers: $a_1 = 10$ ppm Bayer 73; $a_2 = 1$ ppm Bayer 73; $a_3 = 0·8$ ppm Bayer 73; b_1 and $b_2 = 10$ ppm copper sulphate; c_1 and $c_2 = 10$ ppm NaPCP.

molluscicides express the figure for snail toxicity as ppm/h, i.e. parts per million per hour. The relationship between snail mortality and time of exposure for three common molluscicides, copper sulphate, Sodium pentachlorophenate and Bayluscide is shown in Fig. 15 (Gonnert, 1961, 1962). Allowing for the fact that these data have been obtained from different authors, working under different conditions, they clearly reveal the straight line relationship between mortality and time of exposure for different concentrations.

The relationship between concentration and time of exposure is perhaps more effectively presented by plotting concentrations for given mortalities, say 50% and 90%, against time of exposure. When this is done on logarithmic paper a straight line relationship is produced. This has been done with Bayluscide (niclosamine) and with another nitrosalicylanilide compound called PSA (Ritchie and Fox, 1968). The results in Fig. 16 show that with Bayluscide the

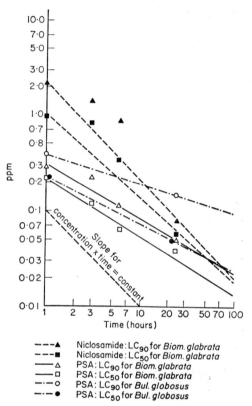

- - -▲	Niclosamide: LC_{90} for *Biom. glabrata*
- - -■	Niclosamide: LC_{50} for *Biom. glabrata*
——▵	PSA: LC_{90} for *Biom. glabrata*
——□	PSA: LC_{50} for *Biom. glabrata*
-·-○	PSA: LC_{90} for *Bul. globosus*
-·-●	PSA: LC_{50} for *Bul. globosus*

FIG. 16. Relationship between concentration and time of exposure for given mortalities of 50% and 90% (after Ritchie and Fox, 1968).

straight line curves for LC_{50} and LC_{90} values are in general nearly parallel to each other and to a base line on which Time × Concentration equals a "constant". However, the results for the 3 h and 6 h exposures are irregular in being considerably off the lines, indicating low efficiency at these particular exposure times. In the case of PSA, flatter curves are produced reflecting the relatively higher efficiency of this compound with shorter exposures. The convergence of the curves for the two compounds indicates that they may be equally effective at long exposures. The curves also reveal slight differences in reaction between the two test species used, *Biomphalaria glabrata* and *Bulinus globosus*.

In the case of N-tritylmorpholine a quite different relationship has been established (Boyce and Williams, 1967). These results have been plotted on logarithmic paper in the same manner as above, *viz.* exposure time against concentration in ppm required to produce 50% and 90% mortality in test snails. It will be seen that this curve (Fig. 17) does not follow the theoretical straight line but appears to

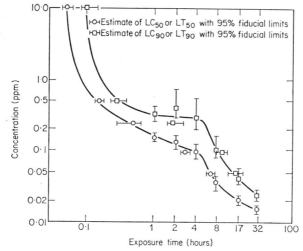

FIG. 17. Relation between exposure time and concentration required to produce 50% and 90% mortality in snails (after Boyce and Williams, 1967).

be two-phased, with a distinct change in relationship at an exposure period of about 4 h. This is particularly marked in the case of LC$_{90}$ data. It should be pointed out that this feature is not necessarily due to the specific properties of the molluscicide in question, as the curve produced in the case of another aquatic snail species, *Bulinus truncatus*, does not show any evidence of being two-phased.

The value of these precise laboratory investigations in terms of field implication are perhaps best brought out if the exposure time is charted against the product of lethal concentration × exposure time (ct), using 90% mortality as a standard as this is closer to the mortality required in field practice (Fig. 18). It will be seen that at the shorter range of exposure the ct value changes rapidly, and indicates — in theory at least — that with exposures of 15 to 30 min the amount of molluscicide needed could be as little as one tenth of that required for longer treatments in running water. With exposures between 4 and 32 h, the ct value is relatively constant and therefore the amount of molluscicide required to control *Biomphalaria glabrata* in a running water system will not vary significantly with exposure time in this range.

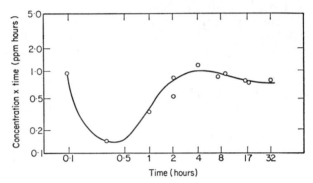

FIG. 18. The product of concentration of N-tritylmorpholine and exposure time required to give 90% mortality of *Australorbis glabratus* (*Biomphalaria glabrata*) (after Boyce and Williams, 1967).

Field evaluation of molluscicides

Owing to the number of variable environmental factors in the field as compared with the laboratory, it is extremely difficult — even in a closely coordinated programme such as that of molluscicide evaluation — to attempt any standardization for procedures at this stage. Even on the vital question of how best to sample snail populations in order to ensure reliable quantitative data, much depends on the species of snail, the nature of the habitat, whether the water is static or flowing, etc. All of these difficulties are by no means peculiar to snail control and are of the kind that crop up continually in quite different areas of pesticide evaluation.

In the case of intermediate snail hosts whose habitat is normally static collections of water such as ponds, dams and lake edges, the phase of comprehensive laboratory evaluation can be followed directly by trials in completely natural habitats in the field. In contrast, where the snail species are more closely associated with rivers, streams and running water in general, and with irrigation systems in particular, there are many advantages in using specially constructed artificial field habitats before attempting the more difficult phase of evaluating the molluscicide in natural water courses or in the entire complex of an irrigation system.

Good examples of field evaluation in static snail habitats have emerged from work in eastern and southern Africa, and in the Middle East. In Tanzania, fish ponds containing natural snail populations proved ideal for comparing the effects of Sodium pentachlorophenate and Bayer 73 (Bayluscide). These ponds measured 75 yd^2 (about 60 m^2) in area and contained abundant vegetation (Webbe, 1961). Snail populations for five weeks prior to treatment were estimated by two methods, firstly by collecting with a hand net for a fixed period of time in a defined portion of each pond, and secondly by the use of snail traps in the form of pieces of hardboard, about 3 ft^2, anchored to float on the surface of the water — assisted by cork floats — near the margin of each pond. These traps not only provided attractive aggregation sites for the snails themselves but also provided a specially attractive substrate for snails to attach their egg masses in numbers of anything up to twenty to thirty egg masses per trap. After addition and mixing in of the calculated dosage of molluscicide, snail population studies were continued until the reappearance of snails in the treated ponds. Snail density was expressed as "total number of snails collected per 10-minute sweep and on the snail traps". Water samples for chemical analysis were taken from each pond immediately after treatment for estimation of the dosage actually applied, and also one, two and seven days later.

These small scale or plot trials showed that with Bayluscide the concentrations applied were quickly reduced to trace amounts, probably due to adsorption by mud and vegetation and to ultraviolet irradiation from the strong sunlight, but that nevertheless the ponds remained free of snails for a period of eight to nine weeks after treatment.

This rapid fall in Bayluscide concentration is by no means a general feature; molluscicide applied to pools with muddy water and with aquatic vegetation in Rhodesia maintained a high level of concentration for 72 h, during which period the sun shone strongly throughout each day (Shiff and Garnett, 1961). The continued activity of Bayluscide after this three-day period was confirmed by introducing test snails in cages made of nylon mosquito gauze, into the pond for 24 h and noting that 100% mortality was produced.

The snail sampling methods used in trials with storage dams in Rhodesia were based on systematic hand searching as well as dredging with a scoop net, the results being presented as "number of snails found per man-half-hour of collecting". Again, a single treatment virtually eliminated the snail population, and repopulation did not take place until about two months afterwards.

In some countries where ponds, swamps and other collections of stagnant water provide ideal habitats for the local snail intermediate hosts, the natural snail densities may still be rather low for conclusive field tests. In Iran, for example, evaluation of the molluscicidal and residual effect of copper compounds was based entirely on the use of caged snails introduced into the treated pond for a period of 24 h immediately after treatment, and again after a period of nine days (Chu *et al.*, 1968).

In areas where the aquatic snails are particularly associated with irrigation systems and with the wide range of habitat provided by irrigation canals and channels, and by drainage channels and ditches, there are many advantages in interposing pilot trials on specially constructed artificial habitats before proceeding to the more complex problem of evaluation in natural sites. In Tanzania, for example, such a series of experimental canals has been specially constructed for field screening of molluscicides (Crossland, 1967). The canals, $3\frac{1}{2}$ ft wide, were designed to support dense populations of several species of snail, including local intermediate host species. Each canal was 560 yd long and 12–18 in deep, graded to produce a water velocity of 220 yd/h (200 m/h). Small measuring weirs enabled accurate measurements of discharge to be made, and mesh screens placed downstream from the weirs prevented re-invasion of snails after each treatment. The particular method of snail sampling adopted in this type of pilot trial was a mud sampling technique (Crossland, 1962) in which a plug of mud, 10·5 cm in diameter was removed from the bottom of the canal with a tube sampler, the mud being washed through a sieve and the snails sorted and counted. The effectiveness of molluscicide treatment is estimated by comparing pre-treatment and post-treatment counts, after making due allowance for mortality in a similar untreated canal. In addition, the technique of caged snails was used to estimate snail mortality at more frequent intervals, and to gain more accurate information about effectiveness at various distances below the point of application of the molluscicide. Estimations of the numbers of snail eggs in the canals were made by collecting by hand for a specified period, and recording the results as numbers collected per man hour. Examination of egg masses in the laboratory enabled further information to be gained regarding the stage of egg development, whether "early" or "late", and also whether egg masses had been killed by particular molluscicide treatments.

The pilot project in question was ideally designed to test the effect of prolonged low dosage of N-tritylmorpholine in order to establish the most effective time/concentration application for field use. For this trial, the period of application selected was sixteen days because field observations in this area had shown that the mean time from egg laying to hatching was twelve and a half days with a maximum of fifteen days, and it could therefore be expected that all snail eggs could hatch and the newly hatched snails be killed before the end of the treatment. A simple automatic dispensing unit (Fig. 19)

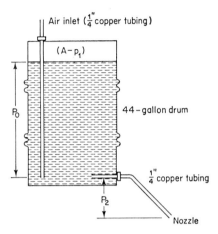

FIG. 19. Diagram of dispenser for continuous low dosage application (after Crossland, 1967).

allowed controlled low concentrations of the molluscicide to be added continuously to the canals over long periods. The results obtained with one of the host snail species — *Biomphalaria pfeifferi* — are shown in Fig. 20 which is particularly illuminating not only in demonstrating the effect of this particular dosing regimen, but also in showing a striking degree of conformity between the data based on snail collection and the data based on caged snails (Fig. 21).

Artificial cement-lined channels have also proved extremely useful as a first stage of field evaluation of molluscicides against snail hosts which live in streams in Puerto Rico (Berrios-Duran *et al.*, 1968). The aim of this work has been the "field-screening" and comparison of several compounds of proved molluscicidal value, rather than an actual "pilot trial" concerned with the complete evaluation of a single molluscicide. The cement-lined channel used in these experiments was $1\frac{1}{2}$ km long and formed the upper part of a stream with muddy bottom and marginal vegetation which formed the natural habitat of the snail in question, *Biomphalaria glabrata*. In this 3 ft wide channel, normal flow of water was confined to a shallow trough 40 cm wide and 12 cm deep. In the channel, forty cages of *Biomphalaria* were exposed at four sites — 5 m, 30 m,

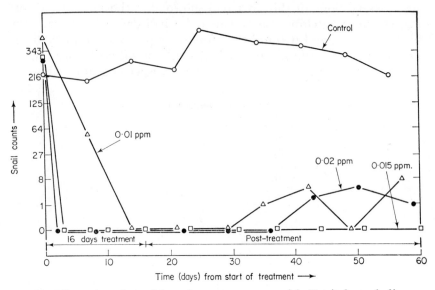

FIG. 20. Effect of prolonged low dosage treatment with N-tritylmorpholine on canal populations of *Biomphalaria pfeifferi* (after Crossland, 1967).

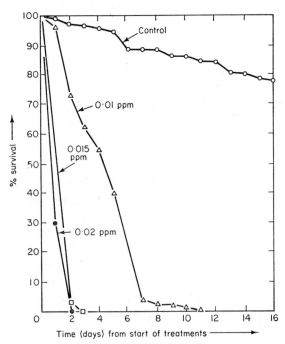

FIG. 21. Effect of prolonged low dosage treatment with N-tritylmorpholine on caged *Biomphalaria pfeifferi* (after Crossland, 1967).

1050 m and 1375 m from the application point. The exposure period corresponded to the application period selected. Observations on recovery in the laboratory were continued until all surviving snails showed normal activity and dead snails could be definitely differentiated by post-mortem discolouration. A careful check on the possible effects of handling laboratory-reared or field snails in the course of these cage tests was carried out in a full routine without using chemical, in order to establish reliable base line data. As this channel contained no mud or vegetation, it is perhaps the closest approach possible to a standardized field screening test for molluscicides.

A further stage in evaluation, using the natural stream habitat with mud, vegetation and exposed to the variable factors such as progressive dilution of chemical likely to occur in nature, could in this particular case be carried out in the lower part of the same water course, using caged laboratory-reared snails. In this way it was possible to work out to what extent molluscicide activity was affected by the progressive dilution of the chemical on the one hand, and the reciprocal increase in exposure on the other hand due to impoundment, marginal vegetation and more rapid water flow at the surface and middle of the stream.

Evaluation large-scale trials in irrigation systems

The pilot trials in Tanzania described above were followed logically by treatment with N-tritylmorpholine (Frescon) to a complete irrigation system in connection with a sugar estate in the same region. This system included not only the main canals, secondary canals and an extensive system of tertiary canals, but also a series of storage reservoirs with a capacity ranging from one to five million ft³ (28,000 m³ to 144,000 m³). The same area had been used a few years previously for field trials with Bayluscide (Crossland, 1962). Evaluation methods therefore had to take into account the nature of the preferred snail habitats within this varied system, and that these habitats occurred both in still water and in association with flowing water. In the reservoirs and secondary canals selected for special study drag scoops were used for sampling the indigenous snail population. At each sampling station a snail count was based on the number collected in three scoops. Each week fifty samples of this kind were taken from one of the reservoirs and from each of the seven canals. In addition, seventy snail cages were set up at intervals throughout the treated area, with special efforts concentrated on the reservoir and on the associated canals. In order to obtain data representing the range of conditions existing in the reservoir itself, twenty cages were placed at intervals around the sides, and five floating cages plus five sunken cages being attached to stakes in deeper water in the main body of the reservoir.

A week before treatment started twenty-five *Biomphalaria pfeifferi* and twenty-five *Bulinus tropicus* were put in each cage. A day or two before the start of the treatment any snails which had died were replaced with live ones, and the cages were subsequently examined at intervals during the course of the treatment. In this large scale trial, the first of its kind, the application time selected was thirty days at 0·025 ppm of molluscicide, although *Biomphalaria* was eliminated from all except a few places after only four to five days, and did not reappear for three months. While the longer application had the advantage of killing snail eggs — which are much less affected by short exposures to higher concentrations — in practice it was concluded that continuous application of molluscicide for five days each month achieved more continuous control.

In the Egypt 49 project in the irrigated delta of the Nile, a large scale field trial for comparing Bayluscide with Sodium pentachlorophenate (NaPCP) was carried out in two areas of 30 km² and 22 km₂, intersected with a variety of watercourses lying between two main irrigation canals. The watercourses included main canals, branch canals and a range of private watercourses consisting of distribution field channels and furrows, collector drains, laterals and sub-laterals, which made up a total length of over 900 km in each of the two areas.

In the evaluation of molluscicide impact, snails were collected by two methods. In the two main canals the drag scoop was used (W.H.O., 1965), thirty scoops being taken every five metres at six collecting stations. In the other watercourses the routine dip-net method was used. The drag scoop is designed to collect all snails in a strip 25 cm wide from the centre of the watercourse to the water's edge. It also collects a sample of the aquatic vegetation on which egg batches of snails may be recovered.

The problems involved in sampling aquatic snail populations have been investigated perhaps more critically than in any other target aquatic organisms (Hairston, 1961; Hairston *et al.*, 1958; Dazo *et al.*, 1966; Ritchie *et al.*, 1962). The question of estimating snail populations at very low densities has also received special attention because the intermediate snail hosts — being hermaphrodite — have immense capacity for rapid build-up of population after near eradication. There seems little doubt that, while many of the conflicting or inconsistent results obtained in molluscicide testing when evaluation extends to the field may be attributed to differences in environmental factors and other local conditions, a great deal of the inconsistency must be attributed to sampling techniques and sampling errors. Snail samples have been recorded in units of area, e.g. "quadrats", "dips" and "scoops", in units of time, e.g. "man hours", or in more or less arbitrary units such as "trap counts". The methods used in some areas are not always suitable in other areas. For example, the methods described for the Egypt 49 project appear to be applicable to conditions in Egypt but unacceptable for general use (W.H.O., 1965). Conversely, evaluation of molluscicide impact by means of cages of laboratory-reared snails has now been widely used in many countries, particularly in rivers, streams and irrigation systems, but has not been used in the Egyptian project.

Many of the basic sampling problems or errors are due to one feature common to many aquatic organisms, namely the patchy distribution and the tendency to aggregate in clumps. In extreme cases, density estimates based on too few samples can give wildly misleading results, and make it almost impossible to arrive at an accurate evaluation of field treatments. The most practicable method of reducing this error is to increase the number of samples. With aquatic snails it is suggested that no less than thirty samples in a habitat are required for the data to be replicable with confidence, and between fifty and one hundred samples would be preferable (Hairston, 1961). Work with both amphibious and aquatic snails has shown that the efficacy of different sampling methods may decline remarkably with increase in the size of each sample. Implicit in the need for a large number of samples therefore is the requirement that the samples be small in size, even though a significant proportion of these samples will inevitably contain no specimens at all.

While some of these essential difficulties in developing sampling procedures for evaluating pesticide impact may prove almost insoluble in many cases, the experience gained in the field of snail control has served a wider function of drawing the attention of field workers to the importance of reporting their data in usable form; this requires that they report not only the total number of snails collected, or the mean number per sample, but also the distribution of snails among samples. Table IV shows the possible arrangement of twenty-four snail specimens among ten samples. Although the mean number per sample is constant, i.e. 2·4, it is evident that another set of ten samples for each kind of distribution would be less and less likely to give the same mean as we proceed from column 1 to column 4, because in ten samples a chance finding or missing of a single clump would make a great difference in the estimate of the mean. The chances of thus incorrectly estimating the mean are best expressed as the variance, which has been included for each column.

TABLE IV

Possible arrangements of twenty-four snail specimens among ten samples (after Hairston, 1961).

Number of snails	Number of samples			
	Nearly uniform (1)	Nearly random (2)	Clumped (3)	Extreme clumping (4)
0	—	1	4	9
1	—	2	2	—
2	6	3	—	—
3	4	2	1	—
4	—	1	1	—
5	—	—	—	—
6	—	1	—	—
7	—	—	1	—
8	—	—	1	—
⋮				
24	—	—	—	1
Mean number per sample	2·4	2·4	2·4	2·4
Variance	0·27	2·9	9·2	57·6

IMPACT OF MOLLUSCICIDES

In most of the countries where molluscicides have been applied regularly for controlling the aquatic snail species which are inter-mediate hosts in human bilharziasis, the overriding public health priorities have perhaps discouraged academic studies on the effect of such treatments on other biota. Apart from observations on fish (Chapter 2, p. 63), few systematic investigations have been carried out on other fauna or on invertebrates. However, one or two of these isolated studies have been carried out by competent freshwater biolo-gists and are noteworthy contributions to the general problem of evaluating pesticide impact.

In Rhodesia, as in many other countries with a long history of snail control operations, the original molluscicide of choice — water soluble copper sulphate — has been replaced in turn by the water soluble Sodium pentachlorophenate, and later by Bayluscide (niclosamide) which is practically insoluble in water and requires formulation. More recently tritylmorpholine or Frescon has been added to this armament.

Snail control in Rhodesia is based on a large scale blanket application of molluscicide covering all natural waters and artificial lakes within a prescribed area (Clarke *et al.*, 1961). This is followed by focal treatment, and in some cases several re-applications may be necessary.

In order to study the short term effects of molluscicides on small biologically stable ponds, a series of small fish ponds 4 × 4 m in area of uniform composition were selected and isolated from each other (Shiff and Garnet, 1961). Six stations were marked in each pond, and 2 l samples of water were collected regularly. One sample of 1 l was taken from the surface to a depth of approximately 10 cm, and 1 l from a depth of approximately 30 cm deeper. The samples were filtered through a fine silk plankton net and the residues preserved for examination. Sampling was carried out in the morning between 10.30 and 11.30 in order to obviate population differences due to diurnal fluctuations. One of the ponds was retained as control, while the other three were treated respectively with copper sulphate at 20 ppm, sodium pentachlorophenate at 5 ppm and Bayluscide at 1 ppm of 70% wettable powder. The results obtained over a period of thirty days following treatment are shown in Fig. 22.

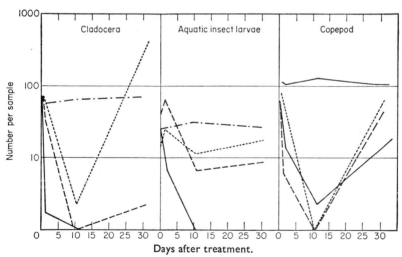

FIG. 22. Fluctuations in numbers of microfauna in ponds treated with different molluscicides, *viz.* copper sulphate 20 ppm, NaPCP at 5 ppm and Bayer 73 (Bayluscide) at 1 ppm (after Shiff and Garnett, 1961). — pond 1 treated with copper sulphate, 20 ppm; – – – pond 2 treated with NaPCP, 5 ppm; - - - pond 3 treated with Bayer 73, 1 ppm; – · – · pond 4 untreated control.

The immediate effect of both sodium pentachlorophenate and copper sulphate is to reduce the overall population of microfauna and microflora very considerably, while only a slight reaction is apparent in the pond treated with Bayluscide. In all ponds except that treated with copper sulphate, repopulation took place within the period of observation.

Cladocera are very susceptible to the effects of molluscicides. In the case of copper sulphate they appear to be completely eliminated, none being recorded after ten days. Sodium pentachlorophenate also produces a very sharp reduction followed by a slow rate of recovery. In the case of Bayluscide the initial short reduction is followed by an enormous increase in population.

This extreme sensitivity of Cladocera — *Daphnia* and its allies — to certain chemicals, as compared with the much greater tolerance on the part of Copepods and Ostracods, is also strikingly evident in the case of the organophosphorus insecticide Baytex(fenthion). Treatment of a pond with Baytex at 0·2 lb per acre ($\equiv 0\cdot025$ ppm) for midge control, produced a complete disappearance of Cladocera from the treated pond, and they did not become re-established for about five months. Under similar exposure Copepods and Ostracods were not affected (Patterson and von Windeguth, 1964; Ruber, 1963).

To return to the molluscicide experiment, copper sulphate also has a severe effect on aquatic insect larvae, and also produces a short-term reduction in Copepods and their nauplii larvae as well as on Ostracods.

In contrast to the distinct effects produced by these three molluscicides on non-target organisms it appears that the most recent, and possibly most effective molluscicide, N-tritylmorpholine or Frescon has very little environmental effect on fauna other than snails (Boyce *et al.*, 1967). Samples of water taken from a dam before and one week after treatment with 0·2 ppm tritylmorpholine showed no significant difference in the number of microfauna and flora (Boyce *et al.*, 1966; Shiff, 1966), the range of organisms including the Cladocera which were so sensitive to the effects of the other three molluscicides.

CHAPTER 5

INSECTS OF PUBLIC HEALTH IMPORTANCE: EVALUATION OF CHEMICAL CONTROL DIRECTED AGAINST AQUATIC STAGES

CHEMICAL CONTROL OF MOSQUITO LARVAE

The control of mosquitoes by destruction of larvae in their breeding places has been practised in many parts of the world since the beginning of the century, and is still being vigorously pursued in many places.

For the purpose of this general review it would be useful to make an arbitrary distinction between three main types of water body involved in mosquito control. Firstly, there is a very wide range of water type, ponds, ditches, marshes, rice fields, grassy river edges, etc., favoured by different species of anopheline mosquito, including the vectors of malaria. Despite this variety of habitat, the majority of these water types contain clear unpolluted water. The widespread application of larvicide to these breeding places, originally from the ground, but latterly by aerial application as well, provides perhaps the earliest example of repeated mass application of chemical to the natural freshwater environment.

In contrast to the extent and varieties of such breeding places of anopheline mosquitoes in general, is the preference of larvae of several species of *Aedes* — vector of urban yellow fever and other virus diseases — for the water in small containers in and around human habitations. Favourite sites are provided by storage jars and the water collections in various domestic utensils, including tins and broken bottles thrown out as refuse. In the chemical control of mosquito breeding in such domestic sites, strict precautions are essential to ensure that any larvicide added to containers of potential drinking or cooking water must be absolutely free of any toxic hazard to the householders.

A third arbitrary category is provided by the urban and suburban mosquito breeding places specially suited for *Culex pipiens fatigans*, the most widespread vector of filariasis in tropical towns and townships. Many of these water collections consist of sullage water or are in other ways heavily contaminated. These water collections are of no particular domestic use, and accordingly there is little restriction

5+

on the type of chemical used in control. The high organic content of such water collections has a strong de-activating effect on many chemical larvicides and their formulations, and this presents a special problem in control.

From the point of view of impact of pesticide treatment on wildlife and non-target freshwater fauna, the latter two categories are of negligible importance. In contrast, the widespread application of larvicide over extensive areas of swamp and marshland — for controlling not only certain anopheline mosquitoes, but also mass breeding of species of *Aedes* which constitute serious biting pests — must be considered a possible hazard to freshwater fish and non-target invertebrates in the sprayed areas.

Interest in larvicidal control of mosquito breeding, and the extent to which larvicides have been employed in different countries, has passed through many different phases in its history. Up till the Second World War, control of mosquito pests, and of disease vectors in particular was based almost entirely on larvicides (in addition to such mechanical methods of habitat control or eradication as drainage, filling, water control, etc.) the larvicides of choice being a range of petroleum oils and Paris Green (copper acetoarsenite) (Soper, 1966). In the few years prior to the war, however, increasing emphasis was placed on chemical attack on adult mosquitoes, particularly in their indoor resting places in human habitations and animal shelters. Pyrethrum was the initial choice for house spraying with insecticide, but in the early 1940s this practice rapidly gave way to the organochlorine compounds DDT, gamma BHC and dieldrin. Side by side with the early successes of DDT house spraying, there was a corresponding fall off in use of larvicides. Where larviciding was continued, it was based essentially on DDT and its allies. In the course of the following ten to fifteen years, the use of larvicides decreased still further, and — with one or two localized exceptions — this method of mosquito control played only a minor part in the Global Malaria Eradication Program from about 1955 onwards.

In the last year or two however there has been a renewed interest in chemical control of mosquito larvae (Pal and Gratz, 1968; Fontaine, 1968; Mulla, 1967). This renewed interest has been due to one or other of several factors. In some areas or regions, continuous conventional measures against adult mosquitoes alone have reduced malaria transmission but have failed to eliminate it completely. This may be due to the development of resistance to the insecticide used on the part of the mosquito, or it may be due to the fact that a significant proportion of the mosquito population feeds outdoors or rests outdoors or both, and thus escapes the full impact of chemical treatment of the inner walls and surfaces of habitations. In Jordan for example, where such difficulties were encountered, both larviciding and adulticiding were reinstated in 1965 with the result that by 1967 only twenty-seven malaria cases — none of which were indigenous — were reported.

Larviciding is once more recognized as a most reliable way of treating mosquito breeding in dense urban areas. This applies particularly to mosquito vectors such as *Culex pipiens fatigans* which from an early phase proved to be highly resistant to conventional house spraying with DDT as well as to several successive chemicals. Larviciding is also regarded as the most effective way of dealing with mosquitoes responsible for outbreaks of urban malaria, for example in Karachi in 1967.

Renewed interest in the application of mosquito larvicides has also been aroused by the continued supply of new synthetic insecticides being produced by the chemical industry, many of which have very high toxicity to mosquito larvae, combined with low mammalian toxicity. In addition, new and more effective methods of applying larvicide from aircraft have been developed, and costs have been greatly reduced by the technique of Ultra Low Volume application (U.L.V.) in which the larvicide is applied from the air in concentrated form in oil solution rather than as a formulation which requires mixing with a bulky volume of water before application.

A further incentive to increased interest in larvicides is due to the fact that in several parts of the world — but not all — mosquitoes have developed resistance to the principal insecticides used, starting with DDT and dieldrin and progressing to several of the organophosphorus compounds which have been used to replace these. While resistance, or increased tolerance, also develops on the part of the larva it is less likely to reach such a degree as to render larvicide treatment completely ineffective.

In view of the world-wide problem, continuous work is going on in several research centres on the screening and testing of new candidate mosquito larvicides. This is a collaborative effort coordinated by the World Health Organization in which the chemical industry provides the new or promising compounds for testing by established research centres. Larvicides which emerge from this initial stage of screening and laboratory testing against three main types of mosquito — *Anopheles, Culex* and *Aedes* — are selected for tests in the field against different types of locally important mosquito under natural conditions (Mulla *et al.*, 1964; Metcalf *et al.*, 1969).

One particular group of synthetic organic pesticides which has been very thoroughly studied is the organophosphorus one, outstanding representatives being Baytex (fenthion), Dursban and Abate. With the increasingly wide use of these compounds as mosquito larvicides, it has been estimated that the average life expectancy of a new OP insecticide is not more than four years (Mulla, 1966b).

Intensification of this resistance problem may well redirect interest to petroleum oils, to which insecticide resistance is unknown, to more scientific and discriminative techniques, or to the development of entirely new compounds which have modes of action other than that of the present insecticides. Even Paris Green (copper acetoarsenite) which was once the mainstay of malaria control and which was shelved for many years with the advent of DDT, has been once more reinstated as an effective larvicide against salt-marsh mosquitoes in Florida (Nat. Comm. Dis. Centre, 1967).

In this intensified testing and evaluation of new chemical methods for controlling mosquito larvae, there is increasing appreciation of the need to consider the environmental aspects of larviciding. An increasing number of reports dealing with this aspect are appearing for example in the annual proceedings of two of the largest mosquito control agencies in the U.S.A., if not in the world, namely the California Mosquito Control Association, and the New Jersey Mosquito Extermination Association. Some of these collateral investigations on fish and non-target invertebrates have provided the first indication about the ecological impact of many organophosphorus compounds from parathion onwards. In the California Mosquito Control Program, OP compounds are widely used for the elimination of mosquito larval populations. The average number of treatments per year is four, but in some areas up to ten may be necessary. Parathion has been widely used for this purpose at the rate of 1 lb/acre. Parathion residues have been recovered from water, mud, fish and plants, and the effects on aquatic life have been evaluated both in the laboratory and in the field (Mulla et al., 1966; Mulla, 1966a).

In the helicopter application of two more recent OP larvicides, Dursban and Abate, crude observations made on the effect on non-target organisms indicated that in the case of Dursban there was no obvious effect at 0·001 to 0·005 lb/acre. However, in the range of 0·01 to 0·02 lb/acre, there was a noticeable die-off of practically all arthropods observed. Abate on the other hand had no noticeable effect on non-target organisms at any of the applications tested (Moore and Breeland, 1967).

These environmental studies on the impact of the new mosquito larvicides are described in more detail in Chapter 6. Suffice to say at the moment that all mosquito control agencies are becoming increasingly conscious of the need to use new larvicides in such a way

as to achieve the main objective of reducing mosquito larval populations while at the same time ensuring the minimal adverse effect
against non-target organisms or on the habitat itself (Travis *et al.*,
1968). In one particular testing laboratory in the United States, 100–
150 new compounds are screened annually for toxicity to mosquito
larvae (McDuffie and Weidhaas, 1967). Out of this programme, or
others similarly orientated, may one day emerge the ideal selective,
non-persistent larvicide, whose impact will be strictly limited to the
mosquito larvae in question.

An integral part of the use and evaluation of new chemical larvicides is to check the susceptibility levels from time to time by means
of a standard W.H.O. test. Marked increase in tolerance on the part
of natural populations of mosquito larvae can be measured in this
way, and it is often possible to tell in advance if this decreased susceptibility is likely to develop into a degree of resistance which would
render the particular larvicide no longer effective against mosquito
populations in that area (Womeldorf *et al.*, 1966).

The methods of applying new larvicides are the subject of continuous investigation, not only with a view to increasing efficiency,
but also in cutting costs. One of the most significant of these trends
is the increasing use of the Ultra Low Volume method of applying
insecticide concentrates themselves rather than previously prepared
aqueous dilutions. As mentioned earlier this has been particularly
advantageous in aerial application (Stevens and Stroud, 1967; Mount
and Lofgren, 1967; Knapp and Gayle, 1967; Mulhern, 1968). These
concentrates or near concentrates which have only oil diluents and
emulsifier added, can be applied at the rate of 6–8 fluid oz/acre as
compared with the more conventional 0·5 gal/acre required with
water-mixed formulations.

The application of larvicide concentrates has also been developed
in another direction to deal with specific situations which are very
familiar to workers in the entirely different field of aquatic snail
control, namely, continuous low dosage of pesticide to irrigation
water. In California, a problem is presented by mosquito (*Aedes* sp)
breeding in irrigated pastures. Under certain conditions larvicide
applied from aircraft fails to penetrate the plant canopy, or produces
undesirable drift and contamination of protected areas. In order to
deal with this, the method evolved is to apply the insecticide in the
form of an emulsifiable concentrate without dilution by continuous
drip to the water emerging from the irrigation well (Mulla *et al.*,
1969). On the basis of accurate data about the output of the well
supplying the irrigation water, the larvicide can be applied on an
accurate parts-per-million basis. As a result accurate comparison can

be made between different larvicides, both as to larval control and to effective distance of carriage. From the point of view of environmental contamination, the drip application method has the advantage of strictly confining the larvicide to the habitat requiring treatment. This method is also more effective in killing the more sensitive newly hatched larvae, whereas most current techniques of larvicide application are aimed at the late instars which in general are more tolerant.

The accuracy with which larvicide can be applied in this direct drip technique is in marked contrast to variables inherent in aerial application of insecticide. While insecticide may be dispensed from the aircraft at a carefully measured rate of say 1 lb/acre or, in the case of swathe treatment of streams, in terms of gallons per flight mile, there are many difficulties in the way of translating this into terms of parts per million in the aquatic habitat. For example, it has been calculated that the application of DDT at 1 lb/acre over water would give a concentration of 0·37 ppm if the water were 1 ft deep, and 0·023 ppm if the water were 16 ft deep. This assumes of course that the chemical will be evenly distributed and that all of it will go into solution. In order to find out what degree of agreement there is between the real and the estimated concentration in the water of salt-marshes, use has been made of the reactions of freshwater copepods (Ruber, 1962). Aerial application of DDT at 1 lb/ acre produced no significant mortality of copepods even though the water was rarely more than 18 in deep. In some marshes, application at 2 lb/acre also had no effect on copepod populations. However, laboratory tests showed that copepods are very sensitive to DDT concentrations down to 0·04 ppm, i.e. at almost one tenth of the concentration which in theory would be reached by 1 lb/acre treatment. It is clear that the actual concentration achieved falls far short of the theoretical figure, and that there must be considerable loss of DDT. This discrepancy may be due to several factors of which the most important would appear to be — in such salt marsh environments at least — colloidal adsorption of DDT.

EVALUATION OF MOSQUITO LARVICIDES

The approach to the question of evaluating mosquito larvicides at laboratory level in the last ten or twelve years has been strongly influenced by the fact that certain aspects of larval susceptibility to insecticides have become of sufficient international concern to necessitate some uniformity in test methods and criteria. The first reports on the resistance of adults of certain species of mosquito to the dominant insecticides used in the Global Malaria Eradication Program, DDT and dieldrin, led to the establishing of standard tests for measuring levels of susceptibility and resistance in adult mosquitoes. In order to provide a more complete picture of the impact of this insecticide pressure on mosquito populations as a whole, standard procedures for mosquito larvae were also laid down at an early stage on the basis of existing empirical screening tests for larvicides (W.H.O., 1958, 1963).

These methods and criteria have formed the basis of much of the subsequent work on the laboratory screening and evaluation of new larvicides. The original test method, as recommended by the W.H.O., was drawn up by a group of specialists who met in Geneva and who — after an examination of different current practices and criteria used in different countries — were able to agree on a completely standard procedure acceptable to all concerned. In order to further ensure complete uniformity of test methods, standard test kits were issued which included ready made-up concentrations of each of the three insecticides involved at that time, namely DDT (p, p', isomer), gamma-BHC or lindane (pure gamma isomer) and dieldrin (HEOD) in ethanol. Exact instructions were laid down for each step, and standard report forms as well as log-probability paper for plotting regression lines were provided.

It was emphasized that the test was designed primarily to establish base-lines on susceptibility to the insecticides, and to measure changes in level brought about by insecticide pressure in the field. The test was not necessarily designed to indicate relative effectiveness in the field.

The salient feature of the standard test was that lots of 20–25 third or early fourth instar larvae are distributed in each of twelve small beakers containing 25 ml of water. Into each of twelve glass vessels (e.g. 500 ml beakers) 225 ml of water is placed. Test concentrations are prepared by adding 1 ml of the appropriate standard insecticide solution under the surface of the water in each of the glass vessels and stirring vigorously for 30 sec. There are two replicates at each concentration, and two control replicates. Within 15–30 min of preparing the test solutions, the mosquito larvae are added by tipping the contents of the small beakers into the vessels. Mortality counts are made after 24 h. Provided that not less than three mortality counts between 10% and 90% have been obtained, a dosage-mortality regression line can be plotted from the data obtained, and the LC_{50} and LC_{90} figures read from the graph. If the mortality in controls is between 5% and 20%, but not more, the percentage mortality can be corrected by a standard procedure.

At the time these standard procedures were being laid down, larval control itself was considered to have limited application in antimalaria campaigns. Since that time the failure of conventional anti-adult mosquito control measures alone to eliminate malaria transmission in certain refractory areas, combined with the rapid development in the field of organophosphorus (OP), carbamates and other insecticides, has revived the possibility of control by means of larvicides and led to the development of an expanding programme for the screening and evaluation of new chemical larvicides.

In these evaluation programmes, the standard routine adopted by different workers or different research centres tends to differ in details, but not in principle, from the original W.H.O. susceptibility test. For example, in the Riverside Laboratories of the University of California, the routine established prior to the W.H.O. test, and retained since then, differs slightly in that it employs 25 fourth instar larvae — with no third instars — tested in 100 ml of test solution — not 250 ml, and the technical material is dissolved in acetone rather than ethanol (Mulla, 1961; Mulla et al., 1964; Mulla et al, 1966; Metcalf et al., 1969). As in the W.H.O. test, the results are expressed in LC_{50} and LC_{90} values in parts per million after a 24 h exposure.

Routine tests of this kind were among the first to reveal the powerful larvicidal action of such new organophosphorus compounds as Dursban and Abate. In addition, these routine tests were normally carried out on three test species of mosquito, *Anopheles, Culex* and *Aedes*, and it soon became clear that — quite apart from any question of resistant strains — larvae of these three indicator species were liable to differ markedly in their reaction to the same compound. Abate for example was found to be fourteen times as active (at LC_{90} level) against the larvae of *Culex pipiens quinquefasciatus* as against *Anopheles freeborni* (Mulla et al., 1966).

While it is convenient to use uniform fourth instar larvae for such screening tests, a critical enquiry into the relative susceptibility of the earlier instars revealed that differences in reaction did exist but that there appeared to be no uniform pattern, at least with the species tested in this case, *Culex p. fatigans*. The first instar larvae were more susceptible than the fourth instar larvae to the majority of the wide range of insecticides tested, but in the case of DDT the reactions were similar (Mulla, 1961).

While the general principles of the W.H.O. test form the basis of most large scale larvicide screening programmes, slightly different criteria have been used to calculate the mortality levels from 90% upwards. On the one hand the conventional LC_{50} and LC_{90} values are retained in the extensive programme for evaluating new larvicides against salt-marsh mosquitoes on the Mediterranean coast of southern France (Gras, 1966; Gras and Rioux, 1969). On the other hand some programmes in the United States continue to use the LC_{50}, but have preferred to replace the LC_{90} either with an LC_{95} value (Nat. Comm. Dis. Centre, 1967; Metcalf et al., 1969) or an LC_{100} value (Keppler et al., 1965; Klassen et al., 1964). In these latter research centres the screening and evaluation programme is closely geared to the practical situation in which mosquito populations have become resistant not only to the chlorinated hydrocarbons, but also to such OP compounds as malathion, parathion and methyl parathion. The LC_{95} and LC_{100} values have therefore been adopted in order that laboratory data may be more directly translated into terms of field dosage adequate for effective larval control. In screening large numbers of candidate chemicals it has been found convenient to use the LC_{95} value as an arbitrary standard for selection or rejection, only those compounds with an LC_{95} of less than 1 ppm being recommended for further evaluation at advanced stages.

As the LC_{50} value is one that is common to all reports on larvicide screening it has the advantage that it can be used to make direct comparisons between results obtained by different groups of workers. On this basis, the range in toxicity of various larvicides is well brought out in the following table which refers to larvae of *Anopheles albimanus* (Metcalf et al., 1969), the chemicals being listed in order of decreasing toxicity.

TABLE V

Compound	Larval LC_{50} in ppm
Dursban	0·006
Abate	0·011
Fenitrothion	0·012
DDT	0·015
Fenthion	0·016
Bromophos	0·034
Decapthon	0·092
Malathion	0·100
Arprocarb	0·230
Carbamult	0·300

In some laboratories it has been found convenient to present — in addition to the LC_{50} and LC_{90} data — the toxicity levels relative to those of Dursban which has been adopted as a suitable base in view of the fact that in general it is the most toxic of known larvicides (Lofgren et al., 1967).

5*

The reasonably close accord between the test procedures used by different authorities in evaluating new chemical larvicides has undoubtedly been influenced by W.H.O.'s standardization of the original larval susceptibility tests. While the value of these tests in establishing relative toxicity levels of a wide range of new compounds is now well established and accepted, one of its most important original objectives has come in for some criticism, namely the validity of the test with regard to DDT itself. Earlier it was noted how the vagaries of DDT and the reactions it produces made it unacceptable as a standard reference pesticide in fish toxicity studies. Many of these peculiar qualities of DDT in high dilution or suspension in water are equally applicable to the standard larvicide test.

One of the difficulties is that although for most practical purposes DDT is considered as insoluble in water, this insolubility is not absolute, and is still high enough — 0·0374 ppm at 25°C — to come within the low range of concentrations used in susceptibility tests. In accordance with this it has been found that at 0·01 ppm — a concentration used in routine tests — no settling of DDT takes place, but does so at the 1·0 ppm level (Bowman et al., 1959). Over the wide range of test concentrations likely to be used therefore, the small volume of solution of DDT in acetone or ethanol added to the greater volume of water in the test container produces a suspension of DDT. Settling of DDT from this suspension, or its deposition on the inner walls of glass or paper containers, may significantly reduce the amount of DDT in suspension, and introduce errors into the test.

In addition, over a period of 24 h, there may be a considerable loss of DDT from suspension by volatilization or codistillation (Weidhaas, et al., 1959). This loss would be further accentuated if the test containers were aerated during the exposure period. This is not normally necessary with mosquito larvae, but has been used in similar types of laboratory tests on more sensitive non-target stream dwelling invertebrates.

There seems little doubt that many of the variations and discrepancies experienced in these tests can be attributed to the uncertain degree and action of these physical factors, included among which is the fact that the size of the test container and the nature of its material, glass or paper cups, may affect the degree of deposition of DDT. In addition, those variables tend to exert a differential effect on the larvae of different types of mosquito, introducing further possibilities of error (Thomas, 1965). This may be due to the fact that the time/concentration relationship determining mortality may follow a different course in different species, or it may be due to behavioural differences on the part of the larvae during the 24 h exposure period. Some larvae, such as those of *Aedes* for example, tend to browse around the inner surfaces of the container rather than on the surface like *Anopheles,* and in this way may be more liable to ingest DDT deposited from suspension (Schmidt and Weidhaas, 1959; Weidhaas and Schmidt, 1966; Busvine, 1968).

Apart from the variables due to the physical state of the DDT itself in suspension, some workers have expressed dissatisfaction with the test procedure and the criteria of mortality (Doby and Corbeau, 1962). By basing the all-important mortality data on counts of dead and live larvae at the end of the standard 24 h exposure period, a degree of error and personal bias is introduced by the fact that after that comparatively short time the status of "moribund" larvae is an uncertain one. Errors can be made both by grouping these along with the number which are definitely dead, or by discounting them from the mortality total. In order to minimize this as well as to allow for slow or delayed action on the part of the larvicide — particularly with strains which have developed some resistance to DDT — it is suggested that observation be continued for several days after the 24 h exposure period.

One of the earlier queries made on the W.H.O. standard test pointed to its limitations in the case of the fast-growing larvae of tropical mosquitoes (Elliott, 1958). The larvae of many tropical mosquitoes develop very rapidly; the larval and pupal development may be complete in seven days. The fourth instar itself may last only 48 h, and the third instar 24 h or even less. When such rapidly growing larvae are exposed for a period of 24 h, it is considered that the test imposes starvation as well as toxic effects. In order to obviate this and to reduce starvation effects to a minimum it was recommended that an exposure period of 1 h would be adequate followed by a further 5 h in insecticide-free water. This method has proved to be a useful supplement to the W.H.O. test in studies carried out in Rangoon, Burma, on the susceptibility of *Culex pigiens fatigans* larvae to chlorinated hydrocarbon insecticides (Rosen, 1967). In keeping with the shorter exposure of 1 h, this method employs higher concentrations of insecticide to establish LC_{50} and LC_{90} levels and to deal with resistant strains, and it is at these higher concentrations that the problem of deposition of DDT from suspension is likely to be aggravated, introducing a further variable in turn (Busvine, 1968).

ADVANCED AND FIELD EVALUATION OF MOSQUITO LARVICIDES

As a useful intermediate between the laboratory phase of testing, and evaluation in the completely natural habitat, it has been found convenient in mosquito larvicide evaluation to interpose plot or container tests. The nature of these intermediate tests and the extent to which they forecast ultimate conditions in the field is influenced by the type of mosquito involved and its breeding habits.

In the case of the classic vector of urban yellow fever, *Aedes aegypti*, whose larvae normally live in a variety of domestic and peridomestic collections of clean water, it is possible to interpose a simulated field test which must give a close approximation to natural conditions by using standard containers of the type which would normally be utilized by this mosquito. For this purpose 55 gal steel drums have been assembled as test containers, each containing 50 gal of water treated with a range of concentrations of different compounds and formulations. Approximately 50 third instar larvae of a uniform strain of *Aedes aegypti* were placed weekly in each drum, and observed at 24 h intervals for mortality. The ability of the treatment to kill within 24 h or to prevent completion of the life cycle was used as a measure of the persistence of the treatment (Brooks and Schoof, 1965; Brooks *et al.*, 1966).

Extended tests of this kind confirmed the great value of the OP compound Abate for treatments of this kind involving water collections or types of water likely to be used for drinking purposes, either by man or domestic animals. Abate has an unusually low mammalian toxicity and its use at 1 ppm in drinking water is approved by the U.S. Public Health Authorities. In bird baths or animal watering devices it can be used at 10–15 ppm (Nat. Comm. Dis. Centre, 1967). The use of standard containers — in the form of concrete water storage jars — has also been used to evaluate new compounds and formulations against the larvae of *Aedes aegypti* in Thailand (Lofgren *et al.*, 1967).

Another type of semi-field test which is also a very close approximation to trials in a completely natural habitat is provided by the use of experimental field plots in California. In studies on the control of the nuisance mosquito *Culex tarsalis*, field plots of 1/16 and 1/32 acre were used and filled to a depth of 8–10 in with canal water. These were treated at precise concentrations, and the effect was evaluated by pre-treatment and post-treatment counts of fourth instar larvae per 10–20 dips per plot, the post-treatment counts being taken 24 h after treatment (Mulla *et al.*, 1964; Mulla *et al.*, 1966).

The value of comparing small plots as a guide to ultimate impact of mosquito larvae has also become evident in investigations carried out in connection with the New Jersey mosquito extermination campaign, mainly directed against the salt-marsh mosquito *Aedes sollicitans*. Attempts to evaluate accurately the effect of mosquito larvicide applied over a large area had met with various difficulties among which was a certain degree of patchiness in distribution of the chemical (Ferrigno *et al.*, 1964). In order to save time and man-power it was found more convenient to restrict tests to small plots $\frac{1}{4}$ acre in area, to which different larvicides and larvicide formula-tions could be applied at accurate dosage. In these plots effects of treatment were based on the average number of *Aedes sollicitans* per ten dips.

The presentation of results obtained is shown below in Table VI (Ruber and Ferrigno, 1964).

TABLE VI

Average number of *Aedes sollicitans* per ten dips in plots treated with three toxicants (simplified after Ruber and Ferrigno, 1964).

Treatment	Pre-application		Post-application Days after treatment					
	Plot for treatment	Control	1		10		45	
			Treated	Control	Treated	Control	Treated	Control
DDT 1 lb/acre	26	27	0	8	0	2	2	3
Endrin 0·5 lb/acre	38	27	0·4	2	0·12	7	0·01	2
Baytex 1·0 lb/acre	39	28	0	6	0	3	0·34	3

In the majority of larvicide control experiments in the field this conventional sampling by periodic dipping for larvae forms the basis for comparison between different field treatments, and is probably a reasonably accurate guide for most practical purposes. As in many other similar types of sampling method for aquatic invertebrates its accuracy will depend on the number of samples and the variation between samples. In practice the usefulness of these unsophisticated methods of larval sampling has seldom been seriously questioned ex-cept on the comparatively rare occasions when the observer is anxious to establish whether larval populations have actually been eliminated. Critical investigations of this kind made in Sardinia in one of the earliest malaria eradication projects based on the use of DDT both as an adulticide and larvicide, revealed that specific differences —

even among anopheline mosquitoes themselves — could determine the relative efficiency of this dipping method under different conditions. *Anopheles* larvae spend a great part of the time at the surface of the water, but tend to dive to the bottom when disturbed. Some species tend to stay down for longer intervals after being disturbed and are therefore less likely to be caught by surface scooping with a pan or dipper.

When patchy distribution of larvae in natural habitats makes the conventional type of evaluation tedious and time consuming, it has been found useful on occasions to use field bioassay in which known numbers of mosquito larvae are exposed in open floating cages made for example by means of a net bag suspended in the water from a floating ring of cork (Schober, 1967).

LARVICIDAL CONTROL OF BLACKFLY (SIMULIUM) LARVAE

The control methods which have long been used for reducing or eliminating larval populations of *Simulium* provide one of the most outstanding examples of direct application of chemical pesticides to streams, rivers and river systems. The need for controlling blackflies has two distinct origins.

In many temperate and subarctic regions such as Canada and the U.S.S.R., dense populations of blackflies constitute a serious biting menace to man and to domestic animals. In contrast, in many parts of tropical Africa as well as more limited areas in central America — particularly Mexico and Guatemala — the interest in *Simulium* is not so much as a biting pest but in its role as vector of human onchocerciasis. In areas of high endemicity of this disease, and continued re-infection of man with the parasite transmitted by the bite of the fly, invasion of the eye with the microfilarial stage of the parasite produces various degenerative changes including blindness. As such areas in Africa are usually associated with large rivers which produce high populations of the main vector, *Simulium damnosum*, the more popular term "river blindness" has been coined directly from the native dialect description of this disease. Although "river blindness" represents the most severe and intractable stage of the onchocercal infection it is not strictly synonymous with the name "onchocerciasis" as there are many areas with a high prevalence of onchocerciasis in the human population not necessarily accompanied by a high blindness rate (W.H.O., 1966).

In the context of the present general appraisal of pesticide impact on aquatic organisms, there are certain unique features of the long-established methods for insecticidal control of *Simulium* larvae in running water. Most striking is the very wide range in size of streams and rivers forming the main habitats of the different species of *Simulium* involved. In the case of onchocerciasis in Mexico and Guatemala, two of the three main vectors concerned — *Simulium ochraceum* and *S. metallicum* — prefer to breed in comparatively small streams, sometimes mere trickles heavily covered with undergrowth. In contrast, *S. damnosum*, the main vector of African onchocerciasis, is associated with some of the largest rivers in that continent such as the Niger, the Congo and the Sudan and Victoria Nile, as well as with some of the largest river systems such as the Volta in West Africa. *S. damnosum* may also breed in smaller rivers or streams in certain localities, but in general high prevalence of onchocerciasis transmitted by this fly is associated with the enormous extent and intensity of breeding in the large rivers.

Direct attack against the aquatic stages of *Simulium* in these rivers still remains the only effective method for reducing blackfly populations and interrupting transmission of the disease. Some idea of the enormous volumes of water which have to be treated in this practice of larval control, and the huge scale on which control operations have to be carried out, can be gained from the following. At one of the dosing points on the River Niger the river was between three and four hundred yards wide (McMahon, 1967), while at another dosage point on the Volta the river was six to seven hundred yards wide (Kuzoe and Hagan, 1967). The discharge rate of these large rivers varies greatly and in times of flood, in the Volta for example, may reach or exceed 500,000 cusec. In contrast, the discharge of the Volta in the dry season varies from 23,000 cusec down to 3300 cusec.

Treatment of such rivers is not normally carried out at times of maximum spate, but nevertheless regular treatments have to be made when the discharge rate is as high as 150,000 cusec. There is one advantage however in the high rate of discharge of these largest rivers, in that they provide more efficient carriage of larvicide and may produce controlling effects on *Simulium* larvae at long distances — sometimes forty or fifty miles — below the application point. The enormous volume requiring treatment with chemical larvicide in these rivers becomes even more impressive and formidable when compared with another well-known public health problem requiring pesticide treatment of running water, namely the control of the aquatic snails in irrigation systems for control of bilharziasis. In Tanzania, for example, the discharge of the main canals ranges from 40–60 cusec, while in the secondaries it varies from 15–30 cusec (Crossland, 1967).

DDT has long been the larvicide of choice in control of *Simulium* larvae (McMahon, 1957, 1967) and there is a vast amount of information about effective dosage rates and treatment regimens, particularly with regard to control of *S. damnosum* in Africa (W.H.O., 1966). DDT is usually applied from the ground in the form of an emulsifiable concentrate containing up to 33% DDT. The period of application is comparatively short, between 30 min and 15 min in different areas, and the application rates vary from 0·3 ppm/30 min to a maximum of 0·5 ppm/30. In the largest rivers with high discharge rates, the more effective carriage of larvicide mentioned above enables efficient control to be produced at lower rates of dosage such as 0·02 to 0·04 ppm/30 min in the Niger. Over the period of several months when *Simulium* larval densities are at their highest, the treatment may be repeated at weekly or ten-day intervals. In the largest rivers the general technique of larvicide application is from an outboard motor-powered boat or canoe driven slowly across the middle of the river, the partly diluted emulsion being discharged at a steady — and known — rate from convenient containers such as 4 gal petrol tins. Some idea of the great quantity of insecticide required for treating a single river may be gained from experience in the Niger (Hitchen and Goiny, 1965). In a fairly typical week in August, at the height of the *Simulium* season, the Niger at Kainji (the site of the dam) required a dose of 310 gallons of DDT emulsion compared with 353 gal of DDT emulsion used in the dosing of twenty-six other streams and rivers. During the following week when the Niger was in high flood, it required a dose of 420 gal of insecticide.

In view of the cost and labour involved in surveying large rivers and in setting up approach routes to a series of application points, more attention is being given to the possibilities of aerial application of larvicide. This method has been found particularly successful in dealing with pest *Simulium* in New York State (Jamnback, 1969a, b). The general technique is to apply the larvicide in one or more swaths at right angles across the breeding stream. For this purpose oil solutions of the insecticide are found to be more effective and less costly than the emulsifiable concentrates used in ground control. This usually takes the form of a 20% insecticide in oil solution with 0·5 to 0·75% Triton X-161 added as a surfactant. The insecticide is applied at the rate of 1 US gal per flight mile. With this technique effective control is produced at lower dosages than quoted above, although the completely different rationale of aerial application makes it difficult to define the dosage in strict terms of ppm/min. The possibility of aerial application of larvicide for control of *S. damnosum* in West African rivers is now undergoing critical trial, but it may be some time before any decision can be made about the implications of this method in the long-term project planned for onchocerciasis control in Africa (Jamnback *et al.*, 1970).

Control of *Simulium* larvae in general, and *S. damnosum* in particular has been dominated for many years by DDT. Despite the well-known drawbacks of this insecticide regarding persistence, accumulation in food chains, toxicity to fish and liability to produce resistance, DDT is still the larvicide of choice in most *Simulium* control schemes and will undoubtedly continue to play a major role until such time as a really effective and more selective substitute is found. One of the alternative possibilities, Baytex (fenthion) has been thoroughly investigated both in the laboratory (Garms and Kuhlow, 1967) and on the Niger in Guinea (Garms and Post, 1967), but despite some advantages in the way of low persistence and less toxic effect on fish, it still falls short of the ideal replacement for DDT.

In New York State the application of DDT to streams has now been suspended in favour of the allied organochlorine compound Methoxychlor. This is considered to be as effective as DDT as a larvicide, but to be less persistent and to have a reduced adverse effect on stream biota in general. It should be pointed out however that much more experimental work will have to be done before this general claim can be fully substantiated. The possibility of Methoxychlor as a replacement for DDT in the African onchocerciasis control projects is now being carefully investigated.

At the moment, the continued massive application of DDT to *S. damnosum* rivers for control of onchocerciasis in Africa remains one of the most outstanding examples of the deliberate application of this chemical to natural water bodies, and is in striking contrast to the complete ban placed on the further use of DDT by Scandinavian countries and in parts of the United States. The situation in Canada is particularly interesting in that some of the earliest and most dramatic results with DDT were produced in that country for the control of the serious blackfly biting pest. The increasing body of evidence about the accumulation and persistence of DDT residues in lakes into which some of these *Simulium* rivers discharge is bringing increasing pressure to bear for the suspension of DDT application. At the same time blackfly continue to be a serious biting pest in developing areas of Canada, and at the moment it is difficult to see how these conflicting interests can be resolved. Methoxychlor would appear to be the most likely *immediate* replacement for DDT in that country, but much more work will have to be done before the general ecological impact of that chemical can be accurately assessed.

At present research towards finding a more selective, less persistent, *Simulium* larvicide is proceeding along two distinct lines.

Firstly, by means of the experimental channel or simulated stream techniques described later, a range of candidate chemical larvicides are being screened in the laboratory to study their effect on detachment and mortality of *Simulium* larvae introduced from natural habitats. So far a wide range of compounds, particularly those organophosphorus compounds which have already shown promise as mosquito larvicides, have been tested either as technical products dissolved in acetone or ethanol, or as emulsifiable concentrates or other water miscible formulations likely to be applied in field practice. One or two promising compounds have emerged, but the best fall short of the ideal replacement for DDT. The powerful organophosphorus larvicide Dursban for example is highly toxic to *Simulium* larvae at very low concentrations but also appears to have an equally lethal effect on many non-target and food chain organisms. Another promising candidate OP larvicide — Abate — is less generally biocidal than Dursban, but has run into formulation trouble, the emulsifiable concentrate formulation designed for field practice proving much less effective than solutions in organic solvents (Muirhead-Thomson, 1970; Jamnback and Means, 1968). However, as solutions in fuel oils are preferred for aerial application, there may still be a future for Abate.

A second and very ingenious approach to the use of more selective *Simulium* larvicides is to use DDT itself formulated in a particulate range in such a way that it is readily ingested by *Simulium* larvae, but less readily available to other stream invertebrates and non-target fauna (Kershaw *et al.*, 1968). *Simulium* larvae show an unusual combination of being particulate feeders, while at the same time living in fast-flowing parts of streams and rivers. DDT was prepared in the range of $4–11\mu$, i.e. in accordance with the range in size of food particles occurring naturally in the gut of various species of *Simulium*. This form of DDT has a low sedimentation rate and also requires no oil solvent or emulsifier. Preliminary tests in small streams indicated that it is possible to select certain time/concentrations of this particulate form of DDT, such as 0·2 ppm for 30 min, which produce a marked reduction in populations of *Simulium* larvae while leaving the bottom fauna undisturbed.

At high dosage of 0·4 ppm for 30 min, sensitive aquatic insect fauna such as nymphs of the mayfly, *Baetis*, are removed and there is also some effect on the freshwater shrimp, *Gammarus*. At that dosage *Simulium* larvae were cleared for distances of 150 yds and 1100 yds respectively below application point, colonization usually occurring within a month. The full potentials of this novel approach have not yet been tested in rivers, particularly against *S. damnosum* in the large rivers of Africa.

It seems clear that situations are likely to arise in Africa which will demand either that DDT be applied in some carefully designed physical form which will exercise some selective action, or that new chemicals, more selective and less persistent than DDT be introduced (Ovazza, 1970). Implicit in the choice of new or candidate chemicals is the absolute need for such larvicides to have the minimal toxicity to man and domestic animals liable to drink or come in contact with river water treated with larvicide. An example of such a situation is provided by the new Niger Dam at Kainji in Nigeria. During dam construction regular DDT treatment of the Niger and some of its tributaries had been carried out for a number of years in order to reduce the *Simulium* population and afford some protection to the immigrant labour against onchocerciasis. The dam was completed at the end of 1968, and from that time onwards, as the Kainji Lake starts to fill, some of these *Simulium* rivers will now flow into the lake itself. As the proposed fishing industry in the new Kainji Lake eventually becomes established, the further use of DDT will be contra-indicated (Kershaw, 1965; White, 1965).

While the development of water resources in Africa, and the creation of man-made lakes, may possibly have the effect of inundating, or rendering stagnant, former foci of *Simulium* breeding, at the same time new problems will undoubtedly be created by the ideal breeding conditions provided by dam spillways and associated rapids (Burton and McCrae, 1965). Until now, the overriding public health consideration of reducing the incidence of *Simulium* and onchocerciasis in Africa has permitted the regular use of DDT with minimum regard to possible undesirable effects on fish, on food chain organisms, or on the general ecology of the aquatic habitat. The increasing world-wide pressure to restrict the indiscriminate application of DDT in a way which might sooner or later be inimical to wildlife may well influence authoritative opinions in the developing countries of Africa (Ovazza, 1970). In addition, the need to exploit to the full the potentialities of large rivers and associated man-made lakes with regard to fish production is almost certain to lead to a reappraisal of long accepted priorities, and to a more coordinated approach in which the interests of fishery and livestock production and wildlife organizations must be considered on the same level as the more obvious and pressing problems of public health (Meschkat and Dill, 1961).

THE EVALUATION OF SIMULIUM LARVICIDES

The larvae of blackflies (*Simulium*) occupy rather a unique position in the freshwater community. Their ability to anchor themselves firmly to the substrate while at the same time retaining their ability to move around by means of silken attachment lines, enables them to survive and flourish in the swiftly flowing current of the streams and rivers which form their habitat. Their remarkable adaptation to life in streams and rivers, and their close dependence on a constant flow of well-aerated water, makes them at the same time peculiarly vulnerable to changes of medium. When moved into still water in the laboratory, they require constant aeration for survival, and the aeration must be vigorous enough to produce agitation and turbulence as well. Even then, a heavy mortality may set in within 48 h or less. In addition, normal handling methods suitable for other aquatic insect larvae or nymphs, such as the use of forceps or pipette for isolating or counting individuals for routine tests, have an adverse effect on the larvae of most *Simulium* species, and result in a high mortality.

These difficulties account in part for the complete failure to date to establish self-supporting laboratories colonies of any species of *Simulium* (Muirhead-Thomson, 1966). Other factors contributing to this failure are the difficulties in inducing laboratory-reared adult female *Simulium* to take a blood meal, to become fertilized, or to lay viable eggs in the laboratory. Although some progress in overcoming these obstacles has been made in the case of a European species, *Simulium erythrocephalum* (Wenk and Schlorer, 1963; Merryweather, 1970), any type of laboratory study on the reactions of *Simulium* larvae is still completely dependent on supplies of live material collected in natural breeding sites in streams and rivers.

It should be pointed out that this dependence on live material from natural habitats is not peculiar to *Simulium*. This also applies to several other stream invertebrates such as mayfly nymphs on which very little work has been done in attempting to establish laboratory cultures or colonies. The case of *Simulium* is noteworthy however in that it has been the subject of intensive study for many years, and that workers in many different countries have tried out a wide variety of methods in attempting to overcome the problem of maintenance and colonization in the laboratory.

Although *Simulium* larvae brought into the laboratory can be maintained in static water vigorously aerated and agitated by means of a jet of compressed air, for a period of 24 to 48 h before heavy mortality sets in, it has become increasingly evident in the last few years that in laboratory methods for evaluating pesticide impact it is essential for the *Simulium* larvae to be exposed to flowing water in an experimental channel or trough. Before discussing these newer techniques, some attention must be given to an earlier method involving static water and compressed air, not only because it was the first technique to produce consistent and reproducible results, but also because some of the principles used in that test have now been utilized as an essential first step in establishing *Simulium* larvae in an experimental channel in the laboratory (Muirhead-Thomson, 1969).

In the earlier technique (Muirhead-Thomson, 1957; 1966), which was actually worked out with larvae of *Simulium damnosum* — the main vector of human onchocerciasis in Africa — and other tropical species, vegetation with attached larvae was collected from swiftly flowing streams which formed the natural habitat, and transported to the laboratory in polythene bags. The vegetation with attached larvae was immersed in 5–10 l of clean water in a large glass jar. A jet of compressed air was directed against the lower part of the inner wall of the jar producing a constant stream of air bubbles up one side of the jar. In the course of a few hours, larvae migrated from the vegetation to this zone of aeration and agitation, and aggregated along the vertical zone on the wall. Vegetation could then be removed, and the contents of the jar gradually replaced with clean water. Larvae remained attached and viable long enough — at least 24 h — to enable tests with various larvicide dosages to be carried out. In an improved version of this technique, the jet of air was directed against a detachable glass plate which could be removed from the jar once the bulk of the larvae had become attached to the plate (Fig. 23). If the plate with attached larvae was very quickly transferred to a jar of clean water and immediately exposed to a stream of air bubbles from a compressed air jet, the majority of larvae remained firmly attached after the swift interchange. The small proportion of larvae which became detached during this operation usually found their way to the original attachment site by means of their silken attachment threads.

Over a period of several years attempts were made by the World Health Organization to utilize these principles in order to devise a completely standard laboratory test for studying the susceptibility of *Simulium* larvae to DDT and other insecticides. In the course of that work certain deficiencies in the original technique described above were pointed out, such as the need to standardize the number of larvae exposed at each test, the need to identify the exact species

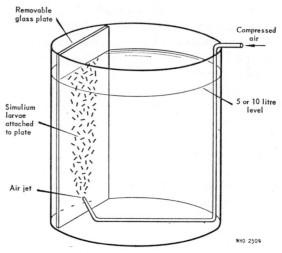

FIG. 23. Original design of closed-circuit aeration system for testing reaction of *Simulium* larvae to insecticides (after Muirhead-Thomson, 1957).

of larvae tested — rather than rely on the more easily distinguishable characters of the pupae produced by control batches of larvae — and also the fact that vigorous aeration during the actual exposure period to the larvicide being tested might produce a significant loss of insecticide concentration due to co-distillation or deactivation.

A static test, combining improvements and modifications made by different workers, is still recommended by W.H.O. as the best provisional method for recording any changes in susceptibility of *Simulium* larvae, and for the early detection of resistance in areas under regular DDT pressure (W.H.O., 1963). It is emphasized that despite its artificialities, it is still the most convenient method for comparative purposes, but it does not necessarily indicate accurately what particular time/concentration application is likely to produce effective mortality in the field. For the latter purpose the newer flowing water trough or channel techniques are considered essential.

In the trough technique developed in the course of *Simulium* control in New York State (Jamnback and Frempong-Boadu, 1966; Frempong-Boadu, 1966) small stones or vegetation with attached *Simulium* larvae are taken from streams and transferred to the laboratory where they are placed in large troughs of a kind originally used for rearing salmon. The troughs are 13·5 ft long and 13 in wide. Water enters through an adjustable valve at the upper end, and flows out the other end over an effluent lip. Most of the introduced larvae soon migrate to the shallow water which flows swiftly over the lip, and a proportion of these become attached there and take up the same position as they do in their natural habitat. In order to enable more tests to be carried out at a time, small troughs 3 ft long and 1 ft wide, and 6 in deep are now used. Larvae surplus to the requirements of each test involving 25–35 medium to large larvae, can be removed by forceps from the lip. Insecticide can be introduced into the trough at the upper end, effectiveness being measured by the larval detachment rate. The recovery of larvae which become detached is studied under favourable conditions in clean water in a well-aerated jar.

The value of such troughs or experimental channels has also been well demonstrated elsewhere in the United States in a technique which is more of the nature of a semi-field test than a strict laboratory one (Wilton and Travis, 1965; Travis and Wilton, 1965). Portable equipment consisting essentially of a reservoir tank and four small V-troughs is set up in a field near a natural *Simulium* stream. The water supply for the experimental channel is pumped from the stream into the reservoir and evenly distributed to the four channels. The particular species of *Simulium* larvae used in these tests — *Simulium pictipes* — are evidently unusually amenable to handling, and can be easily dislodged from the flat rocks on which they frequently occur in masses, and can then be readily established in the troughs. After exposure to chemical metered through the channels, efficacy is measured by the detachment rate. Subsequent survival of larvae remaining attached is checked by transferring them to a nylon bag which is immersed in clean flowing water of the nearby stream for 24–48 h.

It has long been the opinion of many field workers that *Simulium* larvae which become detached by the action of a chemical larvicide and washed downstream, will eventually die, either because they ultimately succumb to the effects of the insecticide, or because they are washed into eddies or other areas of still water where survival is unlikely. In addition, it was long considered that larvae washed from their firm anchorage would be exposed to high mortality due to predators. There are prima facie reasons for examining this assumption much more critically.

The activities of freshwater biologists in the last few years have thrown a great deal of new light on the phenomenon of natural drift of stream benthos, including *Simulium* larvae (Waters, 1961, 1962, 1965; Elliott, 1965, 1967; Elliott and Minshall, 1968). It now appears that invertebrate drift, which in some cases shows marked nocturnal increase, is a part of the natural life and dispersal of many of these stream invertebrates. The fact that drifting *Simulium* larvae not only drift, but can re-attach successfully, has been demonstrated in tropical rivers by suspending strips of cane which are immersed in the water without any contact with the bottom or with any *Simulium* attachment sites. Within a few days dense masses of larvae accumulate on the cane; in the absence of any egg masses, this must clearly be due to colonization by larvae drifting downstream on their fine attachment threads (Muirhead-Thomson, 1970).

In view of the need to examine the factors of detachment and subsequent survival or mortality in a more critical manner it was necessary to devise a more effective way of inducing large numbers of *Simulium* larvae to aggregate in an experimental channel in the laboratory. The method finally worked out is as follows (Muirhead-Thomson, 1969).

In the first phase of this technique which utilizes the previously established principles of inducing aggregation by means of a directed air jet, vegetation with attached larvae from field sources is placed in about 10 l of clean water in an experimental jar. A jet of compressed air directed against the lower part of the inside wall induces larvae within a few hours to migrate to the vertical area of maximum aeration and turbulence (Fig. 24 — 1, 2). When larvae have

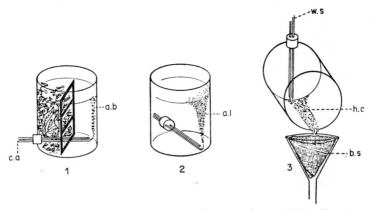

Fig. 24. Flowing water apparatus for testing reactions of *Simulium* larvae in an experimental channel (after Muirhead-Thomson, 1969).

become firmly established, the vegetation is removed. The jar is then smoothly and quickly rotated through 90° decanting the contents, while at the same time a water supply to the inside of the jar is turned on. The vertical strip of dense larval aggregation now takes up a horizontal position with the larvae exposed to a continuous flow of water (Fig. 24 — 3). During this rotation, the majority of larvae remain firmly attached and evenly distributed throughout a narrow channel 1 ft long by 2 in wide. In each experiment several hundred larvae can readily be induced to attach and become established in this way, and on occasions more than 1000 larvae of all stages have become established, giving a density of approximately 40 per sq in.

Owing to the large numbers of larvae exposed at each test, the fractions which detach at intervals after exposure to chemical are sufficiently large to provide a valid basis for data concerning percentage detached and percentage mortality of each detached fraction. Different time/concentrations of chemical can be monitored through the channel from a 60-litre reservoir, usually at a rate of flow of 1 litre/min or approximately 1 ft/sec in the very shallow channel. A 1 h exposure was selected as an arbitrary standard, and fractions detached at various intervals after beginning of application — 15, 30, 45, 60 min, 2 h and 24 h — were collected and recorded separately. After detached fractions of larvae had been exposed to the selected exposure period, they were transferred to clean water vigorously aerated by compressed air for a holding period of 24–48 h.

Once larvae had become established in this channel, the degree of detachment in untreated controls was negligible for several hours afterwards. Overnight however, during the course of 24 h there is a small but consistent degree of detachment — about 5% — among larvae which are live and healthy, and which perhaps represents the degree of detachment which normally takes place in their natural habitat.

By means of this laboratory technique it was possible to build up a much more consistent and accurate picture of the degree of detachment and mortality produced by different chemical larvicides, and by different time/concentrations of the same larvicide. The results expand and amplify the work of other investigators (e.g. Travis *et al.*, 1967; Travis and Schuchman, 1968) in showing firstly that different compounds tend to produce different degrees of detachment; DDT, BHC and methoxychlor for example producing a relatively higher rate of detachment than the organophosphorus compounds. A more critical examination of 24 h mortalities after a 1 h exposure period show three main types of reaction. At one extreme, the pyrethrins produce a high and immediate rate of detachment, but there is a high 24 h survival rate in the detached fractions. Several organophosphorus compounds tested at the minimal larvicide dosage produce very low detachment during the exposure period; thereafter detachment increases, with a subsequent high mortality in all detached fractions. The interpretation put on this is that larvae exposed to this group of compounds only become detached when they have absorbed a lethal dose of chemical (Muirhead-Thomson, 1970).

Between these two extremes are several chlorinated hydrocarbons such as DDT, gamma BHC and methoxychlor which produce an increasing tempo of detachment during the course of the 1 h exposure period; the detached fractions however show a very variable and inconsistent mortality after 24 h, the survival rate under the conditions of this test being as high as 60% on occasions under dosage conditions which are considered adequate for field control.

In the practical control of *Simulium* larvae in their natural habitats, there would appear to be many advantages in inducing a high degree of detachment during the short application period currently used in the field, in that detached larvae, floating downstream along with the wave of larvicide, would be exposed to its effects for a much longer period. With this theoretical consideration in mind, larvae in the experimental channel have been exposed to combinations of pyrethrins or pyrethroids — which produce maximum detachment — and organophosphorus compounds, which produce low detachment but high subsequent mortality. The results of some of these combinations are shown in Fig. 25, and indicate that the theoretical expectation is actually achieved in practice in the experimental channel. The combination of pyrethroid and OP larvicide appears to be the most effective one so far in producing maximum detachment during the exposure period, along with maximum ultimate mortality. Under field conditions this mixture would be expected to have a potentiating effect, reducing the chances of larvae remaining attached throughout the passage of the larvicide wave and subsequently surviving the sub-lethal exposure. The principle has still to be tested under field conditions.

With regard to the eggs of *Simulium*, comparatively little laboratory work has been done on the reactions of this stage to larvicidal chemicals. This has been due mainly to two factors; firstly, are the reports from many countries where DDT treatment of streams and rivers has been carried out that rapid re-population after larvicidal effect of treatment has worn off, indicates strongly that eggs are unaffected by this treatment. Secondly, is the fact that the eggs of some species of *Simulium* are extremely difficult to find, and rarely on such a scale as to justify a screening programme in the laboratory. Recently, opportunities have arisen for studying the reactions of *Simulium* eggs more systematically, using a British species *Simulium ornatum* (Muirhead-Thomson and Merryweather, 1969, 1970). Eggs of *S. ornatum* resemble those of *S. damnosum* — the main African vector of onchocerciasis — in that they are laid at or just below water level in large masses in a gelatinous matrix, each mass representing the combined efforts of a large number of females ovipositing communally. From the experimental point of view this fact presents difficulties in that individual batches can neither be distinguished or separated, nor is it yet possible to count out or isolate known numbers of eggs without serious risk of damage.

Using short exposures — initially 1 h — tests with eggs against a series of larvicidal compounds, confirmed that eggs were quite unaffected by larvicidal dosages of DDT, Baytex, methoxychlor and a range of organophosphorus compounds. They were in fact unaffected by concentrations of 10 ppm DDT, which is up to 100 times higher than used in the field.

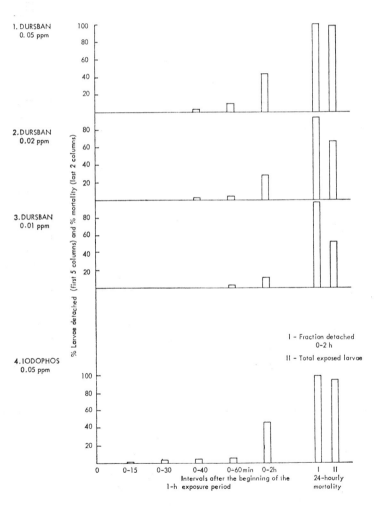

FIG. 25. Continued on p. 146 with legend.

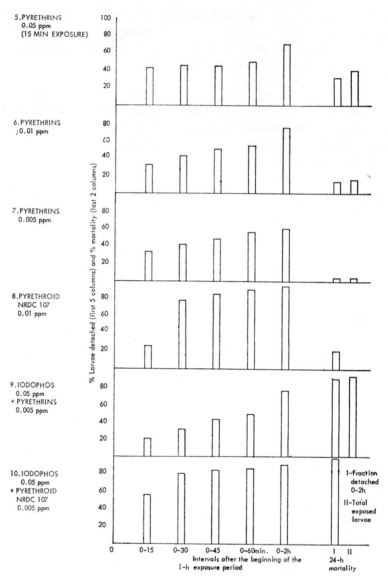

FIG. 25. Chart showing detachment/mortality pattern of *Simulium* larvae exposed to different chemicals and chemical combinations in experimental channel (after Muirhead-Thomson, 1970).

When the exposure period was extended to 24 h, at corresponding lower concentrations, there was still no effect produced by DDT and the chlorinated hydrocarbons. On the other hand, the extended exposure period revealed that one or two OP compounds produced inhibition of hatching. This was particularly marked in the case of Dursban which produced complete inhibition of hatching at 0·1 ppm for 24 h exposure. At 0·05 ppm, many eggs hatched but most larvae appeared to die in the process. This effect was still evident at concentrations as low as 0·001 ppm. This marked increase in ovicidal action with prolonged exposure to proportionately much lower concentrations has a parallel in the case of the effect on snail eggs of the molluscicide Frescon. It remains to be seen how far these reactions of S. ornatum eggs provide an accurate pointer to the reactions of the tropical vectors of onchocerciasis.

EVALUATION OF SIMULIUM LARVICIDES IN THE FIELD

In evaluating the effect of river treatment with larvicides for the control of Simulium larvae, the methods most generally used have been based on the routine collection of larvae at select observation stations sited at various distances below the application point. The observation stations are usually points on the river which are easily accessible and in which — possibly for many months prior to treatment — Simulium larvae can readily be recovered at all times. In smaller streams observation stations may cover a distance of perhaps only one or two miles downstream from the proposed application point. In the larger rivers, particularly those in Africa such as the Niger and the Volta where control operations are directed against Simulium damnosum, observations or collecting sites may be extended up to fifty or sixty miles downstream from the application point, as some treatments can normally be expected to be effective for such long distances.

Entomologists have long been conscious of the comparative crudity of their larval sampling methods in evaluating the effect of larvicide treatment of rivers. In large tropical rivers, often several hundred yards wide, the physical difficulties may make it dangerous or impossible to sample a complete range of larval aggregation sites, many of which may be on rocky outcrops in mid-stream, in rapids, or in inaccessible parts of the river bank. Under such conditions figures attempting to portray percentage reduction or percentage mortality of larvae at various points below application point, or at various intervals after treatment, become rather speculative. Evaluation of effect is therefore usually based on complete elimination of larvae from routine observation sites, and it is generally assumed that these larvae have in fact been killed and not just dislodged or detached. In many cases the assumption appears to be fully justified, especially when supporting evidence from other sites — including those from further downstream — indicate a general disappearance of larvae from the treated river (Burton *et al.*, 1964). However, in view of the number of inaccessible sampling sites in such rivers, together with the fact that little is known about the extent to which larvae can attach, and live at least for a time, in much deeper waters than the surface layers which they normally inhabit, the need has been recognized to examine present sampling methods much more critically (W.H.O., 1965).

In an endeavour to study larval mortality in treated streams by more accurate standards than an "all-or-none" basis, a bioassay method has been devised in Ghana in connection with DDT-treatment of the Volta River (Noamesi, 1964; Burton, 1964). In this method, 25–100 larvae of mixed ages and instars are counted out and placed in a glass tube the ends of which are covered with bolting silk. Two to four of these bioassay tubes are placed in a wire basket which is submerged in the river at points where larvae are collected. After treatment of the river with DDT for 30 min, an immediate check is carried out just below dosing point. Breeding sites at greater distances from this point are checked after intervals of 2, 4, 6 and 24 h. The results indicate that after these various periods there is a variable mortality depending on distance, but that after 24 h the mortality is 100% in all cases, even at the forty mile point below application.

These results appear to support the opinion of many field workers that in treated rivers detachment of larvae is tantamount to death, and that no significant degree of re-attachment takes places. This is further supported by the observation that for several days after treatment of the river with larvicide, the normal attachment sites at the observation points yield only the youngest instar larvae which have presumably hatched from the *Simulium* eggs which are unaffected by normal field larvicide dosages.

Where smaller rivers and streams provide the habitat of local *Simulium*, more quantitative sampling methods have been introduced. Many years ago the Canadian workers used white painted wooden cones as standard attachment or aggregations sites for larvae (Wolfe and Peterson, 1958) and this method is still being used in evaluation of recent larvicides in Canada (Swabey *et al.*, 1967). Recently, a preference has been shown by British workers for using polythene tapes for sampling (Williams and Obeng, 1962; Kershaw *et al.*, 1966). For example in evaluating the possible selective effect of applying DDT in the forms of particles of appropriate size range, a small stream with variable width up to 10 ft, and 6–12 in deep was used for experiment (Kershaw *et al.*, 1968). Strips of polythene 2 ft long and 1½ in wide were fixed to stakes driven into the bottom of the stream. The natural fluctuation, month by month, in numbers of larvae and pupae on these tapes was recorded over several seasons prior to the actual test with larvicide.

Somewhat similar methods have been used in evaluating the effect of aerial application of *Simulium* larvicides in New York State (Jamnback, 1969). Bright orange plastic indicator tags are placed in streams five days before treatment, and counts of larvae on these tags are made four, three and one day before treatment, and one day after.

Those concerned with the evaluation of *Simulium* larvicides are acutely aware of the comparative crudity of the methods used and the extent to which results obtained and interpretations reached may vary enormously according to the observer. However, awareness of these gross variables does not necessarily mean that these errors can be overcome. At present, some of the difficulties in the way of quantitative evaluation seems almost insuperable.

The same acute awareness of possible error also applies to the simulated stream tests described above. As these tests depend on live larval material taken from natural habitats, it follows that there must be many variables in the composition of the larval sample used, in the distribution of age groups among the larvae, in the extent to which they are infected by parasites or weakened by predator attack. In addition, the natural robustness may well vary from season to season, or even from week to week, to a degree which may not be very evident in untreated controls, but which may produce differences when larvae are exposed to the additional stress of larvicide pressure. Feeding activity of larvae in experimental channels may not necessarily duplicate that in the natural habitat, and this may mean that the amount of larvicide ingested could vary from sample to sample or from larva to larva (Travis, 1968). Furthermore, the criteria of mortality, as to length of holding period and conditions under which larvae are maintained, vary greatly according to the different techniques used by different workers.

Obviously a great deal of critical research is required before any one of these points can be satisfactorily dealt with. In this respect *Simulium* larvae present perhaps a greater challenge than most other aquatic organisms, but it is evident that similar difficulties are experienced in other fields particularly where — as in the case with studies on microcrustacea — a great deal of evaluation in the laboratory has also to be based on samples from natural habitats rather than on maintained standard cultures (Ruber, 1963).

CHEMICAL CONTROL OF THE AQUATIC STAGES OF NON-BITING MIDGES AND GNATS

In many parts of the world problems are created by the enormous production of non-biting midges and gnats from various types of water body. At certain seasons of the year a serious nuisance is created by the swarms of these insects which are attracted to light and invade streets and houses in vast numbers, generally making living conditions extremely uncomfortable or even intolerable on occasions. The problem is by no means a rural one as the swarms are just as liable to invade urban and suburban areas, particularly areas of rapid expansion, interfering with the comfort and amenities of life in such places, and seriously affecting the value of property. Because of their small size they can penetrate conventional mosquito screens, and their high density makes them liable to be easily inhaled producing health problems quite apart from the nuisance and irritation caused.

In many warm countries local names exist for these midge pests, such as the "nimitti" which infest Khartoum and other parts of the Nile (Brown *et al.*, 1961 and the "sayule" at San Carlos, Nicaragua (Bay, 1964).

The majority of these non-biting midges with aquatic early stages belong to two groups of two-winged flies, the true non-biting midges, Chironomidae (Tendipedidae) and the non-biting gnats (Chaoboridae). Various members of the Chironomidae such as *Chironomus* and *Tanytarsus* are responsible for the majority of non-biting midge problems in many parts of the world. Problems created by the Chaoboridae are rather rarer or more localized, but are equally important where they occur. The larval stages of these midges and gnats are usually associated with the soft bottom mud of lakes and ponds, but they may also inhabit the bottom muds of rivers, such as the Nile. At certain stages and at certain times larvae may leave the bottom mud and move freely in the open water.

With regard to the Chaoboridae, one of the best known representatives of this group is the Clear Lake gnat — *Chaoborus asticopus* — of California which has been the subject of classical studies not only from the direct pest control point of view, but also because of associated pioneer work on the accumulation of TDE — an analogue of DDT — in freshwater habitats (Lindquist and Roth, 1950; Lindquist *et al.*, 1951; Hunt and Bischoff, 1960; Cook and Conners, 1963).

Clear Lake, the largest natural freshwater lake in the State of California is located in the inner coastal range in the northern part of the country about 100 miles north of San Francisco, at an altitude of about 1320 ft. It has a surface area of 42,000 acres and is generally shallow, the depth being mainly under 30 ft, with a maximum of 50 ft in a few localized spots. Due to the shallowness there is little indication of a thermocline, and bottom temperatures are frequently close to those of the surface. The long existing problem created by the Clear Lake gnat (*Chaoborus*) to the residents in that area was one of the first to be tackled by means of the then recently discovered chlorinated hydrocarbons, DDT and its allies. Following laboratory tests as well as trials in small lakes in that area, it was found that TDE (DDD) was highly effective against gnat larvae, and much less harmful to fish than DDT (Lindquist and Roth, 1950). The first large scale treatment of the lake took place in September 1949 at a time of the year when larvae were still migrating from the mud into the water each night. Many of the problems posed by treatment of such a large water area with the requisite amount of insecticide (14,000 gal producing 1 part of TDE in 70,000,000 parts of water) are equally pertinent today and in other spheres of lake treatment, such as with toxaphene in fish eradication. For example, in order to prevent insecticide concentration near the shore and possible injury to littoral fauna, none was discharged within 0·75 miles of one shore and 0·5 miles of another (Lindquist *et al.*, 1951). Wave action and water currents were considered effective in rapidly distributing the chemical throughout the water. Application was made by surface craft in the form of swaths, markers being used to establish the boundaries of each sector. Treatment was also extended to ponds, reservoirs and small lakes within fifteen miles of Clear Lake.

Gnat larvae rise to the surface when they are affected by TDE or other chlorinated hydrocarbons. After treatment, a sheet of floating larvae — at the density of hundreds per square foot — covered large areas of the lake surface. The operation was highly successful and it appeared that by April 1950 the gnat population had been almost completely eliminated. This striking success may have been partly due to the habit of the gnat larvae of making nocturnal migrations from the soft bottom mud to the surface, especially in warm weather. During daylight, the larvae are embedded in the soft mud, and laboratory experiments indicated that little control could have been achieved unless the larvae migrated into the open water.

As complete eradication of the Clear Lake gnat was not achieved, it was anticipated that re-infestation would occur and that further periodic treatments would be necessary. By the summer of 1954 the gnat had once more risen to nuisance levels, and a further treatment with TDE was given which, however, was not successful. By this time it was also becoming evident that this ally of DDT was being accumulated in the main food chains of the lake to a degree sufficient to poison fish and aquatic birds (Hunt and Bischoff, 1960). This collateral investigation on the ecological impact of TDE provided one of the earliest convincing demonstrations of the insidious build-up of DDT and chlorinated hydrocarbons in freshwater ecosystems, and was the forerunner of a great proliferation of work on DDT residues in aquatic plants and animals, and the concentration of these residues at the peak of food chains both within and outside the freshwater habitat.

In subsequent control operations against the Clear Lake gnat therefore, attention has been concentrated on the organophosphorus compounds in which there is no problem of persistence or accumulation within the habitat. Methyl parathion at 3 ppb was found to be highly toxic to early instar larvae, this level of concentration being considerably below the LD_{50} for bluegills, the most sensitive fish species in Clear Lake (Hazeltine, 1963; Cook and Conners, 1963). A considerable measure of selective control was therefore achieved, with minimal effect on the other biota of the lake. Despite the advantage of the organophosphorus insecticides over the chlorinated hydrocarbons it appears that treatment must be more frequent, and that no permanent control can be hoped for. Continuous pressure from one chemical insecticide introduces the likelihood of resistance developing on the part of the target gnat larvae, and the search for more effective replacement compounds must therefore continue. In this connection it appears that the effect of organophosphorus compounds on gnat larvae may differ considerably from those reported either on Chironomid midge larvae or on mosquito larvae. Two of the most effective of the latter for example, viz. granular formulations of Baytex(fenthion) and Abate, have been reported ineffective against *Chaoborus* larvae at normal larvicide dosages (von Windeguth and Patterson, 1966). Conversely, the successful use of methyl parathion to suppress *Chaoborus* in Clear Lake has had little adverse effect on the Chironomid population of the lake, the number of the latter having actually increased according to some reports (Bay, 1964).

With regard to the aquatic larvae of the non-biting Chironomidae such as *Chironomus* and *Tanytarsus*, their control is a matter of concern in many different countries ranging from temperate to tropical. The larvae of Chironomidae, of which the familiar "blood worm" is an example, are much more closely associated with the muddy bottom of their habitat than those of the Clear Lake gnat. For this and other reasons their control involves rather different problems, in particular the need to use larvicides or formulations which will concentrate in the mud or its vicinity, rather than in the open water. This is particularly relevant in large water bodies, and may prove a major obstacle in some such cases.

As in the case of the Clear Lake gnat, early control measures based on DDT and on TDE (DDD) were very successful in some areas. Along the Blue Nile in the Sudan, particularly where it flows through and near Khartoum, measures against the nuisance midge, "nimitti" — principally *Tanytarsus lewisi* — were initially based on DDT treatment of the river at a calculated dosage of 0·11 ppm over a period of 1 h, 50 min (Brown *et al.*, 1961). Because of the injurious side-effect on fish TDE (DDD) was substituted, the main operation being carried out in 1957 by treatment of the Sennar Reservoir, with a wettable powder formulation. By 1959 the midge population in Khartoum had been reduced to a low level. The larvae of *Tanytarsus* live in the bottom mud of the river, but use the surface at night. This fact, together with the thorough mixing and penetration of chemical produced by the flow and turbulence of the water, probably contributed to the success of this operation. A similar success with TDE for dealing with a chironomid problem on a small scale in England was achieved by treatment of ponds (Edwards *et al.*, 1964).

In the United States a variety of treatments have been used for chironomid control. In Florida, BHC and EPN were used extensively in midge control in the early 1950s, but were only partly successful. Baytex(fenthion) however has proved rather more effective, and when applied to a lake with an average depth of 17 ft at the rate of 0·20 to 0·25 lb/acre to give a concentration of about 4 ppb, was effective in controlling larvae of *Glyptotendipes* (Patterson and von Windeguth, 1964a and b).

The successful control of chironomid larvae however, still poses a problem in many places, and a variety of organophosphorus compounds such as malathion, dipterex and DDVP have been found to have possibilities, while at the same time producing the least mortality with fish (Hilsenhoff, 1959). The efficacy of these new compounds has been improved by applying them as granular formulations which penetrate the main body of water and release the toxicant in close proximity to the larval populations (von Windeguth and Patterson, 1966; Whitsel *et al.*, 1963). The ever-threatening possibility of resistance developing on the part of the target species under regular pressure from a single organophosphorus compound, together with the fact that the effects of even the best larvicides do not last for more than three to four weeks after each treatment, has prompted the continued search for more effective compounds (Mulla and Khasawinah, 1968; Anderson *et al.*, 1965). These laboratory tests and field trials have revealed that different chironomids may differ in reaction to the same chemical. This difference appears to be partly determined by differences in larval habit. The tube-dwelling forms closely associated with the mud are more susceptible to OP larvicides than are the non-tube dwellers which are only exposed to the concentration of the chemical in the water.

Despite the increasing armament of new and powerful organophosphorus and carbamate chemicals of possible value in midge control, there appears to be no easy solution to the problem. This applies even in areas such as Florida, Wisconsin and California where vigorous research programmes have been encouraged for a number of years. In some instances the problem appears to be of sufficient magnitude as to be beyond chemical control. For example, "sayules" or Chironomid midges have long been a serious nuisance in and around the town of San Carlos, Nicaragua during the annual dry season. The principal midge source is the bottom of Lake Nicaragua, and to a less extent in the mud of river bottoms. In the lake bottom chironomid larvae have been recorded at densities as high as 100,000 per sq m (Bay, 1964). Lake Nicaragua is the largest and southernmost of the two great lakes of Nicaragua, and is 160 km long by 72 km wide, with depths of over 40 m recorded. The vast scale of this particular midge control problem is such that there appears to be no possibility of control by aquatic pesticides.

LABORATORY EVALUATION TECHNIQUES FOR LARVAE OF NON-BITING CHIRONOMID MIDGES

In many parts of the world, in both temperate and tropical climates, swarms of Chironomid midges become a serious nuisance. Although these insects are non-biting their sheer density can cause serious discomfort and annoyance. For many years the most effective method of reducing these insect populations has been the larvicidal treatment of the lakes, ponds and other water bodies which form the larval habitat. The question of the most effective chemical for treatment is continually under review. With the increasing range of new potential larvicides, a need has arisen for more critical methods for evaluating different chemicals and different formulations in the laboratory.

The larvae of most species — but not all — of pest Chironomids live in the bottom mud of water bodies and construct mud tubes for their protection. Many of these muddy water habitats occur in polluted water with a low oxygen content. Larvae deprived of these conditions in the laboratory may show a high mortality or exhibit cannibalistic tendencies. Development of valid laboratory evaluation techniques is dependent on the extent to which these natural requirements can be met, while at the same time maintaining some degree of standardization in the tests and in the test medium.

According to the habits of the different species involved, the problem has been tackled in different ways by different investigators. In England swarms of non-biting midges — mainly *Chironomus riparius* — have for several years given rise to complaints in parts of the Colne Valley, near the Hertfordshire Main Drainage Authority Sewage Works (Edwards *et al.*, 1964; Learner and Edwards, 1966). On occasions larvae has been recorded at densities exceeding 100,000/m² of river bed. The larvae, which are detritus feeders, build tubes in mud, and fourth instar larvae penetrate to a depth of about 10 cm.

In the laboratory test method, aquaria of about 25 litres capacity were used, provided with a layer of rich organic mud at the bottom which Chironomid larvae were allowed to colonize. In addition two other dominant mud-dwelling invertebrates were used in the same test aquaria, namely the isopod *Asellus* and the worm *Tubifex*. Wettable powder formulations of the chlorinated hydrocarbons DDT and TDE (DDD) were applied over the surface water, and the animals were recovered from the mud one week later by sieving. The type of results obtained are shown in Fig. 26.

Essentially the same technique was used for a quite different pest species, *Tendipes plumosus*, in the United States (Hilsenhoff, 1959). Fourth stage larvae were put into slate bottomed aquaria and allowed

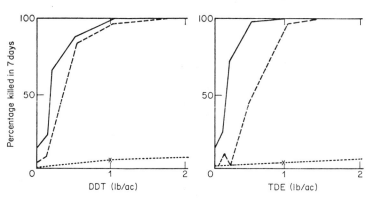

FIG. 26. Chart showing toxicity of DDT and TDE (DDD) wettable powder formulation to *Chironomus riparius* larvae, *Asellus* and *Tubifex* (after Edwards *et al.*, 1964). ——— = *Chironomus riparius*; – – – = Asellus; - - - - = *Tubifex*.

1 h to burrow into mud. Each test lasted five days, after which the mud was strained through mesh, and larvae recovered. Those tests showed that several organophosphorus compounds such as Dipterex, DDVP and malathion were highly toxic to midge larvae, and had least mortality for fish.

In the earlier campaign against chironomid larvae, emphasis had been on the chlorinated hydrocarbons, particularly TDE (DDD), because it was less toxic to fish than DDT. Since that time, problems of resistance to that group of compounds, together with their persistence and accumulation in food chains, has reduced the value of these chemicals and led to a need for a more critical approach to test methods used both for screening larvicides and for detecting resistance. Valid data for LC_{50} and LC_{90} can only be obtained by means of a large number of tests and duplicates, for which the aquarial type of test described above is not suited. Tests were therefore carried out in standard 40 ml wax paper cups containing 100 ml of tap water and 4–5 g of white sand. In each of these cups twenty uniform fourth stage larvae were placed which had been reared under standard conditions from egg masses of laboratory colonies (Mulla and Khasawinah, 1969).

In view of the fact that chironomid larvae under these conditions may show increased mortality and cannibalism, the first essential step in establishing a valid evaluation technique was to find out by experiment how these unnatural and unfavourable effects could be minimized. The experiments were therefore designed to study all combinations of three of the main factors concerned, namely aeration or no aeration, exposure period of 24 h or 48 h, and test with sand and without sand. The results obtained with two species of tube builders, *Chironomus* sp and *Goeldichironomus holoprassinus* show that the most suitable combination for test purposes is to have sand in the cups, avoid aeration of the water, and assess mortality after 24 h.

As with tests with many other aquatic organisms, the criteria for establishing whether larvae were dead or not had to be defined, as estimating mortality requires some skill and is therefore liable to introduce a human error into interpretation of results. Screening tests using this technique showed that the non-tube building species, *Tanypus grodhausi* appeared to be the least susceptible in the field to most of the insecticides tested, and this was attributed to the fact that it was only exposed to the actual concentration of toxicant in the water, whereas the tube-dwelling forms were exposed to additional amounts of chemical absorbed in the mud (Edwards *et al.*, 1964).

CHAPTER 6

IMPACT OF PESTICIDES ON AQUATIC INVERTEBRATES IN NATURE

DDT AND CHLORINATED HYDROCARBON INSECTICIDES

Reference has already been made to studies carried out in the United States and Canada on the effect of widespread aerial spraying with DDT of freshwater fish in exposed streams and surface water. These studies also stimulated investigations on the effect of this spraying on stream invertebrates.

Aerial spraying of forest areas with DDT was particularly intense in the middle fifties, the main target being the spruce budworm. The dosage used at that time was a heavy one of 1 lb DDT/acre. In that extensive spraying over hundreds of thousands of acres, no attempt was made to avoid contamination of non-target areas or environments such as freshwater bodies. As part of the intensive studies started in forest areas of Montana in the Yellowstone National Park on the relation of DDT spraying to fish kills, a systematic attempt was made to study stream bottom organisms before and following spraying (Graham, 1960). Bottom organisms in small streams were sampled with a standard square-foot sampler, while in larger streams a square yard unit was used. In two experimental streams, the volume of drifting insects was found to increase one hundred times from before spraying to 1 h after spraying. Bottom samples showed that reductions of over 90% of the volume within a week after spraying were common. Downstream, the effects generally decreased within a few miles below the sprayed area.

In another area exposed to the same heavy aerial treatment with DDT at 1 lb/acre investigations were extended over four years following a single spraying operation. Streams were sampled eight days after the spray application in 1955, and again six weeks later, with a follow-up in each subsequent year (Hastings et al., 1961). These observations showed that there was a drastic reduction in all forms immediately after spraying, especially in the aquatic insect larvae and nymphs of Ephemeroptera (mayflies), Trichoptera (caddis flies) and Plecoptera (stone flies). In the case-bearing caddis flies of the Leptocera type the effect was particularly marked. These were numerous before spraying, but after spraying no live specimens were found in the four-year post-spraying period. During that time Ephemeroptera and Trichoptera in general took about three years to reach steady normal levels, and there were also considerable differences in the composition of the post-spraying population.

Similar types of study have been carried out in woodland areas exposed to aerial spraying with DDT for the control of the gypsy moth, a comparison of stream samples being made one week before and one week after spraying (Hitchcock, 1960). In that investigation the effect of DDT treatment appeared to vary from stream to stream, several genera of aquatic insects being eliminated from some but not from others. The Ephemeroptera as a group were not eliminated, while on the other hand the carnivorous genera of Plecoptera (*Isoperla, Acroneuria*) suffered greater mortality than the non-carnivorous *Nemoura* and *Peltiperla*, possibly due to the habits of predaceous species of wandering in more exposed conditions.

Reference has already been made to the intensive studies on the effect of DDT spraying — as well as of water contamination by heavy metals from mines — on fish in the Miramichi River system in northern New Brunswick. Equally intensive studies have been made on the effect of this spraying on aquatic insects in the streams after a forest-covered watershed had been aerially treated at the rate of 0·5 lb/acre (Ide, 1957, 1967). These observations were carried out on a long-term basis in order to follow the course of events right through the year of spraying itself, and subsequently through the first and second years after spraying. The sampling method used was the 1 yd² emergence trap which was emptied at approximately 24 h intervals. The results are presented in Fig. 27.

Spraying was carried out on 14th–17th June, and in the three weeks following this, emergence was almost negligible. From the middle of July until the middle of August there was a great increase in the number of insects emerging, but not a correspondingly great increase in volume, indicating that most emerging insects were small, e.g. minute Chironomids. The increase in volume of emerging insects could be attributed mostly to caddis flies and larger insects which may have been in the pre-pupal or pupal stages when spraying was done.

In the years following spraying, it became evident that the Trichoptera (caddis flies) as a group had been most severely affected. They were almost eliminated by the spraying, and did not reappear to any appreciable extent in the second year. The decrease in the number of Trichoptera — mainly predaceous species — may account

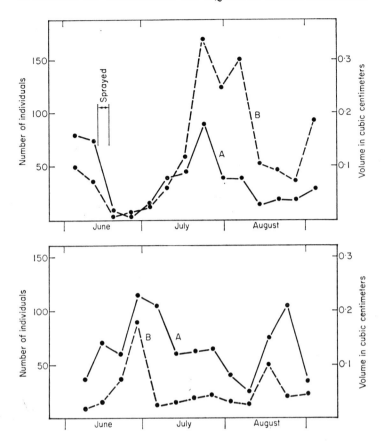

FIG. 27. Weekly changes in numbers (B) and volume (A) of insects emerging daily into 3 yd² cage traps in Trout Brook in 1955 — the year before any spraying had been done in the area — and in 1956, the year in which the stream was sprayed with DDT (after Ide, 1957).

for the increased abundance of small insects, mainly *Chironomids*, on whose larvae they usually feed.

This long-lasting effect of DDT treatment on predaceous caddis larvae, as well as on the predaceous nymphs of stoneflies (Plecoptera) may well have some bearing on the observations made in Canada many years previously on the long-term effects of DDT applied deliberately to streams for the control of *Simulium* larvae (Davies, 1950). In the years following treatment of a stream with DDT, the *Simulium* population — after initial drastic reduction — showed a phenomenal increase as demonstrated by cage traps. By three years after spraying, emergence had increased to about seventeen times

6*

the pre-spraying figure, up to 80,000 *Simulium* emerging from 1 yd²
during the summer of 1947.

Control measures against *Simulium*, whether purely as a biting
pest or as a vector of human disease, have been carried out in
many countries for over twenty years. In the vast majority of cases
the basis of control has been the regular application of larvicides to
the streams and rivers in which the immature stages develop. Control
operations were originally based on the use of DDT, and DDT is
still the larvicide of choice in the absence of a suitable replacement. Although it has been recognized for many years that
DDT treatment of rivers was liable to have a drastic and devastating effect on the ecological balance, systematic investigations on
this problem have been few and far between, and most of these have
been mainly concerned with the effect of DDT treatment on the
freshwater fish fauna. Reference was made earlier to the side
effects of *Simulium* control operations carried out on the Victoria
Nile at Jinja, Uganda, before and after March 1956 when the
river was dosed with DDT (Corbet, 1956). The treatment — which
was probably much heavier than the calculated dosage — was considered to have almost completely eliminated the lithophilous insect
fauna, with subsequent drastic effect on those species of fish dependent on this food supply.

In those *Simulium* control programmes in Africa the overriding
public health demands have completely dominated any other ecological considerations, and the pleas for caution expressed by a few far-
seeing biologists (e.g. Hynes, 1960) were clearly too much in advance
of the times to receive due attention. A systematic attempt to study
the ecological effects of DDT treatment of streams was made in the
River Manafwa in eastern Uganda in 1960, at a point where the
stream is about 12 ft wide flowing over stones and boulders (Hynes
and Williams, 1962). DDT was applied at the rate of 0·1 ppm for
30 min, and sampling at eight stations was carried out from 29–31
days after treatment, i.e. after an interval long enough for unaffected
eggs to hatch and re-populate the stream. The most drastic effect
appeared to be in three insect predators, *Neoperla*, *Hydropsyche* and
Cheumatopsyche, which were reduced both in numbers and size.
This in turn had led to an increase in prey organisms such as mayfly
nymphs (*Baetis*) and *Simulium* larvae below the dosage point. Many
Ephemeroptera were noticeably smaller below dosage point than
above, indicating that the exposed generation had been killed and
had become re-established from eggs. There is other evidence that
despite the immediate marked effects of *Simulium* larvicide dosages
on many non-target organisms, recovery — once treatment has been

suspended — may be very rapid. In the case of the Victoria Nile described above, the populations of aquatic mayflies and caddis flies recovered rapidly when treatment was discontinued (Corbet, 1958).

In North America it was found that a somewhat similar dose of DDT — 0·1 ppm for 20 min — appeared to have very little effect on riffle inhabiting arthropods other than blackfly larvae (Jamnback and Eabry, 1962). In that part of New York State DDT has been used regularly for a number of years, and the question arose as to whether there might have been a cumulative effect on the stream ecology. Square foot samples were taken from streams which had been regularly treated two to three times annually for the previous five to ten years, and compared with those with no history of treatment. Despite a careful statistical analysis of the data, making full allowance for differences between samples within streams, differences between samples of streams treated alike, and differences between samples in groups of streams treated differently, it was not possible to demonstrate convincingly that the DDT treatment had any adverse effect on stream arthropods.

From the select examples discussed above as well as from many other scattered observations which have not been quoted in detail, it is rather difficult to get anything other than a rather confused picture about the impact of DDT on stream invertebrates. Much of this may be attributed to the wide range of conditions in rivers and streams under observation, and it is clear for example that this widely differential effect can exist between different streams in the same study area (Hitchcock, 1960). In addition there are wide differences in the periods of observation. Some observers have concentrated their attention on the immediate — and often drastic — effects of DDT spraying produced in the few days immediately following exposure. Others have extended their observations over much longer periods of up to two to three years after a single exposure to DDT. Those longer term observations have shown that some genera of stream invertebrates which appeared to be almost entirely eliminated within a few days of treatment, do in fact make a very rapid recovery to normal populations within a few weeks or months, while others appear to be more permanently affected.

Many of the apparently anomalous results must be attributed however to the well-known difficulties in quantitative sampling of stream bottom organisms (Macan, 1958, 1963) and to the fact that in some investigations results have been based on bottom samples alone while others have relied on an entirely different type of sampling technique by means of emergence traps. With regard to methods of bottom sampling many investigators have used the Surber sampler

(Surber, 1936) for sampling bottom fauna of rapids and riffles. This is a square foot sampler operated so as to collect aquatic invertebrates from the enclosed area of bottom. The catch gives a measure of the "standing bottom crop" and may be expressed as number or volume or weight of organisms. This method is considered particularly suitable for obtaining total weight or volume, but may give rise to serious errors if the sample is expressed as number of individuals, this error increasing with increase in number of small animals in the population (Ide, 1940). With this method, results must be based on a large number of samples. For example, it is reported that even in a single riffle 194 samples would be required to give significant figures on total weight and seventy-three samples for total numbers (Needham and Usinger, 1956; Hitchcock, 1960). In this connection it is worth noting that equally strong emphasis on large numbers of small samples has been stressed in the entirely different field of sampling aquatic snail populations.

In view of these sampling variables and of the different type of information yielded by bottom sampling and by emergence traps, the range of evaluation methods used in another investigation is particularly instructive. This study was concerned with the fluctuation in populations of certain aquatic insects following aerial application of aldrin granules over 23,000 acres of farmland in Sugar Creek, Illinois (Moye and Luckman, 1964). A six-mile stretch of stream through this area was sampled up to nineteen months after treatment. Sampling was carried out in four shallow rubble-bottomed riffles. A series of pre-treatment samples were taken, and these were followed by collections one week after treatment and again at more or less weekly intervals up to nineteen weeks. Three 1 ft² samples were taken from each riffle at each sampling, and in addition a modified emergence trap (Ide, 1940) was used to collect adult forms emerging from the stream. The emergence trap measured 2 × 2 × 2 ft, and was held 2 in above the bed of the stream to allow free access of larvae and nymphs. A plastic cover to the trap was treated on the undersurface with oil-additive STP, a viscous sticky material for catching insects coming in contact with it. Each trap was placed over a large submerged rock in each riffle, and the top plates of the traps were removed each week for examination. This method was particularly valuable for sampling adult mayflies, caddis flies and midges.

The bottom sampling technique was supplemented by the use of standard 4 × 8 in bricks placed in each riffle for mayfly nymphs and caddis larvae. Immediately following treatment, and for about five days afterwards, drift nets were used to sample the massive flow of dead and moribund insects. Using the bottom sampling methods it was shown that no immature mayflies were collected from the second to the seventh week after treatment with aldrin. Caddis larvae recovered quickly from the effects of treatment, and in fact there was a great population increase in the summer following treatment, perhaps due to removal of predator populations. Brick collections confirmed the bottom sampling and showed that nine months after treatment the mayfly population in the treated portion of the stream was at a very low level, and that in contrast to this the population of caddis larvae had recovered to a higher density than untreated controls. Following an initial adverse effect, midges also recovered quickly and there were more *Chironomus* in the treated riffles than in the untreated controls; by the following spring numbers were back to normal. Apparently the removal and continued absence of mayflies from the stream did not have any effect on the fish populations, which — after an initial high kill — were once more abundant seven months after treatment.

IMPACT OF ORGANOPHOSPHORUS PESTICIDES

In mosquito and non-biting midge control programmes based on chemical attack on the immature stages, DDT and the organochlorines have been almost completely superseded by the organophosphorus insecticides, and to a lesser extent by the carbamates and others. These changes have coincided with an increasing awareness of the need to assess the impact of such chemical treatments on the non-target section of the freshwater community. Many of the new organophosphorus compounds are lethal to target species such as mosquito larvae at such low concentrations that it would seem *a priori* that other aquatic forms could prove equally sensitive. To offset this is the increasing weight of evidence, based on extensive physico-chemical analysis of water, mud, aquatic flora and fauna of treated habitats, about the non-persistence of these compounds in the environment, and the fact that they may disappear completely in a matter of days after application.

One of the first OP compounds to be thoroughly investigated from the point of view of general ecological impact on fresh water was methyl parathion which was used from 1962 onwards as a replacement for TDE (DDD) for the control of the clear lake gnat (*Chaoborus ascictopus*) (Cook and Conners, 1963). Methyl parathion was applied to this huge body of water at the rate of 3 ppb, in three treatments within three months during 1962. Although this compound is known to have a much higher mammalian toxicity than any other used as an aquatic pesticide, the very low dosage —

adequate for control of early instar *Chaoborus* larvae — was found to be well within the safety margin of the most sensitive of the local fish, bluegills. Studies on the short-term effects of these treatments on lake plankton and benthos were facilitated by the fact that complete records for the previous pre-treatment year were available for direct comparison. The dominant plankton — which were sampled by plankton tow net at different levels — were cladocerans (*Daphnia* spp) and Copepods (*Cyclops* spp, *Diaptomus* spp), with the Copepods slightly in excess of the Cladocerans. The benthos — sampled by Eckman dredge — consisted mainly of Oligochaetes and Chironomid larvae.

Although this treatment was completely effective in controlling the early instar larvae of *Chaoborus*, the general ecological impact appear to be minimal, with the possible exception of the zooplankton. In the treatment year, there was an immediate decrease in plankton following the second and third treatment, and there was no indication of the population explosion in September and October such as had occurred in the previous pre-treatment year. However, rapid and unpredictable changes in zooplankton population levels are liable to occur normally, and consequently the observations were not considered to provide conclusive evidence that these changes were entirely due to the organophosphorus treatment. It is emphasized that the selective effect of this treatment of clear lake is very likely associated with the extremely low concentration of toxicant found adequate for control of the target species. The possibility of long term effects was almost eliminated by the fact that there was a 50% deterioration of methyl parathion within 48 h, and complete disappearance of the chemical within two weeks of treatment.

One of the earliest OP compounds to replace DDT on an extensive scale was Baytex(fenthion) which has been widely used in control of mosquito larvae and aquatic larvae of non-biting midges. In Florida Baytex was found to be much more promising in midge control than either BHC and EPN which had been used extensively in the early fifties (Patterson and von Windeguth, 1964b). Application of a granular formulation to small ponds showed that at a concentration of 0·025 ppm — at which concentration it was lethal to Chironomid larvae (*Glyptotendipes paripes* and *Chironomus fulvipilus*) — it was non-toxic to such aquatic organisms as Copepods, Ostracods, Hydra, Annellid worms (*Tubifex* spp), snails and clams. However, this concentration was lethal to Cladocera (Patterson and von Windeguth, 1964a).

The likely impact of Baytex treatment on the actual lakes in which the midge larvae abound was further investigated by means of laboratory tests on organisms normally present in the shore-line areas of the lake, since the initial concentration of the toxicant would be highest in this shallow water area. The dosage of Baytex used in midge control was 0·20 to 0·25 lb/acre calculated to give a concentration of 0·1 ppm in water 1 ft deep and 0·01 ppm in water 10 ft deep. This dosage of Baytex(fenthion) was found to exceed the toxic limits for shrimp (*Palomonetes*) and Amphipods (*Hyalella*) commonly found in the shallow water area of the lake. However, although these organisms would be killed in the shallow waters of the lakes, in actual practice it was found that shrimps and amphipods continue to abound in treated lakes, and this appears very likely due to survival in the deeper waters of the lakes and rapid re-population of the shore area when the effects of Baytex treatment had declined.

One of the most interesting aspects of the impact of Baytex on freshwater life is the extreme sensitivity of the microcrustaceans belonging to the Cladocera — *Daphnia* and its allies — as compared to the relative insensitivity of the other microcrustaceans belonging to the Ostracods and Copepods. This was demonstrated not only in the investigations above, but also in studies on salt water mosquito control in New Jersey (Ruber, 1963). Baytex is lethal to Cladocerans down to levels of 0·00065 ppm or lower, while it causes little mortality to Copepods and Ostracods at concentrations up to 0·5 ppm and sometimes higher (Figs. 26–28). In this connection it is worth noting that the high sensitivity of Cladocera to Baytex is of much less ecological significance in these salt marshes — in which the microcrustaces are dominated by Copepods — than in freshwater environments where Cladocera such as *Daphnia* and its allies may be vital components of the food web.

Some idea of the impact of OP compounds other than Baytex on Cladocera can be gauged by field observations on the Cladoceran *Moina rectirostris*. This was found to be a common species in the highly polluted waters of sewage oxidation ponds which were used in field studies on the evaluation of new larvicides for control of chironomid larvae. The abundance of *Moina* was assessed at four different levels before and after treatment. A range of OP insecticides, Dursban, parathion, methyl parathion, Abate and Akton, at practical rates all proved highly toxic to *Moina* which indeed was more susceptible to these compounds than the target midge larvae themselves (Mulla and Khasawinah, 1969). The adverse effect of one of these compounds, Abate, has also been confirmed from other sources (Porter and Gojmerac, 1969).

Among other invertebrates it appears that nymphs of dragonflies (Odonata) are more affected by Baytex used in mosquito control operations than most other non-target species (Whitsel *et al.*, 1963). In areas treated with Baytex at 1/10 lb/acre damsel fly nymphs (*Libellula*) proved even more sensitive than the target mosquito larvae, being reported dead soon after application as compared to the mosquito larvae which did not begin to die until about 2 h after application. Other dragonfly nymphs were slightly less susceptible, not dying until 10 h afterwards (Warnick *et al.*, 1966).

In mosquito control a variety of organophosphorus compounds are commonly in use such as parathion, Baytex, Dursban and Abate. Perhaps owing to different dosages, different formulations and different environmental conditions, results do not always agree closely. The general impression is that the majority of non-target invertebrates are either unaffected or only temporarily reduced in numbers (Warnick *et al.*, 1966).

In the case of Dursban — one of the most powerful of the new OP larvicides — it has been clearly shown that at a certain critical range comparatively small increases in concentration may determine how lethal the impact of this chemical is on freshwater forms. In experimental ponds *Culex tarsalis* larvae can be controlled by dosages of Dursban as low as 0·005 lb/acre, at which concentration no ill-effects could be observed on such non-target fauna as corixids and diving beetles and their larvae. At higher dosages of 0·01 to 0·05 lb/acre, mayfly nymphs — which are also highly sensitive to several other OP larvicides — were noticeably affected (Mulla *et al.*, 1966). The same general conclusions about Dursban have been reached on the basis of aerial treatment with Dursban against mosquito larvae. At dosages of between 0·001 and 0·005 lb/acre, no obvious ill-effect on non-target invertebrates was evident. However, at 0·01 to 0·02 lb/acre there was a noticeable die-off of practically all arthropods (Moore and Breeland, 1967).

This generally biocidal effect of Dursban at such concentrations on a wide range of freshwater invertebrates is well in keeping with the results of controlled laboratory tests on freshwater shrimps (*Gammarus*), mayfly nymphs (*Baetis, Ecdyonurus*) and caddis larvae (*Hydropsyche, Limnephilus*) (Muirhead-Thomson, 1970).

With regard to another highly successful OP larvicide, Abate, reports on its impact on non-target organisms are rather more inconsistent, although here again the all-important question of actual dosage or concentration has to be taken into account. On the one hand Abate has been reported as having no noticeable side-effects over a wide range of larvicide dosage used (Moore and Breeland,

1967), and field application of 0·25 lb/acre have also been reported to have no noticeable mortality on Odonata, *Chaoborus* larvae, Copepods, Ostracods or fairy shrimps (von Windeguth and Patterson, 1966). At the other extreme, treatment of a lake at the rate of 0·039 lb/acre for the successful eradication of midge larvae (*Chaoborus*) proved toxic to nearly all other insects in the lake (Fales *et al.*, 1968).

The impact of Abate — and also of another OP larvicide bromophos — has been carefully examined in connection with mosquito control of temporary pools along the shore line of Lake Michigan, Wisconsin (Porter and Gojmerac, 1969). Abate was applied at 0·03 lb/acre which proved to be an effective larvicide dosage. This treatment also eliminated larvae of the caddis fly *Limnephilus indivisus*, and proved toxic to early instar Libellulid naiads (Odonata) but did not harm mature naiads of another odonatan, *Lestes dryas*. The Abate treatment also eradicated Cladocera. Amphipods, Isopods, Ostracods and Copepods were all unaffected by the Abate treatment, as well as by bromophos. In the case of Abate, some of the inconsistent results reported from other sources (Mulla and Khasawinah, 1969) may be due in part to the variable behaviour of the EC formulations of Abate used at that time.

The few OP compounds discussed above represent only a small proportion of a rapidly increasing number of new organophosphorus larvicides which are now available for laboratory tests or field trials (Mulla *et al.*, 1966; Mulla, 1966b). Some of these compounds issued under code names or numbers are liable to be withdrawn or replaced by other closely allied compounds whose exact chemical nature may remain undisclosed. In others, the question of formulation is constantly under review, new formulations rapidly superseding old ones. As a result, information about even the most widely used organophosphorus larvicides such as Baytex, malathion, Dursban and Abate is still very patchy and incomplete, and few investigators have the time or the energy to spare for the many new and more recent compounds scheduled for field trials, and whose likely impact on the environment can only be a matter for conjecture. Our knowledge about the ecological impact of such recent compounds will continue to lag far behind until such time as the problem is tackled in a much more systematic and coordinated manner.

IMPACT OF VARIOUS INSECTICIDES ON CADDIS FLIES, MAYFLIES AND STONEFLIES

While there is a great deal of information from the field about the effects of spraying with DDT and other insecticides on populations of stream-dwelling stoneflies (Plecoptera), mayflies (Ephemeroptera) and caddis flies (Trichoptera), there is a remarkable scarcity of laboratory investigations on the reactions of these insect larvae and nymphs to different time/concentrations of insecticide under controlled conditions. This may possibly be due to the fact that in general the question of laboratory maintenance and culture of many of these stream-dwelling forms has been rather neglected by freshwater biologists (Macan, 1963; Craig, 1966). There is a great deal of evidence to show that many of these aquatic stages react badly when transferred to artificial laboratory conditions from their natural rapidly-flowing, well-aerated habitat. Difficulty is frequently encountered in keeping control mortalities down to acceptable levels, and this in turn has introduced some uncertainty as to the extent to which observed mortality and other reactions can be attributed directly to the pesticide itself, and how much is due to the additive effect of pesticide acting on an already weakened test insect.

There are several reasons why the aquatic stages of this group of insects merit more serious and systematic investigation by means of refined laboratory methods. Firstly, this group contains species which form an important source of food for many freshwater fish, including food fish. Secondly, the group includes several members which appear to be extremely sensitive to certain pesticides, and which can provide very effective indicators of contamination in natural waters. Thirdly, among both stonefly nymphs (or naids) and caddis larvae, there are predaceous species which play an important role in regulating natural populations of several dominant stream-dwellers such as *Simulium* larvae.

The three considerations above usually put this group of invertebrates high on the list of non-target organisms. However, there are times and places where mass production of adult caddis flies and mayflies from natural habitats causes a serious nuisance in cities and towns in their neighbourhood due to the swarms of insects. Such nuisances for example have been caused by swarms of mayflies (*Hexagenia*) produced from freshwater lakes in Florida (Hoffmann, 1960; Lieux and Mulrennan, 1955) and New York State (Jamnback, 1969b), while in other cases rivers — such as the Upper Mississippi — have been the origin of swarms of both mayflies (*Hexagenia*) and caddis flies (Carlson, 1966).

From these various aspects it is not surprising that such laboratory methods which have been developed for evaluating impact of pesticides have developed independently and quite unconnected with each other.

Following the extensive spraying of forest in the Yellowstone area in the United States, it is estimated that about 99% of the aquatic insects along a 100 miles stretch of the river were killed. The destruction of the bottom fauna led to a more critical investigation about the tolerance limits of that group as represented by two species of stonefly naiads (Jensen and Gaufin, 1964a). Tests were carried out in 2 gal glass aquaria (measuring 11 in × 7 in × 6 in) submerged in a constant temperature water tank. The general test methods were those recommended by the American Public Health Association (1960) in which ten naiads were allowed to become acclimatized for 24 h in each jar containing 2250 ml of dilution water, after which the volume was made up to 3000 ml with dilution water containing a series of insecticide concentrations. Exposure was continuous over a four-day period. The mortality was noted each day, and provided data for 24 h, 48 h, 72 h and 96 h TL_m values. The test species selected *Pteronarcys californica* and *Acroneuria pacifica* were important food organisms for trout and other sport fish.

These tests provided a wealth of information about the reactions of these two species to ten organochlorine and organophosphorus compounds, comparisons being made not only on the basis of 48, 72 and 96 h TL_m in ppm, but also by comparing the reactions through the four-day exposure period of test species exposed to the same concentration of different insecticides. The series of responses noted at each 24 h period were as follows, (i) no observable effect, (ii) hyperactivity, (iii) loss of equilibrium, (iv) tremor and convulsions and (v) death. The results showed that at one end of the scale the chlorinated hydrocarbon endrin was by far the most toxic to both species, while at the other end DDT and aldrin were the least toxic (Table VII).

TABLE VII

96–hour TL_m values for two species of stonefly naiads arranged in decreasing order of toxicity (after Jensen and Gaufin, 1964)

Acroneuria pacifica		*Pteronarcys californica*	
Insecticide	96-h TL_m (p.p.m.)	Insecticide	96-h TL_m (p.p.m.)
Endrin	0·00039	Endrin	0·0024
Parathion	0·00280	Guthion	0·0220
Bayer 29493	0·00510	Bayer 29493	0·0265
Malathion	0·00700	Di-syston	0·0285
Di-syston	0·00820	Parathion	0·0320
Guthion	0·00850	Dieldrin	0·0390
Dylox	0·01650	Malathion	0·0500
Dieldrin	0·02400	Dylox	0·0690
Aldrin	0·14300	Aldrin	0·1800
DDT	0·32000	DDT	1·8000

In all tests *Acroneuria pacifica* was more sensitive to chlorinated hydrocarbons and organophosphorus compounds than *Pteronarcys californica*, showing earlier response and ultimately higher mortality. These tests also revealed a size differential in sensitivity, particularly in the case of *Pteronarcys* in which specimens of 4–5 cm in length were resistant to five times the concentration of DDT as compared to specimens 2–3 cm in size. In addition, larger specimens which had already displayed DDT tremors, frequently recovered completely on removal to fresh water.

When similar tests were extended to two species of caddis larvae, *Arctopsyche grandis* and *Hydropsyche californica*, it soon became evident that these organisms were less suitable for laboratory testing than the more robust stonefly nymphs (Gaufin *et al.*, 1961, 1965). The caddis larvae were more susceptible to handling and mechanical injury in the laboratory. They were also highly susceptible to the fungus *Saprolegnia* when maintained at 65°F in contrast to the stonefly nymphs kept in association. Both species of caddis larvae were more sensitive to DDT than either of the stonefly naiads, *Hydrophyche californica* showing the greatest sensitivity with a TL_m of 0·048 ppm.

Basically similar test methods, viz. those of the U.S. Public Health Association, were used with nymphs of the mayfly (*Hexagenia*) and larvae of the caddis fly (*Hydropsyche*) in quite unrelated studies arising from the need to control the nuisance caused by swarms of adult caddisflies and mayflies in the upper Mississippi area (Carlson, 1966). The total observation period in this case was limited to 24 hours, with conditions recorded after 2, 4, 8, 12 and 24 hours. Again *Hydropsyche* was found to be rather an unsuitable subject for laboratory tests, with high control mortalities beyond 48 h. The *Hydropsyche* larvae were found to be much more sensitive than *Hexagenia* nymphs to all compounds tested.

As the object of these investigations was the effective control of aquatic stages, emphasis was on the organophosphorus compounds because as a group they are less toxic to fish than chlorinated hydrocarbons, and they also undergo relatively rapid hydrolysis in water to non-toxic substances.

Laboratory investigations on the reactions of stonefly nymphs or naiads have also been carried out in a quite different context from either of the studies discussed so far, namely, the possibility of resistance developing under continuous DDT pressure (Sprague, 1968). The study area in New Brunswick was one whose streams had been exposed to direct aerial spraying with DDT in four out of seven years, 1952, 1953, 1956 and 1957. In the three other years, 1954, 1955 and 1958 the stream was also contaminated to a reduced degree by DDT spraying upstream. In the last years of DDT treatment no stoneflies were taken in streams in the sprayed area (Webb and Macdonald, 1958), but in 1958 — a year of moderate DDT exposure — stoneflies of the genus *Nemoura* appeared in moderate numbers, and again in 1959 (Webb *et al.*, 1959).

Tests were therefore devised to check the possibility of resistance to DDT, and although the information required was essentially the same as that in the studies discussed above, viz. the establishing of tolerance limits of the test organisms, the criteria adopted provide an interesting and illuminating contrast. In this case tests were carried out at only two concentrations, 1 ppm and 0·1 ppm DDT, and differences in reactions were measured on a time basis in order to establish a figure representing the median mortality time, i.e. the time in minutes taken to produce 50% mortality. In order to reduce handling and transport mortality, tests were carried out near the collecting stream, either eight or ten nymphs being tested in each of the test containers. These were plastic cups containing 1·4 litres of test solution which was kept aerated by a stream of air bubbles from a small aquarium pump. Mortality was recorded at appropriate intervals over the next 11,400 minutes (7 days, 22 h). By the end of that period half of the nymphs in the untreated control had died, and this had to be allowed for in calculating median lethal times, and in comparing the reactions of test animals from sprayed and from unsprayed streams. As the tests failed to reveal any difference in susceptibility between *Nemoura* from sprayed streams and those from control streams with no history of DDT exposure, it was concluded that the apparent return of stoneflies in the face of continued spraying was most likely due to the existence of a dormant stage — possibly the egg — during the spraying in late May and early June.

Laboratory tests for measuring the impact of pesticides on stream invertebrates have also been used in connection with the successful development of TFM in practical control of sea lamprey (Smith, 1967). Tests were carried out in 6 l of solution in 10-l jars at a constant temperature of 55°F. Dissolved oxygen was maintained by means of compressed air delivered through a stone air-breaker in each jar. Mortality was determined at the end of the test period of 22–24 h. The number of specimens tested at each concentration of TFM from 2 ppm to 20 ppm varied from twenty to twenty-five in the case of caddis larvae and non-burrowing mayfly nymphs, to around fifty with the burrowing mayfly nymphs. In the case of stonefly nymphs or naiads the number was usually less than twenty. Occasionally very large numbers of test animals were exposed at particular critical concentrations, e.g. 1950 burrowing mayfly naiads to 10 ppm TFM. The results were recorded simply as percentage mortalities of test animals exposed to different concentrations, and no attempt was made to calculate TL_m or LT_{50} values.

This extensive test series, which covered a very wide range of invertebrates in addition to the stoneflies, mayflies and caddis flies, was particularly interesting in revealing a sharp distinction between the reactions of burrowing mayfly nymphs (*Hexagenia*) and non-burrowing species (*Ephemerella, Stenonema* and *Isonychia*). With the former, mortality reached 96% at 8 ppm TFM, and 100% at concentrations of 12 ppm of TFM and over. With non-burrowing mayflies — and also case-building caddis — no consistently high mortalities were produced up to concentrations of about 18 ppm. Net-building caddis, e.g. *Hydropsyche* and stonefly nymphs, *e.g. Isoperla, Chloroperla*, tended to show an increasing mortality at concentrations of 10 ppm upwards.

In studying the reactions of such highly sensitive stream-dwelling invertebrates to pesticide exposure, the limitations of the short-term static test soon become obvious. Although, with careful handling, these stonefly and mayfly nymphs and caddis larvae appear to survive in well-aerated water, this laboratory environment is a highly unnatural one as compared to the continuous current in their normal habitat. In addition, loss of insecticide in well-aerated, static water produced by such factors as adsorption and co-distillation may well produce test results which cannot readily be applied to exposure to the same insecticide in a continuous flow.

These limitations become increasingly vital when any attempt is made to extend the duration of the test beyond the four-day (or 96-h) period widely adopted. In order to deal with these difficulties, and at the same time provide much-needed information on the chronic and less obvious effects of long-term exposure to pesticide, increasing attention has been given to continuous flow laboratory tests (Gaufin *et al.*, 1961, 1965; Jensen and Gaufin, 1964, 1966). In the apparatus used, 1% emulsifiable insecticide-acetone solutions were diluted with metered quantities of water to provide stock concentrations which were pumped through Pyrex tubing to each aquarium. Twenty-five stonefly naiads were placed in each aquarium for a 48 h acclimatization period prior to addition of insecticide. The need for some natural attachment for the naiads was early recognized, and attempts were made to provide a standard in the form of perforated steel plates. This proved unsuitable because of difficulty in decontamination after each test, and finally a more natural substitute in the form of natural granite stone had to be re-introduced even though it was recognized that unmeasurable differences between stones might introduce possible variations. Daily observations were made on the stonefly naiads, and these were used to compile TL_m values from four days to thirty days.

In addition to providing a wealth of information about changes in reaction with increasing length of exposure, these tests also enabled a comparison to be made between the reactions in static and flowing water over an equal period. This is best illustrated by the organophosphorus compound Guthion. Following exposure for four days Guthion was much more toxic to both *Pteronarcys* and *Acroneuria* in flowing water than in static tests. With *Acroneuria* the four-day TL_m figures in mg/1 were 0·0085 and 0·0020 respectively, while with *Pteronarcys* they were 0·0220 and 0·0046 respectively. That is to say that over that period Guthion was roughly four to five times more toxic in flowing water than in static water. However, this relationship is certainly not a universal one with all insecticides. In the case of the chlorinated hydrocarbon Aldrin for example, the toxic effects after four days were less in flowing water than in the static tests.

With regard to longer exposures between four days and thirty days, the results are exemplified by those of *Acroneuria* which show that the rapid toxicity of Guthion continues up to fifteen days at which time 50% of the naiads were dead in solutions of Guthion which were almost thirty times less concentrated than those which produced the same percentage kill in four-day static tests. Between fifteen and thirty days the lethal toxicity of Guthion did not increase significantly.

As an example of the less obvious effects of prolonged exposures which do not actually kill the test insects, is the effect on moulting. With Guthion for example the moulting rates of *Acroneuria* were reduced at concentrations between 0·001 and 0·005 ppm. After five days' continuous exposure to Guthion, moulting ceased at all concentrations. It was also noted that after prolonged exposure to many of the insecticides tested, nymphs of *Acroneuria* became swollen and distended due to absorption of large quantities of water.

A rather different approach to laboratory evaluation of the impact of pesticides on non-target organisms has arisen in the course of studies on *Simulium* larvicides. At present, it is the practice in *Simulium* control to apply the larvicide — DDT in most cases — for relatively short periods of 30 min or less to the streams and rivers which are the larval habitat (McMahon, 1967; W.H.O., 1966). At increasing distances below the dosage or application point there will be an increasing tendency — due to mixing, eddying and differential flow — for larvae in those places to be exposed to insecticide for rather longer periods, but also at progressively decreasing concentrations. In designing laboratory tests to evaluate the effect of this treatment on non-target organisms, this comparatively short exposure period has to be taken into account. With this in mind a series of laboratory tests on various stream invertebrates was carried out using an arbitrary 1 h exposure period as standard, followed by a holding period of 24 h in clean water (Muirhead-Thomson, 1970). Mayfly nymphs and caddis larvae from a small *Simulium* stream in southern England were maintained in the laboratory in 5 l tanks of tap water vigorously aerated with a jet of compressed air, and then exposed — ten at a time — to a range of larvicide concentrations in acetone. Prior to the test, and during the subsequent holding period, mayfly nymphs were provided with a flat stone to cling to and shelter under, as this seemed to be a vital requirement for their well-being. In controls with acetone alone at 0·1 ppm for a 1 h exposure period, mortality after a 24 h holding period remained consistently at zero.

The results showed distinct differences between the reactions of the three main test invertebrates used, i.e. the nymphs of the mayflies, *Baetis* and *Ecdyonurus*, and the web-spinning larvae of the caddis *Hydropsyche*. The results with two well-known organophosphorus larvicides, Dursban and Abate, showed that *Baetis* was the most sensitive, especially to Dursban which produced 100% mortality at a range of concentrations from 0·01 ppm down to 0·0005 ppm. With Abate, 100% mortality was produced at 0·01 ppm, but the mortality was reduced to about 28% at concentrations between 0·005 and 0·001 ppm. With *Ecdyonurus* there was no striking difference between the effects of Abate and Dursban, mortality at 0·01 ppm being 10–20%, rising to 70–80% at 0·1 ppm. Larvae of *Hydropsyche* were apparently unaffected by concentrations of 0·01 ppm of either compound.

From these static water tests, nymphs of *Baetis* appeared to be much more sensitive to the organophosphorus larvicides than either of the other two test species, and perhaps even more sensitive than *Simulium* itself to the effects of Dursban. However, beyond giving a preliminary indication of the comparative susceptibilities of these stream invertebrates to a range of pesticides, the value of these static tests is rather limited. Comparisons between the reactions of *Simulium* larvae in static tests — in which the water is vigorously aerated — and the more natural flowing-water tests show consistently that higher concentrations of chemical are required to produce the same mortality in flowing water. It appears therefore that laboratory evaluation of the effect of various pesticides on stream invertebrates which are normally exposed to a flow or continuous change of water, should preferably be based on flowing water tests, even when the indicator species appear to thrive in the artificial environment of aerated static water in the laboratory.

LABORATORY EVALUATION TECHNIQUES FOR MICROCRUSTACEA AND CRUSTACEA

In measuring the effects of industrial effluents and metallic poisons, one of the most widespread microcrustaceans, *viz.* the water flea, *Daphnia*, has long been recognized as a particularly suitable indicator species for laboratory tests. As one of the most abundant invertebrates in ponds, always available in numbers and easy to maintain in laboratory culture, it seemed the obvious representative of the microfauna in general, and one whose role as an indicator of pollution would prove complementary to that of fish. The value of *Daphnia* was further supported when one of the earlier investigations revealed that it was more susceptible to many poisons than trout, one of the most sensitive species of fish to pollution (Ellis, 1937).

Daphnia become well established as an ideal indicator species for laboratory tests concerning the toxicity thresholds of various chemical compounds found in industrial wastes (Anderson, 1944, 1946) and is also widely used in Europe as an indicator of water pollution levels (Bick, 1963). It is not surprising that with the increasing development and use of pesticides, *Daphnia* would be one of the first non-target invertebrates to be studied systematically in the laboratory.

In accordance with early practice, standard laboratory tests with *Daphnia* were based on standard fish toxicity methods adopted in the United States (Doudoroff *et al.*, 1951; American Public Health Association, 1960) with mortality noted after a 24 h exposure period to a range of insecticide concentrations. However, some difficulties in determining the exact death point of *Daphnia* have in some cases dictated the need to adopt different criteria for evaluating the effect of pesticide. This has led in one direction to an extension of the exposure period to 48 h as the standard for calculating the EC_{50} (Cope, 1966). In another direction it has led to the adoption of a rather different criterion, *viz.* the "estimated concentration required to immobilize *Daphnia* in 50 h" (Anderson, 1960).

In the first of these investigations, very full data have been obtained on the relative tolerance of *Daphnia*, and a related Cladoceran, *Simocephalus*, to a range of insecticides, with the results shown in Table VIII.

TABLE VIII

48-hour EC_{50} in parts per thousand million (parts per billion of Cladocera to different insecticides, at 21°C (after Cope, 1966).

	Daphnia	*Simocephalus*
Endrin	20	26
Toxaphene	15	19
Dieldrin	250	240
DDT	0·4	2
Heptachlor	42	47
Lindane	460	520
Ethyl guthion	3	4
Malathion	2	3
Diazinon	0·9	2
Pyrethrins	25	42
Sevin (Carbaryl)	6	8

The reactions of these two species of water flea follow a very similar pattern, and show that they are extremely sensitive to DDT and to the organophosphorus compounds listed, but much more tolerant to lindane and dieldrin.

The latter investigation showed that *Daphnia* is much less susceptible to endrin than are fish or stonefly nymphs, but much more susceptible to parathion.

Laboratory and field studies on another Cladoceran, *Moina rectirostris*, a common species in highly polluted ponds used in field tests on Chironomid larvae, have confirmed the high sensitivity of this group of microcrustacea to a range of organophosphorus compounds, Dursban, parathion, methylparathion, Abate and Akton, to all of which they were more susceptible than midge larvae (Mulla and Khasawinah, 1969).

The Cladocera, as represented by *Daphnia* and its allies, have been studied in more detail and for a longer period than any other group of microcrustacea. However, its reactions to pesticides are by no means representative of microcrustacea in general. In fact, one of the most striking features to emerge from work in recent years on other groups of microcrustacea is the very wide difference in reaction which may be shown by different groups to one and the same insecticide. These differences have emerged from both field observations and laboratory studies. For example, after treatment of a pond with the organophosphorus insecticide Baytex (fenthion) at 0·2 lbs/acre (equivalent to 0·025 ppm) in midge control, Cladocera disappeared almost completely from treated ponds and did not become re-established for about five months. Under the same conditions Copepods and Ostracods were not affected (Patterson and von Windeguth, 1964a).

A more exact measurement of this difference in reaction was revealed by laboratory tests comparing the reactions of the Cladoceran, *Daphnia* and the Copepod, *Cyclops*, after a 24 h exposure. With *Cyclops*, Baytex produced 100% mortality down to 1 ppm, while with *Daphnia*, 100% mortality was produced down to the remarkably low concentration of 0·00009 ppm (Ruber, 1963, 1965).

Difficulties in the culture and maintenance of Copepods, together with their very small size relative to such robust creatures as *Daphnia*, which may grow up to 5 mm, have had some discouraging effect on adopting this group for routine laboratory evaluation in pesticide studies. However, two entirely different lines of approach have greatly increased our knowledge of this group in recent years. The first of these concerns studies on the effect of estuarine Copepods of various insecticides used for control of salt-marsh mosquitoes in the United States (Ruber, 1962, 1963, 1965, 1967; Ruber and Baskar, 1968).

The other entirely different line of approach is concerned with the laboratory evaluation of chemicals for the control of those tropical species of *Cyclops* which act as intermediate hosts to the human parasitic guinea worm, *Dracunculus medinensis* (Nugent *et al.*, 1955; Gretillat, 1965; Muller, 1970).

In the course of work on the control of the salt-marsh mosquito *Aedes sollicitans* in the New Jersey tidal marshes, the search for some indicator non-target organisms eventually pointed to a particular Copepod— *Cyclops* (*Metacylops*) *spartinus* — which occurs in the summer months almost to the exclusion of other Copepods and microcrustacea. Its very high densities are closely correlated with the occurrence of *Aedes sollicitans* both as to time and location. At the same time, both laboratory and field studies showed that this species was sensitive to DDT at similar concentrations in the case of the mosquito. This species of microcrustacean was successfully maintained in laboratory culture for four months and probably an equal number of generations. In addition, laboratory tests were carried out on another Copepod, *Cyclops vernatus*, which tends to replace *Metacyclops* at the end of the summer, when floods reduce the salinity of the marshes. These tests revealed a very similar pattern of sensitivity for the two species.

Experience gained in these laboratory tests is very instructive. For various technical reasons it was found extremely difficult to establish EC_{50} and LC_{50} values on conventional lines. The sensitivity of the test animals was liable to vary according to unknown factors such as age and previous history, unless cultures were available which had been reared under carefully controlled conditions. Difficulty was also encountered in accurately evaluating the effect of chemical poisons, particularly those which were slow-acting, and in deciding the relative importance to be attached to such responses as mortality, moribundity, immobilization, etc. Also important is the question of how long a test should be run in order to meet all requirements. The practice finally adopted was a 24 h exposure test, extended on occasions up to six or seven days.

The results of a series of laboratory tests comparing the reactions of representative species of Cladocera, Copepods and Ostracods are shown in Figs. 28–30. It will be seen that each group reacts differently to the three insecticides tested. In the Copepods, endrin is

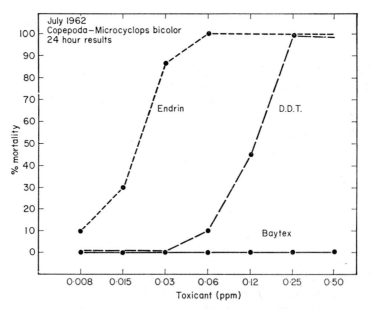

FIG. 28. Twenty four-hour mortalities of Copepods exposed to different concentrations of endrin, DDT and Baytex (after Ruber, 1963).

more lethal than DDT, which in turn is more lethal than Baytex. In fact Baytex appears to have little adverse effect at the ranges used — up to 0·5 ppm. In the case of Cladocera, Baytex is about ten times more lethal than endrin, which in turn is more lethal than DDT.

In later experiments with additional larvicides, Copepods proved to be the least affected by two of the most toxic mosquito larvicides known, namely Abate (organophosphorus compound) and Sevin (carbamate), whereas Dursban (OP) proved to be about as toxic as DDT (Ruber and Baskar, 1968).

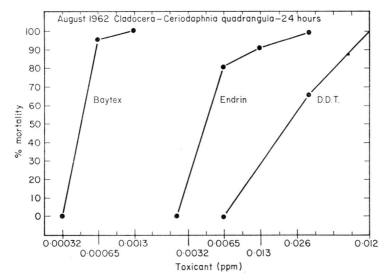

FIG. 29. Twenty four-hour mortalities of Cladocera exposed to different concentrations of Baytex, endrin and DDT (after Ruber, 1963).

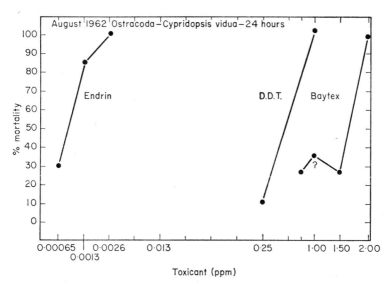

FIG. 30. Twenty four-hour mortalities of Ostracods exposed to different concentrations of Baytex, endrin and DDT (after Ruber, 1963).

CHAPTER 7

INFLUENCE OF CHEMICAL AND PHYSICAL FACTORS ON PESTICIDE IMPACT ON FRESH WATER

TEMPERATURE

Water temperature is one of the most important factors in the environment of aquatic organisms and plays a vital role in determining their distribution, growth, reproduction, metabolism and behaviour. Because it is one of the most easily measurable factors in the natural environment, and one which can be readily controlled in the laboratory, perhaps more is known about the reactions of freshwater animals to this one factor than to any other in the environment.

In the laboratory phases of evaluating pesticide impact, due recognition is given to this major role of water temperature by carrying out all tests at controlled temperatures, either at one constant temperature for all tests, or at two or three constant temperature ranges according to the conditions to which the different test species are normally exposed. The importance of evaluating pesticides under temperature conditions related to those of the test animals in their natural environment is well illustrated by test procedures adopted in the United States where fish in the northern part of the country are tested at lower ranges (12°C) than the warm water fish from the south (17°C).

In trying to assess the effect of temperature on the impact of pesticides on freshwater life it is important to recognize some of the many different facets which have to be taken into account. Differences in temperature, or changes in temperature, can affect the general activity, metabolism and behaviour of freshwater forms in ways which expose them to a greater or less degree to pesticides present in the water. Temperature also influences the chemical and physical state of the pesticide, the extent to which it remains in solution or suspension, its persistence and the extent to which it is broken down or de-activated. In addition, the actual rate of uptake of the toxic chemical by the freshwater organisms may be strongly influenced by the prevailing temperature conditions. In view of the very great range of chemical compounds used as pesticides it would seem unlikely from the start to expect any uniformity of reaction or any clear-cut pattern to emerge.

Some of the variations and vagaries of temperature effect on pesticide impact are well brought out in the extensive fish toxicity studies carried out in different laboratories. For example, in the evaluation of Antimycin carried out at three temperatures, 12°C, 17°C and 24°C, the results shown in Fig. 6 reveal clearly how different species of test fish can react very differently to temperature change. Goldfish are particularly affected, the toxicity of Antimycin increasing tenfold at 17°C as compared with 12°C. Among the catfish the toxicity was enhanced about twofold at 17°C.

In the case of the selective lamprey larvicide TFM however, it appears that the activity of this compound shows little difference in effect over a wide range of temperatures from 35°F to 55°F either on larval lampreys or on rainbow trout (Applegate et al., 1961).

In fish toxicity studies on a wide range of insecticides it is found, not altogether surprisingly, that most of these compounds are increasingly toxic at higher temperatures. However, there are notable exceptions, DDT once again appearing in an enigmatic role. In an extensive series of tests at the Fish Laboratory, Denver, Colorado, involving rainbow trout (*Salmo gairdnerii*) and bluegills (*Lepomis macrochirus*) tests were carried out at three different temperature levels (1·6°C, 7·2°C and 12·7°C for trout, and 12·7°C, 18·3°C and 23·8°C for bluegills), and the criteria adopted for evaluation was the LC_{50} value after 24 and 96 h exposure. With most compounds susceptibility increased with increase in temperature. In the case of lindane and azinphosmethyl (Guthion) however, bluegills showed no change in reaction over the temperature range tested. With methoxychlor, susceptibility decreased with increase in temperature, both at 24 and 96 h. The general range of reaction produced by different temperatures is best brought out by comparing the "relative increase in susceptibility" rather than comparing the original LC_{50} data (Tables IX and X) (Macek et al., 1969).

The unusual temperature relations of methoxychlor are somewhat similar to those already recognized as characteristic of DDT, to which methoxychlor is closely related. Tests with DDT on the same two test species, rainbow trout and bluegills, showed that DDT was more toxic at the lower temperatures — 13°C — than at the high temperatures used — 18·5 and 23°C (Cope, 1966). The increasing toxicity at lower temperatures appears to level off below 7°C and above 29·5°C (Johnson, 1968).

In the test series at Denver described above it was also found that in general the effect of temperature on susceptibility of both species of test fish was less after 96 h exposure than after 24 h. This may be related to the higher rate of uptake at higher than at lower temperatures; because of the limited amount of pesticide in the test containers this would be more marked after 24 h than after 96 h.

TABLE IX

Relative increase in susceptibility of rainbow trout tested against a range of pesticides at 1·6, 7·2 and 12·7°C, based on 24 h TL_{50} (Macek et al., 1969).

Compound	"Relative increase in susceptibility"
Dursban	10·37
Dibrom	5·41
Endrin	5·35
Dieldrin	4·19
Thiodan	4·15
Aldrin	3·52
Trifluralin	3·24
Guthion	1·92
Heptachlor	1·31
Methoxychlor	0·82

TABLE X

Relative increase in susceptibility of bluegills (*Lepomis macrochirus*) tested against indicated pesticides at 12·7, 18·3 and 23·8°C, based on 24 h TL_{50}.

Compound	"Relative increase in susceptibility"
Trifluralin	4·15
Aldrin	3·60
Endrin	3·50
Diuron	2·78
Dieldrin	2·60
Chlordane	2·31
Malathion	2·00
Toxaphene	1·46
Lindane	1·05
Guthion (azinphosmethyl)	1·00
Methoxychlor	0·69

The effect of temperature on susceptibility to pesticide impact has also received a great deal of attention in molluscicide studies. In the case of copper sulphate, the dominant molluscicide in the earlier years of aquatic snail control, it was recognized that activity was greatly influenced by temperature (Hoffman and Zakhary, 1954). In Egyptian canals for example, there are wide seasonal variations in the water temperature. The toxicity of copper sulphate was therefore tested on the local vector snails at temperatures between 14°C and 26°C over this range. At temperatures of 14°C, 17°C, 20°C, 23°C and 26°C the corresponding $LC_{50's}$ were 13 ppm, 4·8 ppm, 1·4 ppm, 0·58 ppm and 0·25 ppm respectively, demonstrating the greatly enhanced effect of copper sulphate with rise of water temperature. Subsequent molluscicides, sodium pentachlorophenate (NaPCP) and Bayluscide (niclosamine) have also been shown to have a more direct relationship between increase in temperature and increase in susceptibility of test snails. In this case the effects of temperature have perhaps been accentuated or magnified because of the very wide range of temperatures used, from 30°C down to 5°C. With the standard test species of snail, *Biomphalaria glabrata*, a solution of 0·3 ppm Bayluscide gave 100% mortality at 30°C, 76% mortality at 15°C and 12% mortality at 5°C, after 8 h exposures. In a 24 h exposure, 0·3 ppp was sufficient to kill all snails at 20°C, but the concentration had to be raised to 0·5 ppm to produce the same 100% mortality results at 5°C (Strufe and Gonnert, 1962). It will be seen that with the longer exposures, the temperature differentials are much less marked. The noticeable fall in molluscicide activity at the lowest temperatures is very likely accounted for by the reduced metabolism of snails at lower temperatures.

The same general trend in temperature relationships exists with Frescon (N-tritylmorpholine) and marked differences are evident within a smaller range of temperatures than above, the range in this case being 15–28°C, Table XI (Boyce *et al.*, 1967).

TABLE XI

Temperature	LC_{50} (ppm)	LC_{90} (ppm)
15°C	0·14	0·28
21°C	0·10	0·17
28°C	0·05	0·10

HARD AND SOFT WATER

It has long been recognized that the action of toxic chemicals on freshwater animals such as fish may be influenced by the quality of the water with regard to such characters as pH, alkalinity and hard-

7+

ness, and that different natural waters may differ widely in respect of these properties. In recognition of this the majority of laboratories concerned with routine studies on fish toxicity or routine screening of potential piscicides, either carry out tests at consistently uniform conditions of water quality, or duplicate all tests in hard as well as in soft waters. The general concept of what is understood by the terms "hard" and "soft" water is exemplified by the composition of the dilution water used in standard tests with insecticides in the U.S.A. (Henderson *et al.*, 1960; American Public Health Association, 1960a) and in molluscicide studies in South Africa (Meyling *et al.*, 1962b, Table XII).

TABLE XII

		Dissolved O_2 ppm	pH	Alkalinity, ppm	Hardness ppm
(a)	Soft water	8·0	7·4	18	20
	Hard water	8·0	8·2	360	400

		Conductivity (micromhos)	Alkalinity (as $CaCO_3$)	Total hardness (as $CaCO_3$)	pH
(b)	Soft water	64	33	26	7·7
	Hard water	950	488	408	8·4
	Tap water	144	66	71	8·2

Between these two extremes of hard and soft water, which encompass all conditions and differences likely to be encountered in natural waters, some fish control laboratories interpose a "medium" dilution water, as follows in Table XIII (Marking and Hogan, 1967).

TABLE XIII

	pH Range	Concentration in parts per million expressed as total $CaCO_3$	
		Hardness	Alkalinity
Soft	6·4–6·8	10–13	10–13
Medium	7·2–7·6	40–48	30–35
Hard	7·6–8·0	160–180	110–120

The actual ingredients of this re-constituted water, according to the degree of hardness or softness, are as follows in Table XIV.

TABLE XIV

Salt added in mg/l

	NaHCO$_3$	CaSO$_4$	MgSO$_4$	KCl
Soft	12	7·5	7·5	0·5
Medium	48	30·0	30·0	2·0
Hard	192	120·0	120·0	8·0

A good example of the way in which water hardness may affect pesticide impact is provided by observations on the molluscicide Bayluscide, especially in view of the fact that studies were made at both laboratory and field levels in quite different contexts in different countries.

In South Africa evaluation of the effect of Bayluscide on aquatic snails and on other aquatic fauna was carried out in two different types of stream, *viz.* soft and moderately hard (Harrison, 1960). In soft water streams fish began to jump out of the water within minutes of spraying the molluscicide, all dying within 5–10 min even after treatments as low as 0·10 ppm. In hard water, fish kill was much slower and some fish did not begin to die until after 2 h, even although most water samples contained 0·2 ppm Bayluscide. In South Africa the reduced performance of Bayluscide in hard water is considered to be a serious disadvantage, and may well be responsible for a number of reports on failure of molluscicide treatment in the field (Meyling *et al.*, 1962).

The reactions of Bayluscide with regard to soft and hard water have also been studied in its role as a potential piscicide (Marking and Hogan, 1967). This was tested in soft, medium and hard waters made up accurately according to Tables XIII and XIV. At all exposure periods the chemical was found to be more toxic to rainbow trout and other test fish in soft water than in hard, which is in agreement with the observations above. The greatest increase in toxicity is between medium and hard water and suggests degradation of Bayluscide at high pH levels and at higher alkalinities.

The toxicity of TFM to both larval lampreys and to rainbow trout is strongly influenced by water hardness and pH. This chemical is most effective in soft acid waters in which minimum lethal concentrations can be as low as 0·5 ppm. As pH, conductivity and alkalinity of the water increase, the dosage requirement of TFM to effect 100% kill of larval lampreys increases. In the hardest and most alkaline waters tested, the minimum lethal concentration for the larvae was 8·0 ppm. Changes in the toxicity of TFM to rainbrow trout were comparable and the differential toxic effect of this compound was retained regardless of its level of activity in any given water. Treatment of any stream with TFM is not precluded because of variations in hardness and pH, but the quantities of TFM required for effective treatment may be considerably greater in hard, alkaline waters than in soft and acid waters (Applegate *et al.*, 1961).

The discovery of the synergistic action of Bayluscide on the lamprey larvicide TFM necessitated re-examination of the effect of soft and hard waters following on the studies on TFM alone (Howell *et al.*, 1964). In order to determine the effect of these factors on the relative toxicity of TFM and TFM-2B (98% TFM plus 2% Bayluscide), comparative tests were run using dilution waters from twenty-six different sources representing the wide range of streams infested with sea lamprey larvae. The pH of these streams ranged from 7·3 to 8·5, the alkalinity (as ppm $CaCO_3$) from 68 to 250, and the conductivity from 99 to 544 (μ mhos/18°C). Both TFM and TFM-2B were more effective in the softer waters with the lower pH values. As conductivity, alkalinity and pH increased, the MLC_{100} — i.e. the minimum concentration sufficient to produce 100% mortality — became greater. In the softer waters with lowest pH, the MLC_{100} was 1·0 ppm for both TFM and TFM-2B. In the hardest waters this had increased to between 9–10 ppm for TFM and 4–5 ppm for TFM-2B. This differential increase in toxicity of the two compounds indicates that the rate of decrease of toxicity of TFM alone is about twice that of TFM-2B when proceeding from the softer to the harder waters.

The interrelations beween pH, alkalinity and hardness, and their role in determining toxicity of certain toxic chemicals is well brought out in studies on the piscicide Antimycin (Walker *et al.*, 1964). As part of the comprehensive evaluation programme, the basic laboratory studies were followed by semi-natural tests in 1000 gallon wading pools, provided with bottom soils of sand or loam, and furnished with various introduced plants. As a further stage in evaluation the trials were carried out in natural hatching ponds, about $\frac{1}{2}$ to $\frac{3}{4}$ acre in area. In the latter ponds Antimycin at 10 ppb was effective in killing fish, but in contrast there was a lack of consistency in the wading pool results. This was attributed to chemical changes in the wading pool water accelerating de-toxification of the Antimycin. As the mass of plant growth increases in the pools, the relatively hard well water which was used to fill the pools was gradually softened because of the decrease in calcium. There was a shift from bicarbonate (methyl orange alkalinity) to free hydroxide (phenolphthalein alkalinity). pH — as an indicator of the acid-base shift — rose from 7·5 upward to a value of 10 or more, with highest pH values in the late afternoon in the presence of abundant plants and sunshine. As calcium ions are removed, magnesium prevails and results in the sort of alkaline shift observed in softer waters. In contrast, the relative success in the hatching ponds was attributed to the fact that the water had high buffer capacity and little reserve alkalinity in the form of hydroxide. Even on occasions when the pools had the same pH and total alkalinity as the hatching ponds, there was more free hydroxide present. Degradation of the toxicant was therefore more rapid, and the pools required 20–40 ppb to achieve effective fish kill.

In contrast to these relationships established above, it appears that hardness, alkalinity and pH have no major effect on the toxicity to fish of chlorinated hydrocarbons (Henderson *et al.*, 1960). This also applies to most organophosphorus compounds with the exception of Dipterex which is converted by mild alkali into the water-insoluble and highly toxic DDVP.

pH

The pH of the water has been recognized as a factor which by itself can affect the impact of some pesticides. One of the earliest examples investigated was copper sulphate which was the dominant chemical used for many years in the control of aquatic snails. The solubility by copper sulphate falls sharply at pH 6·9 and above resulting in loss of copper precipitation in alkaline waters. Because of this, and other factors, the molluscicide has had to be applied in some areas at much higher rates than the normal 30 pm, the minimum effective treatments reported ranging from 48–300 ppm/h (W.H.O., 1965).

The influence of both pH and water hardness on copper sulphate has been well brought out in studies on the oligochaete worm, *Nais*, quite unconnected with snail control (Learner and Edwards, 1963). These worms have been reported as infesting slow and rapid sand filters and water distribution systems from time to time. Tests on the controlling effect of copper sulphate were conducted in hard and soft waters with total hardness of 320 and 18 ppm (as $CaCO_3$) respectively. In the hard water the pH range was 7·0 to 7·7, while in the soft water the pH was adjusted to two different levels, *viz.* 3·4–4·3, representing soft acid water, and 6·5–7·3, around neutrality. The results are shown in Fig. 31.

These results show that around pH 7 copper sulphate is more toxic to species of *Nais* in soft water than in hard water; at 1 ppm copper

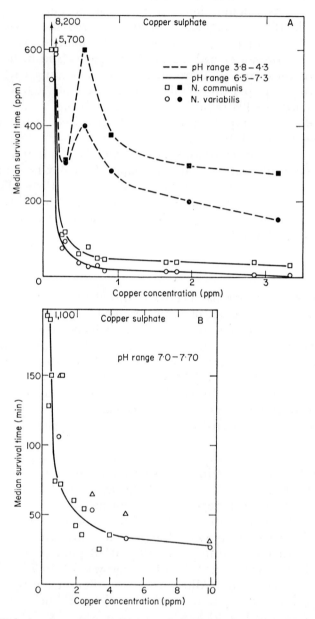

Fig. 31. Relation between median survival time of *Nais* (Oligochaeta) and concentration of copper in a soft water (A) and hard water (B) (after Learner and Edwards, 1963).

the average median survival time is reduced from about 70 min to 35 min. (In soft water copper sulphate is much less toxic at pH 4 than at pH 7. The figures also show that of the two species tested, one is much more resistant to copper sulphate than the other.) At pH values below about 5·5, the copper-concentration/survival-time curve is most unusual in that it shows over part of the concentration range that an increase in copper concentration brings about an increase in survival time.

In contrast to the experience with copper sulphate as a molluscicide, the solubility of one of the major molluscicides in present use — Bayluscide (niclosamine) — increases in alkaline waters, and there is a sharp fall in solubility with consequent precipitation below about 7·0 (Meyling and Pitchford, 1966). In practice, in snail control in Africa for example, this is only rarely a serious drawback as the majority of snail habitats have pH levels of 7·5 or above.

The most recent molluscicide of note, Frescon (N-tritylmorpholine), has also been closely studied with regard to pH relationships. At pH 5·0 molluscicidal activity of suspensions was lost within an hour; at pH 6, the suspension was active for approximately 12 h, while at pH 6·5, the compound was still active up to 40 h (Boyce et al., 1967). The reactions of Frescon to pH became even more important when the prolonged low-dosage technique is used. Studies in this connection were carried out on the rate of hydrolysis at concentrations of 0·5 ppm or less (Beyman et al., 1967). The rate of hydrolysis increased at pH values below 7·5. Above this level, when applied to most African waters, prolonged low dosage is likely to be effective, but at pH 7·0 to 7·5, the use of high initial concentration times and shorter application times is indicated. pH levels below 7·0 are uncommon in areas where molluscicidal control is necessary, but where this does occur Frescon is unlikely to be sufficiently stable for prolonged molluscicidal activity.

The selective piscicide Antimycin has also been closely examined with regard to pH relationships (Berger et al., 1969). The concentration required to produce a complete kill of fingerling goldfish in 96 h at 12°C was 0·20 ppb at pH 5, 1·10 ppb at pH 8 and 60 ppb at pH 10. In the field it is suggested that an application of Antimycin to soft water would be more effective if treatment were made at daybreak. This would allow substantially greater exposure times before the rapid diurnal rise in pH begins to cause degradation of the Antimycin (Burress et al., 1969).

ADSORPTION AND PENETRATION OF SILT

Numerous references have already been made in this review to the well-known characteristic of DDT to deposit out of suspension and to be adsorbed on mud, organic matter or plant surfaces. Because of its slow rate of degradation, this adsorption is a powerful factor in determining the persistence and accumulation of DDT in static water bodies. At the same time, where DDT is applied deliberately as a pesticide, the amount of DDT actually found in suspension is usually much less than the calculated dosage. Reference has been made to a method of demonstrating this considerable loss from suspension by means of the reactions of sensitive copepods to DDT (Ruber, 1962).

The adsorption and retention of DDT, and TDE, on muds, and the effect of this phenomenon on mud-dwelling fauna has been closely studied in connection with chemical control of Chironomid midges (Edwards *et al.*, 1964). TDE was found to be present in mud, and still toxic, ten months after spraying. The effect of this on mud-dwelling fauna is interesting and varied. In the case of Chironomid larvae these tend to leave the mud and move around on mud surfaces after treatment with DDT or TDE, and in this way they become more available to fish or other predators. In the case of the mayfly, *Cloeon dipterum*, the effect varies according to the particular generation involved. Nymphs of the first generation are killed while overwintering in the mud. The second generation of *Cloeon* however develop mainly on filamentous algal mats and macrophytes during spring and early summer, and thus escape the effects of the toxic sediments on bottom muds.

The capacity of DDT in suspension to attach on to mud and silt particles in natural freshwater habitats is considered to have played a vital role in determining the success of one of the earliest uses of DDT against *Simulium* larvae in large rivers (Fredeen *et al.*, 1953; Fredeen, 1962). The most effective larvicide treatments in the Saskatchewan River in Canada were obtained when the river water was turbid, in some instances larvae being eliminated as far as 115 miles downstream from the application point. Other aquatic insects which do not feed on suspended particles were less affected by the larvicide.

The importance of this adsorption factor was confirmed by comparing the effects of applying DDT at the rate of 0·1 ppm and 0·2 ppm for 15 min to canals with different turbidities. When the water contained 521 ppm of suspended solids larvae were almost completely eliminated by the DDT treatment. With 322 ppm of solids, larvae were partly eliminated, while at 25 ppm of solids, the DDT treatment proved ineffective. These experiments suggested that the larvicidal effect in clean water streams might be improved by addition of finely divided material with marked DDT-adsorptive properties, and for this purpose a finely divided diatomaceous earth, Celite, was found to be most effective.

The problem of adsorption on muds, organic matter and aquatic plant surfaces has received a great deal of attention in molluscicide studies. Copper sulphate in particular has long been recognized as being particularly prone to de-activation and precipitation out of solution. This is also a factor influencing the effect of sodium pentachlorophenate (NaPCP). When this molluscicide was applied to a river with a sandy bed the loss of active ingredient over a distance of 1 km was only 10%. Under comparable conditions, the loss of active ingredient in muddy waters amounted to as much as 80% in a river stretch of only 600 m. The results of adsorption tests in the laboratory show that Bayluscide too is adsorbed by organic matter and by water plants, especially those with large surface areas. The adsorption curves for both molluscicides are largely parallel, and the adsorption by mud in both cases is completely irreversible (Strufe and Gonnert, 1962).

In contrast to this the molluscicide Frescon is not de-activated by suspensions in silt (Boyce et al., 1967) nor does it penetrate mud and silt in the natural habitat. Snails that remain beneath the mud in treated water bodies can survive to repopulate (Shiff, 1966).

FORMULATIONS AND PHYSICAL FORM OF PESTICIDE

Comparatively few chemical pesticides are directly soluble in water, among these being the molluscicides copper sulphate and sodium pentachlorophenate and the aquatic herbicide diquat. Water soluble compounds like this can be applied direct to water bodies, or reach them indirectly, in the form of the almost pure chemical.

In contrast, the majority of pesticides in use have very low water solubility, many being for most practical purposes almost completely insoluble. However, these compounds are soluble in varying degrees in different kinds of oils, and on this basis they can be formulated in such a way that when added to water they produce a very fine suspension of particles distributed throughout the water. According to the nature of the chemical pesticide and the particular use to which it is being put, these formulations can take various forms such as oil solutions, wettable powder formulations, emulsifiable concentrates, water miscible formulations as well as sand and

7*

granular formulations. The object of all this is to ensure the maximum dispersion of the pesticide in a fine state of suspension at the most economic rates.

From comparatively simple beginnings, the nature and composition of many of these formulations has become increasingly complex, particularly with regard to the auxiliary ingredients such as emulsifiers, spreaders, stickers, wetters, dispersants, etc. as well as naturally occurring and synthetic fillers, e.g. anti-oxidants and water scavengers, and solvents (W.H.O., 1965). In the case of the molluscicide Frescon for example, the emulsifiable concentrate (EC) is based on tetrachloroethylene with a mixture of hydrophobic and hydrophilic emulsifiers, particularly suitable for flowing water. The commercial success of a particular pesticide may be determined by the ease or difficulty with which it can be formulated, and consequently there is considerable trade secrecy about the exact nature of emulsifiers and auxiliary surface-active agents used in particular formulations. Among these various additive chemicals there is a possibility that some chemical companies are using PCB's or polychlorinated biphenyls, compounds which are being increasingly recovered from the tissues of birds. The function of such chemicals would be to increase the "kill life" of pesticides; arochlors for example are reported to trap and hold volatile ingredients, and to prolong the life of these and of any repellent ingredients (Reynolds, 1969).

For many pesticides, the particular formulation preferred by manufacturers is the emulsifiable concentrate or EC. This formulation can be readily adapted, by dilution with water, to a wide range of agricultural uses and is in general the most effective formulation for direct application to water bodies. In the emulsifiable concentrate the suspension produced on mixing with water is composed of fine particles of smaller size than those produced by wettable powder formulations, and as the smaller particles are more active biologically, toxicity is increased. Some pesticides such as DDT and gamma BHC can easily be formulated as either emulsifiable concentrate formulations or as wettable powders. However in other cases considerable difficulty has been encountered in formulating a stable EC, and there has been no choice but to develop the slightly less satisfactory wettable powder formulation instead. Two of the best examples of this particular problem are the molluscicide Bayluscide and the insecticide carbaryl (Sevin).

In view of the important part played in EC formulations by the variety of solvents used as well as emulsifiers and other auxiliary chemicals, many workers have become increasingly aware of the possibility that some of these components may contribute to the toxic effects attributed to the pesticide itself. This could be an important factor in the correct interpretation of experimental results, and when comparing the effects of different pesticide treatments in the field. For example, pure methoxychlor has been found to be only slightly harmful to *Daphnia magna* in concentrations up to about 3 ppm. But a methoxychlor formulation Metox, 8 ppm — containing 2·4 ppm actual methoxychlor — killed 50% of test organisms in 24 h. The sharp difference was attributed to the effect of the organic solvent, a petroleum product (Cabejszek *et al.*, 1966).

In connection with *Simulium* control in West African rivers, laboratory tests were carried out on the reactions of fish to the two larvicides being compared, DDT and Baytex. In addition to tests with the pure technical grade insecticide, tests were also carried out on the reactions of fish to the solvents and to the other chemical components of the emulsifiable concentrate. In the case of the DDT formulation the solvent and the emulsifier were found to be highly toxic to fish on their own account; at 15 ppm, fish were affected by the ingredients alone after 20 m exposure, but recovered after being transferred to clean water (Post and Garms, 1966).

One of the recent and most powerful OP larvicides, Abate, has produced some inconsistencies in its EC formulations, with widely different results reported by different workers. On the one hand, Abate in acetone solution has been reported as much less toxic to fish than fenthion, with LD_{50} for *Micropterus*, *Lepomis*, *Gambusia* and *Lebistes* greater than 200 ppm, as compared with 1·75–2·0 ppm for fenthion. However, a 25% EC formulation of Abate produced 100% mortality in the fish in 2 h at 50 ppm, all fish being killed at 12·5 ppm in 24 h (von Windeguth and Patterson, 1966).

On the other hand, the situation appears to be completely reversed in the case of *Simulium* larvae both on the basis of laboratory tests and field observations. In laboratory tests with the technical material dissolved in acetone, Abate proved as toxic to *Simulium* larvae as Dursban, the most effective compound tested. Comparisons of the EC formulations however showed that the Dursban EC formulation was about five times as effective as Abate, the minimum lethal dose being 0·02 ppm (1 h) for Dursban as compared with more than 0·1 ppm for Abate (Muirhead-Thomson, 1970).

This superiority of the oil solution of Abate in *Simulium* control is supported by field practice in which oil solutions have been tested as a more convenient form for application from aircraft. In aerial application of Abate against blackfly larvae in New York State, under identical conditions, Abate applied as 20% in oil solution with Triton X-161 added as a surfactant or emulsifier, was completely effective in eliminating 84–98% of larvae from a stretch 500–800 yd below dosage point, while 18% EC had no effect at all (Jamnback and Means, 1968; Jamnback, 1969a).

As these apparently conflicting experiences refer to two entirely different types of test organisms, fish and *Simulium* larvae, direct comparison is difficult and there appears to be no simple explanation of these differences.

Although the EC formulations in general have been preferred for ground application pesticide, recent increase in the scope of aerial application of insecticides has emphasized the great saving in the use of undiluted or concentrated pesticide for area control. This Ultra Low Volume (ULV) method of application refers to treatment in which the total volume of solution applied is less than $\frac{1}{2}$ gal per acre, volumes exceeding this rate being classified as conventional spraying (Mount and Lofgren, 1967; Mulhern, 1968; George *et al.*, 1968). Naled, fenthion and malathion for example have all been used as undiluted concentrates for some rates of application, but for other rates they have had to be diluted.

The increasing value of oil solutions or oil concentrates has produced some problems, especially for the manufacturers. Many of the oil solutions of the newer insecticides, including Abate, require particular kinds of oil for formulation and dilution, and these are not always available except on special order.

Closely tied up with the question of formulation is the particle size of the active pesticide in suspension. Experiments with insecticides have established that biological performance is dependent, among other factors, on particle size. As mentioned above, the general superiority of EC formulations in preference to wettable powder formulations is due to the particles being in a finer state of suspension in the emulsion and therefore being more active. This is well illustrated in a recent example concerning Frescon (N-tritylmorpholine). When adult snails, *Biomphalaria glabrata*, are exposed to 0·06 ppm suspensions of the toxicant ground to different particle sizes, the mortality was as follows (W.H.O., 1965):

Particle size in microns	1–2	2–6	6–10	10–25
% kill	100	70	40	0

A very interesting example of the influence of particle size, and possible practical application of these findings, is provided by work on the effects of DDT on larvae of *Simulium* (Kershaw *et al.*, 1968).

Simulium larvae, which are uniquely adapted to life in fast running water, are particle feeders. Measurement of the size range of particles in the gut of *Simulium* larvae indicated that formulation of larvicide — DDT — in a similar range of particle size might result in the insecticide being ingested only by the *Simulium* larvae and not by other non-target species. A particulate formulation of 4–11 μ was prepared and applied to *Simulium* streams at three dosage ranges, 0·04, 0·2 and 0·4 ppm for 30 min. The lower dosage was not completely effective against *Simulium* larvae, while the highest dosage showed some effect on certain bottom-dwelling non-target invertebrates. The middle dosage emerged as one which showed real indications of selective action, causing *Simulium* larvae to disappear from the stream for at least 150 yd below the dosage point, while leaving the bottom fauna quite undisturbed.

DISPERSAL AND DISTRIBUTION OF PESTICIDES IN WATER

Improved analytical methods in recent years — particularly gas chromatography — have made it possible to detect various pesticides in microgram quantities, and to build up a much more complete picture of the distribution of pesticide in water, mud, aquatic plants and animals. It is such methods for example which have established the continuous presence in some American rivers of DDT and dieldrin and have enabled DDT, gamma BHC and dieldrin to be detected in sewage effluents in England at the following microgram levels (Water Pollution Research, 1967):

gamma BHC	0·018–0·039 μg/l
dieldrin	0·007–0·018 μg/l
DDT	0·005–0·026 μg/l

Information of this kind, based on numerous spot checks, has been particularly illuminating in detecting or confirming continuous low-grade contamination of the environment — including freshwater ecosystems — with pesticides commonly used in agriculture.

However, when pesticide is applied deliberately to a water body for control of some undesirable organisms, it is necessary to have more precise information about the distribution and dispersion of the pesticide from known application points at regular time intervals. This is particularly important in two different types of water body, viz. large static collections of waters such as lakes, and in running water bodies, streams, rivers and canals. The distribution of pesticides in lakes has been particularly important in fish eradication programmes based on the use of Toxaphene, where it is essential to know at what period after treatment the decrease in Toxaphene residues makes it safe to re-stock with trout and salmon.

A good example of this kind of investigation was that carried out in two Oregon lakes (Terriere et al., 1966). One of these had a surface area of 565 acres, an estimated volume of 50,265 acre/ft, and a depth of 147 ft. The other had a surface area of 3207 acres, an estimated volume of 15,830 acre/ft, and a maximum depth of 20 ft. Extensive analysis using gas chromatography showed that after a sharp initial decline to 2 ppb from the application rate of 40–88 ppb, the Toxaphene levels remained at or near this point for approximately one year in the shallow lake, which was rich in aquatic life, and for up to five years in the deeper, biologically sparse lake.

A rather different problem of pesticide dispersal in large water bodies is posed by the control of aquatic snails round the margins of large African lakes, including man-made lakes. In this case the problem is to ensure that the chemical molluscicides applied to the shallow margins — with abundant aquatic vegetation — remain in that area for an effective period and are not dissipated by wave action, underwater currents and diffusion into the great bulk of water in the lake.

It is generally assumed that pesticide applied to comparatively shallow water diffuses fairly rapidly and becomes more or less uniformly dispersed. Critical investigations of dispersion confirm this, but also reveal that the picture is not always a simple, straightforward one. In experiments with the molluscicide Frescon in Rhodesia, the molluscicide in the form of an emulsifiable concentrate was sprayed as a concentrated suspension of 1 : 10 in water on to the surface of a large pond 100 m long, 10 m wide and 2 m deep (Shiff, 1966). Photographs taken at 20 min intervals after spraying showed that the cloud of emulsion sinks completely through the habitat. However, chemical determinations of samples from various levels showed that the behaviour of the emulsion is dependent on several factors. In the absence of vegetation, the emulsion cloud sinks rapidly from the surface but in its downward movement it is attentuated, and this movement can be arrested by some barrier such as a thermocline. In one pond the molluscicide took 10 min to penetrate 24 cm. When vegetation is present, this may act by holding up the release of molluscicide.

A similar problem regarding penetration in depth has been studied in the case of the fish toxicant Antimycin. For practical use this compound is coated on the outer surface of a sand carrier which can be easily spread over the area to be treated. The coated sand sinks to the bottom while the Antimycin is uniformly released. Formulations can be made in such a way as to release the Antimycin at a uniform rate at different depths. The most readily available formulation, Fintrol-5, releases the Antimycin within the first 5 ft. Formulations releasing up to 15 ft (Fintrol-15) and 30 ft (Fintrol-30) are planned. However, in certain shallow fish ponds with a depth of 3·5 ft, and with the bottom completely covered with soft mud, a substantial percentage of the Antimycin is not released before the sand sinks into the mud, and this particular sand formulation is no longer completely effective (Burress *et al.*, 1969). In order to determine the uniformity and strength of Antimycin released by the sand formulation at selected depths, a plexiglass (perspex) column 8 ft high and 1 ft in diameter was set up and filled with re-constituted water. Fintrol was applied at the surface and allowed to sink to the bottom; water at various depths was siphoned off and analysed for toxicant by 96 h bioassay with rainbow trout and goldfish (Berger *et al.*, 1969). The release of Antimycin from Fintrol-5 is apparently uniform, but not complete, within the first 5 ft of depth. Sand formulations are found to work well in the presence of aquatic plants as the sand sinks through the submerged weeds, and sifts effectively through dense patches of emergent vegetation.

Formulations releasing Antimycin at uniform rates up to 15 and 30 ft are being tested (Gildenhaus *et al.*, 1969). In deeper ponds it was found that the existence of a thermocline at about 5 ft, below which the water was stratified and uncirculated by wind or other factors, further slowed down the penetration of Antimycin. It has been suggested that for trash fish such as crappie (*Pomoxis annularis*), which inhabit deeper waters, formulations might be devised for introduction well below the surface of the pond (Burress and Luhning, 1969).

The behaviour of pesticide applied deliberately to running water bodies is a matter of common concern in at least four different fields of applied aquatic biology, namely the control of blackfly (*Simulium*) larvae in streams and rivers; the control of larval lampreys in streams; the control of aquatic snail populations in canals and irrigation systems and the control of mosquito larvae in irrigated pastures.

The application of pesticide to large rivers is a problem almost exclusive to control of *Simulium* larvae — although large rivers like the Nile have on occasions been treated with insecticide in midge control. In one of the earliest demonstrations of *Simulium* control by means of DDT applied to large rivers, namely the Saskatchewan

River in Canada (Arnason *et al.*, 1949), the course of the insecticide movement and the dispersion downstream after aerial application was followed by incorporating in the DDT formulation used, a red dye to indicate when treated water was passing sampling stations. Samples of water were taken at various points downstream and the DDT detected by the best method of analysis available at the time, the Schecter-Haller method. As might be imagined on theoretical grounds, it was clearly shown that while the concentration of DDT became progressively lower as the distance increased from the point of application, at the same time the exposure period progressively increased with the distance.

In current practice *Simulium* control is carried out by applications of larvicide — commonly DDT — at the rate of 0·1 ppm for 30 min in ground application, or the equivalent in short application periods from aircraft. In evaluating the impact of the chemical not only on *Simulium* larvae but also on fish and other non-target organisms, this matter of decreasing concentration coupled with increased exposure has to be taken into account, especially at the long distances downstream — fifty or sixty miles or more — at which larvicide effects have still been recorded. Although the product of time of exposure × the concentration of pesticide may remain much the same for long distances below the application point, different organisms may prove to be more sensitive to prolonged exposure to low concentrations than short periods to high concentrations, and vice versa. In order to examine this aspect critically, there would be advantages in developing laboratory methods of evaluation in which the test organisms are exposed to a gradually increasing concentration of pesticide followed by a gradual decrease, simulating the form of the chemical wave at different points downstream from application point (Fig. 32). Current practice of exposing test animals to a fixed concentration for a standard period may only be providing one aspect of a complex situation. In this connection it should be pointed out that this picture of progressive dilution coupled with increasing length of exposure can be completely disrupted if the river does not pursue a steady uninterrupted course, and is not heavily diluted by tributaries. Areas of rapids in rivers or riffles in streams, alternating with areas of slack or slow-moving water, may result in loss of pesticide by deposition and adsorption on bottom muds in the stagnant pools or backwaters.

The pattern of chemical dispersion in flowing water has received a great deal of attention in aquatic snail control. The dispersion of molluscicide in the flowing waters of canals and irrigation systems has been followed not only by regular analysis of water samples, but also by bioassay with caged snails. For most practical purposes the bioassay method has been the most widely used as it gives a direct indication of the biological effect of whatever time/concentration of molluscicide is present at that point. The use of dyes and tracers, including a salt dilution method by incorporating sodium chloride with the molluscicide, has been tried from time to time. While this

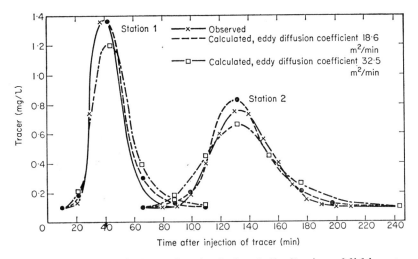

FIG. 32. Comparison of observed and calculated distribution of lithium tracer in a river at two stations below point of application (after Water Pollution Research, 1967).

method has been considered to provide a rough indication of likely dispersion according to the nature of different streams, it cannot be assumed that the attenuation of tracer exactly coincides with the progressive dilution of molluscicide as the latter is subject to various de-activating forces according to its chemical nature and formulation. However, the use of dye can still play an important part in indicating the general flow pattern in a river system, and has been used for this purpose in chemical control of lamprey larvae in streams (Applegate et al., 1961). In treatment of streams which eventually flow into each other, preliminary treatment with dye provided the necessary information as to when two treated water masses would reach the confluence of the streams simultaneously, ensuring that below the point of confluence the same concentration of chemical would be maintained. The two streams in this case had discharge rates of 37 cusec and 5·7 cusec respectively.

The use of bioassay, combined with chemical analysis of water samples, has also been widely used in studies on the dispersion of

TFM in larval lamprey control. The use of caged test animals has probably been used on a greater scale in this work than in any other similar problem of pesticides in running water. In one river, for example, a total of 1205 larval lampreys were placed in the river in fifty cages distributed among five stations. The conditions of these larvae and the numbers dead were recorded at hourly intervals during treatment.

In view of the fact that TFM and TFM-2B are selective lamprey larvicides whose concentration levels have to be maintained within

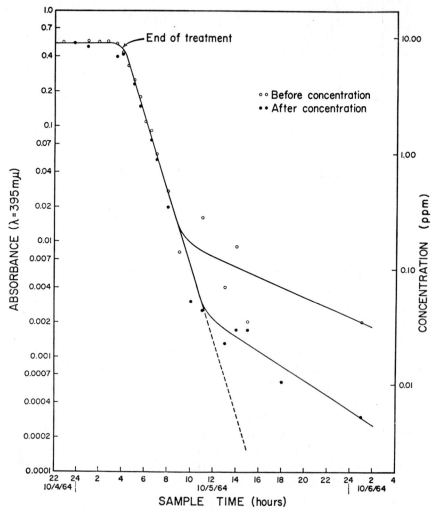

FIG. 33. Disappearance of the lamprey larvicide, TFM, from river after treatment (after Billy et al., 1965).

certain safety limits for the protection of trout, considerable attention has been given to the question of TFM residues in rivers by the
Great Lakes Research Division (Daniels *et al.*, 1965; Billy *et al.*,
1965). In the Lake Michigan area analyses for TFM residues were
made before, during and after treatment of two rivers, the Pentwater
and the Muskegon Rivers. On 17th April the Pentwater River was
treated with 3480 lb of technical grade TFM (33·2% active ingredient), the flow at the sampling point being 93 cusec. The minimum effective concentration required to kill sea lamprey larvae,
and the maximum allowable concentration that would not harm
other fish were 2 ppm and 6 ppm respectively. Chemical analyses
showed a rapid decrease in concentration after treatment. The TFM
had almost disappeared three days after treatment, and no lamprecide could be detected 112 days after treatment.

The Muskegon River was treated with 78,100 lb of technical
grade TFM within the maximum allowable concentration of 15
ppm and the minimum effective level of 6 ppm for 12 h. A plot of
the logarithm of absorbence versus time is shown in Fig. 33 and
shows a straight line, indicating that the loss of TFM follows first
order kinetics, assuming a constant stream flow. It will be noted that
at the lower values there is more scattering of data, and this has been
attributed to a number of factors: (1) possible fluctuations of temperature, dissolved O_2 and pH, which could cause desorption of TFM
from bottom sediments; (2) fluctuations in flow rate; (3) intermittent
flushing of TFM trapped in pools, eddies and backwaters; and
(4) instrumental limitations at low levels. TFM values dropped from
approximately 9 ppm at the conclusion of treatment to less than 0·2
ppm in 6 h, and less than 0·02 after 8 h.

COMBINATIONS OF PESTICIDES

The widespread use of sensitive gas chromatography methods for
detecting pesticide residues has provided abundant evidence that
at low levels of contamination, in the microgram range, it is not
uncommon for several pesticides to be present simultaneously. At
this low level of contamination, emphasis for many years has been
on the dominant DDT, but gamma BHC, dieldrin and others are
frequently present as well, even in the waters of some British rivers.

At the much higher concentrations produced by deliberate application of pesticide to water, or in the aerial application of pesticide
to agricultural or forestry land in which water bodies are unavoid-
ably included, there is an increasing tendency in some areas to apply
two or more pesticides simultaneously, or within very short intervals

of each other. In the cotton growing areas of El Salvador in Central America, at least half-a-dozen insecticides may be applied in the course of the intensive aerial spraying during the cotton growing season. The selection of which insecticides or combinations of insecticides to be used on a particular day is very often a matter of random choice. Faced with a wealth of new chemicals and new formulations for control of cotton pests, the cotton growers tend to use anything available rather than rely on one particular proprietary brand of insecticide.

In the cotton growing areas of the southern United States there is the same tendency to use several insecticides simultaneously, and the same likelihood of these mixtures making an impact on freshwater bodies and freshwater life within the treated areas. The impact of these combined insecticides has been critically examined with regard to mosquito fish (*Gambusia*) in the cotton-growing areas where some populations of these fish exhibit high levels of resistance to one or other of the dominant insecticides, DDT, Toxaphene, endrin and methylparathion (Ferguson and Bingham, 1966a; Ferguson *et al.*, 1966). In view of the extreme difficulty in trying to evaluate the impact of such pesticide combinations ·or mixtures under field conditions, a comprehensive series of laboratory tests was carried out in which mosquito fish were continuously exposed, for up to 36 h, to various combinations of chemicals. Mortality was recorded at 15 and 30 min intervals early in the test, followed by one-hourly observations, and subsequently by 6 h checks. In all tests the sum of the mortalities caused by individual insecticides exceeded that for the same insecticides in combination, and accordingly there was not evidence of any additive effect (Ferguson and Bingham, 1966b).

An example of the more scientific simultaneous use of two pesticides is provided by the employment of mixtures of the organophosphorus compounds, Baygon and Baytex, for ultra-low volume aerial application in mosquito control in parts of the United States (Stevens and Stroud, 1967). The Baygon component contributes to the rapid knockdown of adult mosquitoes, but in itself would fail to control larvae. The larval control is provided by the Baytex component.

In the control of aquatic snails which are intermediate hosts of bilharziasis, there is a wide range of molluscicides available. Some of these are highly lethal to snails but have little effect on snail eggs, while others, less effective, have the advantage of killing eggs at molluscicide dosage. The possibility of using combinations of different molluscicides to produce the most effective mixture for killing both adult snails as well as eggs has been investigated at laboratory level (Paulini, 1965). The molluscicide Molucid (ICI 24223, a compound since withdrawn from production) was taken as representing a chemical with high toxicity to the adult snail, but with no ovicidal action. Sodium pentachlorophenate (NaPCP) and Gramoxone (paraquat) were chosen at representing highly ovicidal compounds. Combinations of Molucid and NaPCP gave lower mortality than either of the more toxic components alone, suggesting that this combination produces some antagonism. In the case of Molucid and Gramoxone, the kills produced were at least equal to, and occasionally higher than either of the individual compounds alone, suggesting some potentiating action.

When assessing the effect of these chemical combinations on aquatic organisms it is important to distinguish between synergism and potentiation (Brown et al., 1967). Potentiation is the term used when two effective compounds give an effect greater than the sum of their individual activities. Synergism is the term used when one of the components is non-insecticidal or non-pesticidal by itself. One of the best known examples of the completely non-insecticidal synergist is piperonyl butoxide which is a methylene dioxyphenyl compound, which has a synergistic effect on pyrethrum and DDT, but rather limited application with other insecticides. A good example of potentiation — although it is frequently referred to as synergism — is provided by the mixture in certain propositions of the molluscicide/fish toxicant Bayluscide and the lamprey larvicide TFM. Clearly there must be cases where it is difficult to make a precise distinction between these two actions, where for example the less active component is not completely non-pesticidal by itself.

In interpreting the impact of pesticide combinations, the usual criterion is that of mortality, the investigator being mainly concerned with finding out what combinations of pesticides produce direct mortalities greater than that produced by the sum of the individual components. However, the possibility must be considered that a potentiating or synergistic effect might be produced in an indirect and less obvious way, particularly if one component of the chemical mixture affects the behaviour of freshwater organisms in such a way as to bring them into longer or more effective contact with the other — possibly more lethal — component. An example of this kind of situation is provided by recent work on the effect of insecticide combinations on Simulium larvae (Muirhead-Thomson, 1970). Some insecticides such as pyrethrins and pyrethroids have a sharp irritant effect on Simulium larvae causing them to detach and drift downstream at concentrations which do not ultimately produce a high mortality. The organophosphorus compounds on the other hand are highly lethal at very low concentrations, but detachment of larvae is slow and does not take place until larvae have absorbed a lethal dose. The idea of combining these two compounds is a logical follow up, and laboratory studies have shown that there is no or very little antagonistic effect. The mixture of pyrethrins and OP larvicide produces a high degree of detachment during the short (1 h) exposure period due to the pyrethrin component, and a high mortality due to the OP component. In the laboratory, it is only possible to demonstrate an additive effect which, however, is not absolute, the final mortality produced by the combination usually being below that produced by the more lethal OP larvicide alone. However, when used under field conditions in natural streams or rivers, a very different effect would almost certainly be produced, an effect difficult to demonstrate completely under laboratory conditions. Application of this chemical combination in the field would — as in the laboratory — produce a high degree of larval detachment within the short application period. The detached larvae would then float downstream with the bolt or slug of insecticide and in this way they would continue to be exposed to the more lethal OP compound for a much longer period than the specified application time. In this way high mortalities would continue to be produced by concentrations lower than the application dosage, and the final outcome of combining these two ingredients would be one of potentiation.

The possibility remains that a non-insecticidal irritant might be found to replace the pyrethrin or pyrethroid and produce the same final effect by prolonging the exposure of larvae to the lethal component for periods much greater than the specified application period. Should this be possible, then the effect produced would indirectly be one of synergism.

APPENDIX

GRAPHICAL FORMULAE OF REPRESENTATIVE PESTICIDES

PISCICIDES

Toxaphene

Chlorinated camphene containing 67–69% chlorine.

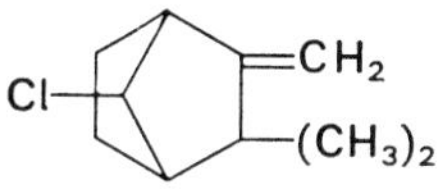

TFM

3-trifluoromethyl-4-nitrophenol.

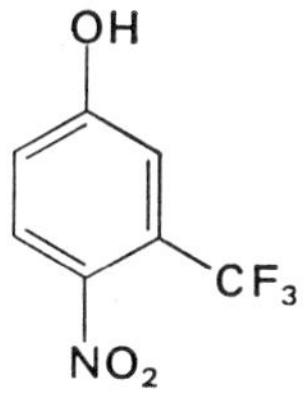

Antimycin A

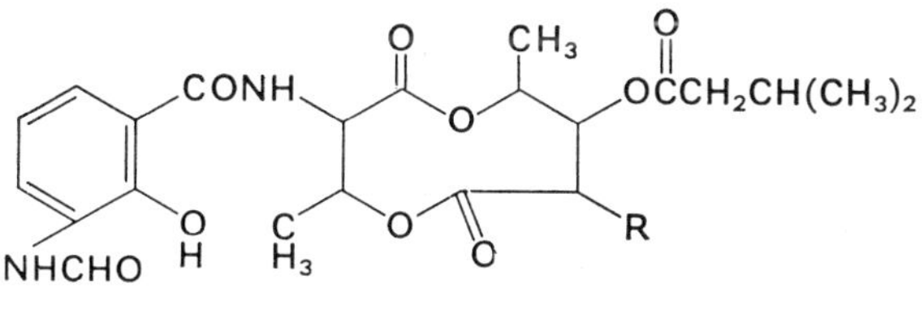

Antimycin A_1; $R = n-$hexyl: $C_{28}H_{40}N_2O_9$
Antimycin A_3; $R = n-$butyl: $C_{26}H_{36}N_2O_9$

INSECTICIDES

I CHLORINATED HYDROCARBONS

DDT

Dichloro diphenyl trichloro = ethane.

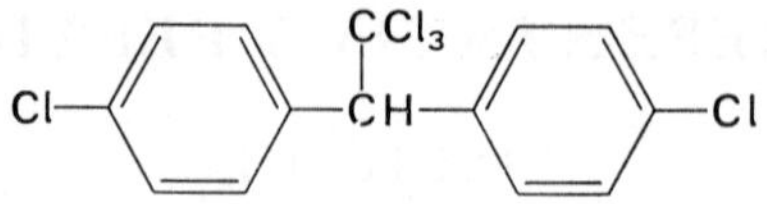

$$Cl- \text{(phenyl)} -CH(CCl_3)- \text{(phenyl)} -Cl$$

TDE (DDD)

Dichloro diphenyl dichloro = ethane.

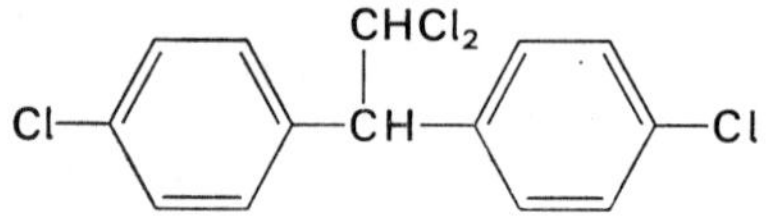

$$Cl- \text{(phenyl)} -CH(CHCl_2)- \text{(phenyl)} -Cl$$

PCB (Polychloro biphenyls)

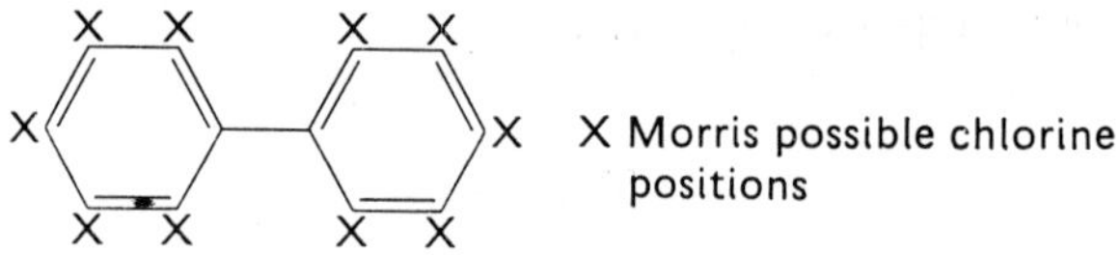

X Morris possible chlorine
positions

Methoxychlor

1,1,1-trichloro-2,2-bis = (*p*-methoxyphenyl) ethane.

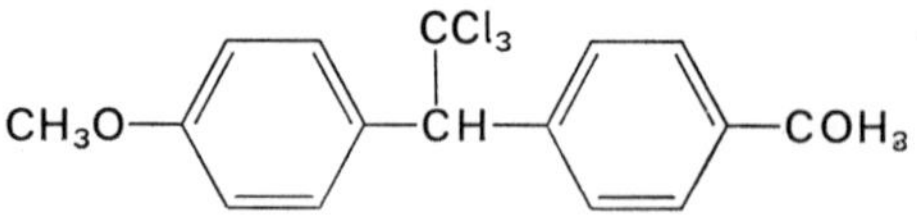

$$CH_3O- \text{(phenyl)} -CH(CCl_3)- \text{(phenyl)} -COH_a$$

Lindane (gamma BHC)

1,2,3,4,5,6-hexachlorocyclo = hexane.

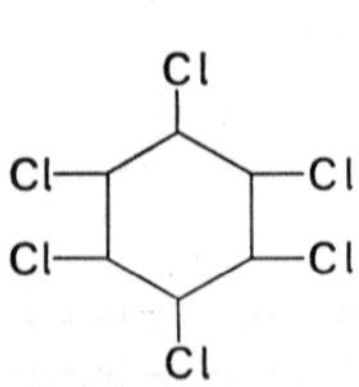

Heptachlor

1,4,5,6,7,8,8-heptachloro-3a,4,7,7a-tetrahydro-4,7-methano **indene.**

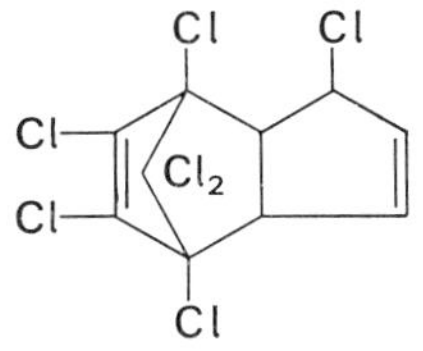

Dieldrin

1,2,3,4,10,10-hexachloro-6,7-epoxy-1,4,4a,5,6,7,8,8a-octahydro-1,4-endo-exo-5,8-dimethano-naphthalene.

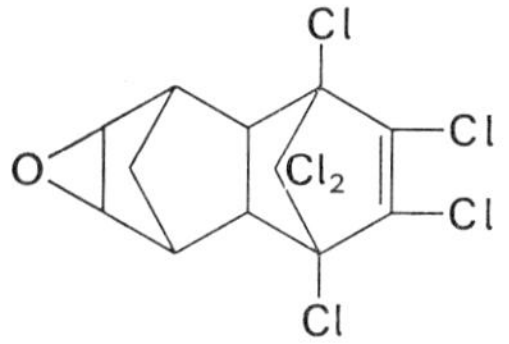

Aldrin

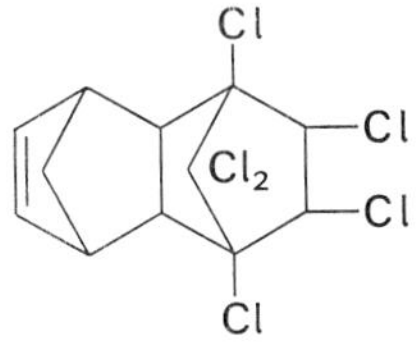

Endrin

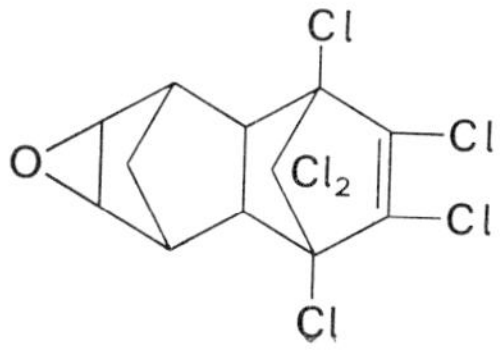

II ORGANOPHOSPHOROUS INSECTICIDES

Dursban

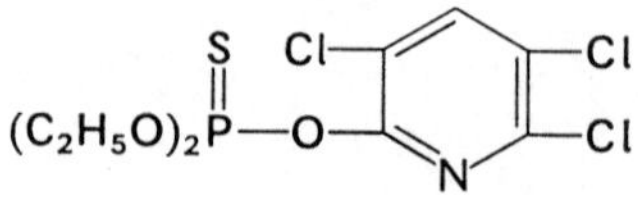

Abate

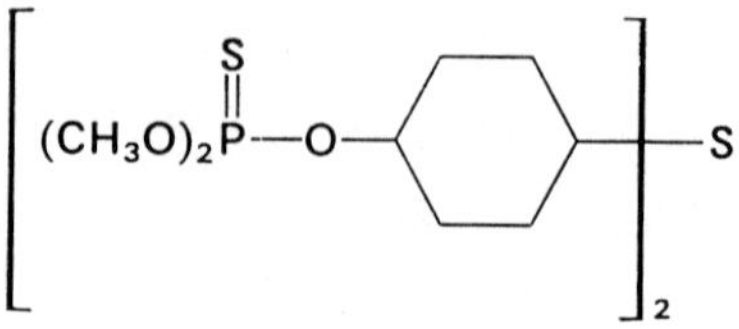

Malathion

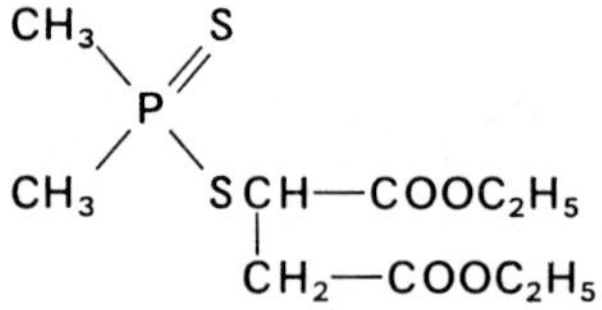

Parathion

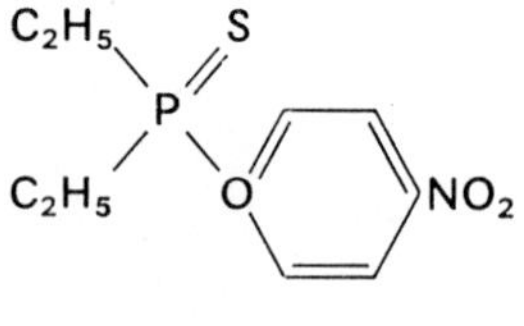

III CARBAMATES

Sevin (Carbaryl)

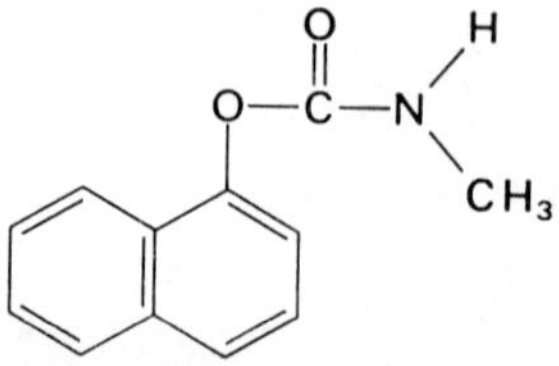

1—naphthyl—N—methyl carbamate

MOLLUSCICIDES

Sodium pentachlorophenate

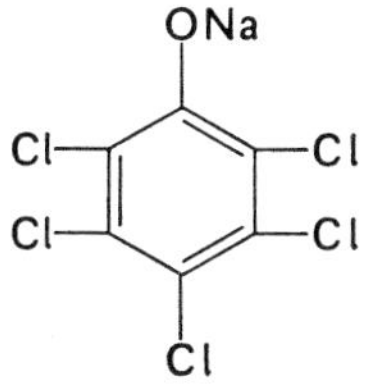
ONa
Cl
Cl
Cl
Cl
Cl

Copper sulphate

$$CuSO_4 5H_2O$$

Bayluscide (Bayer 73. niclosamine)

Ethanolamine salt of 5.2′-dichloro-4′-nitro-salicyl-anilide.

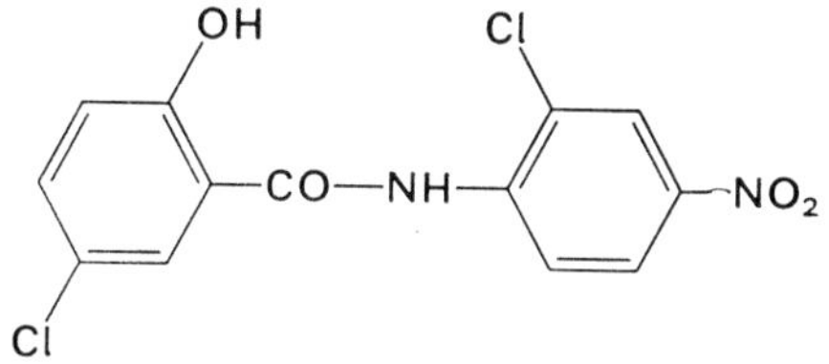
OH
Cl
CO—NH
NO2
Cl

Molucid (ICI. 24223)

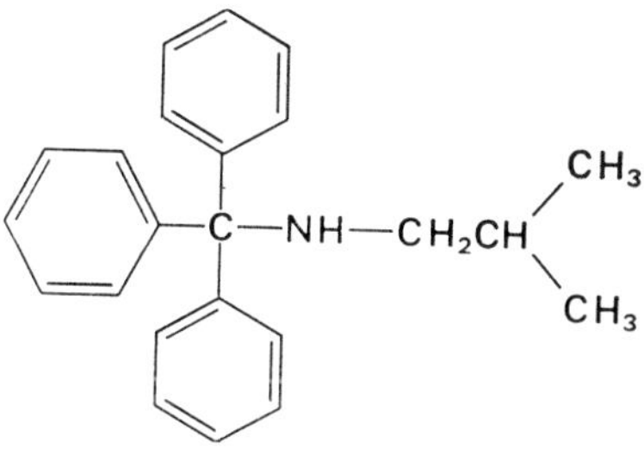
CH3
C—NH—CH2CH
CH3

Isobutyl–triphenyl–methylamine

Triphenyl tin acetate

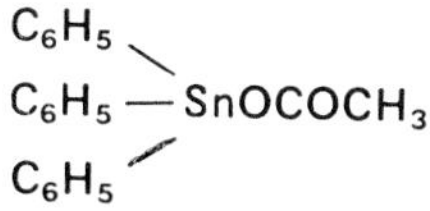
C6H5
C6H5 —SnOCOCH3
C6H5

Frescon (WL. 8008)
N-Tritylmorpholine.

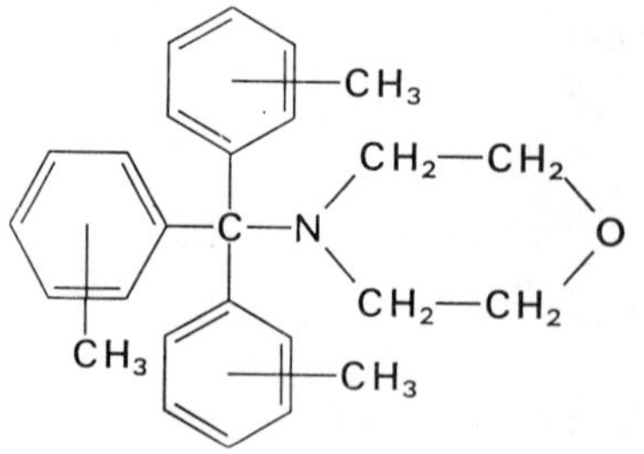

HERBICIDE/MOLLUSCICIDE

Acrolein (Aqualin)

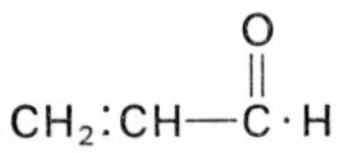

$$CH_2:CH-\overset{\overset{\displaystyle O}{\displaystyle \|}}{C}\cdot H$$

Paraquat (Gramoxone)

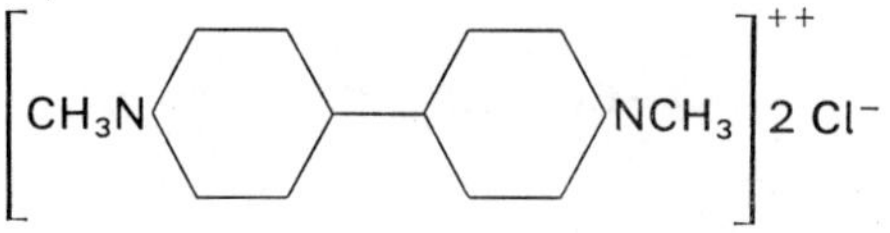

1, 1-dimethyl-4, 4-dipyridilium dichloride

Herbicide
2,4-D.
2,4-dichlorophenoxy acetic acid.

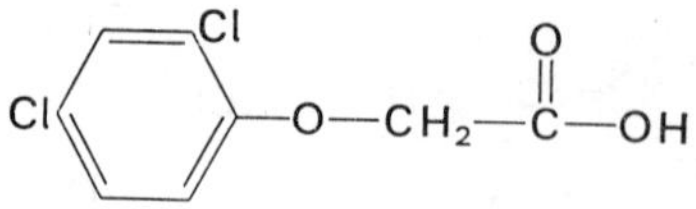

Diquat (Reglone)
1,1'-ethylene-2,2'-di-pyridylium dibromide.

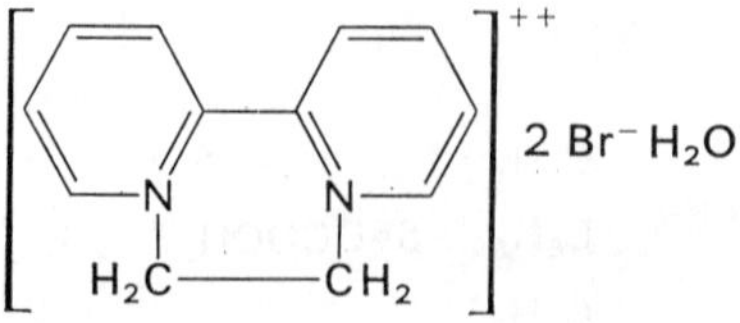

BIBLIOGRAPHY

Alabaster, J. S. and Abram, F. S. H. (1964). Development and use of a direct method of evaluating toxicity to fish. *J. Wat. Pollut. Res.*

Alabaster, J. S. and Abram, F. S. H. (1965). Estimating the toxicity of pesticides to fish. *P.A.N.S.* 11, 91–7.

Alabaster, J. S., Herbert, D. W. M. and Hemens, J. (1957). The survival of rainbow trout (*Salmo gairdnerii*, Richardson) and perch (*Perca fluviatilis*, L) at various concentrations of dissolved oxygen and carbon dioxide. *Ann. appl. Biol.* 45, 177–88.

Allison, D., Kallman, B. J., Cope, O. B. and van Valen, C. (1964). Some chronic effects of DDT on cutthroat trout. *Res. Rep. U.S. Fish. Wildl. Serv.* No. 64.

American Public Health Association (1960). Standard methods for the examination of water and waste water. New York. 626 pp.

Anderson, B. G. (1944). The toxicity thresholds of various substances found in industrial wastes as determined by the use of *Daphnia magna*. *Sewage Wks. J.* 16, 1156–65.

Anderson, B. G. (1946). The toxicity thresholds of various sodium salts determined by the use of *Daphnia magna*. *Sewage Wks. J.* 18, 82–7.

Anderson, B. G. (1960). The toxicity of organic insecticides to *Daphnia*. Biological Problems in Water Pollution. *Trans. 2nd Semin. Biol. Problems in Wat. Pollut.* 1959, Cincinnati, pp. 94–5.

Anderson, J. M. (1968). Effect of sublethal DDT on the lateral line of brook trout, *Salvelinus fontinalis*. *J. Fish. Res. Bd. Can.* 25, 2677–82.

Anderson, J. M. and Peterson, M. R. (1969). DDT: sublethal effects on brook trout nervous system. *Science, N.Y.* 164, 440–1.

Anderson, L. D., Bay, E. C. and Mulla, M. S. (1965). Aquatic midge investigations in S. California. *Proc. Calif. Mosq. Control Assn.* 33, 31–3.

Andrews, A. K., Van Valin, C. C. and Stebbings, B. E. (1966). Some effects of heptachlor on bluegills (*Lepomis macrochirus*). *Trans. Am. Fish. Soc.* 95, 297–309.

Applegate, V. C. (1950). Natural history of the sea lamprey (*Petromyzon marinus*) in Michigan. *Spec. sci. Rep. U.S. Fish Wildl. Serv.* (*Fisheries*) No. 55, 237 pp.

Applegate, V. C. and Moffett, J. W. (1955). The sea lamprey. *Scient. Am.* 192, 36–41.

Applegate, V. C., Howell, J. H., Hall, A. E. and Smith, M. A. (1957). Toxicity of 4346 chemicals to larval lampreys and fishes. *Spec. sci. Rep. U.S. Fish Wildl. Serv.* (*Fisheries*) No. 207.

Applegate, V. C., Howell, J. H., Moffett, J. W., Johnson, B. G. H. and Smith, M. A. (1961). Use of 3-trifluoromethyl-4-nitrophenol as a selective Sea lamprey larvicide. *Tech. Rep. Gt. Lakes Fish. Commn.* No. 1, 35 pp.

Arnason, A. P., Brown, A. W. A., Fredeen, F. J. H., Hopewell, W. W. and Rempel, J. G. (1949). Experiments in the control of *Simulium arcticum* Malloch by means of DDT in the Saskatchewan River. *Scient. Agric.* 29, 527–37.

Baldwin, N. S. (1963). A review of the activities of the Great Lakes Fishery Commission 1956–1963. Great Lakes Fish. Comm., University of Michigan, 13 pp.

Baldwin, N. S. (1969). Sea lamprey in the Great Lakes. Great Lakes Foundation. *Lemnos Mag.* 1, No. 3, 8 pp.

Bartsch, A. F. (1966), in "formal discussion" to paper by Elson and Kerswill, 1966.

Bay, E. C. (1964). An analysis of the "sayule" (*Diptera: Chironomidae*) nuisance at San Carlos, Nicaragua, and recommendations for its alleviation. WHO/EBL/20, WHO/VC/86, 18 pp.

Bay, E. C. and Anderson, L. D. (1965). Chironomid control by carp and goldfish. *Mosquito News* **25**, 310–16.

Berger, B. L., Lennon, R. E. and Hogan, J. W. (1969). Laboratory studies on Antimycin A as a fish toxicant. *Invest. Fish Control* **26**, 1–19. U.S. Dept. of the Interior, Fish and Wildlife Service, Bureau of Sports, Fisheries and Wildlife, Washington D.C.

Berrios-Duran, L. A., Ritchie, L. S. and Wessel, H. B. (1968). Field screening tests on molluscicides against *Biomphalaria glabrata*. *Bull. Wld. Hlth. Org.* **39**, 316–20.

Beyman, K. I., Crossland, N. O. and Wright, A. N. (1967). The rate of hydrolysis of the molluscicide N-tritylmorpholine. *Bull. Wld. Hlth. Org.* **37**, 53–63.

Bick, H. (1963). A review of central European methods for the biological estimation of water pollution levels. *Bull. Wld. Hlth. Org.* **29**, 401–13.

Billy, T. J., Daniels, S. L., Kempe, L. L. and Beeton, A. M. (1965). Field application of methods for recovery of the selective lampricide, 3-trifluoromethyl-4-nitrophenol. *Great Lakes Res. Div. Pub.* No. 13, 17–22.

Bitman, J., Cecil, H. C., Harris, S. J. and Fries, G. F. (1969). DDT induces a decrease in eggshell calcium. *Nature, Lond.* **224**, 5214, 44–6.

Bond, C. E., Lewis, R. H. and Fryer, J. L. (1960). Toxicity of various herbicidal materials to fish. Biological Problems in Water Pollution. *Trans. 2nd Semin. Biol. Problems in wat. pollut.* 1959, Cincinnati, pp. 96–105.

Bowman, J. S. and Orloski, E. J. (1966). Abate insecticide residues in streams and ponds treated for control of mosquito larvae. *Mosquito News* **26**, 557–61.

Bowman, M. C., Acree, F., Schmidt, C. H. and Beroza, M. (1959). Fate of DDT in larvicide suspension. *J. econ. Ent.* **52**, 1038–42.

Boyce, C. B. C. and Williams, D. A. (1967). The influence of exposure time on the susceptibility of *Australorbis glabratus* to N-tritylmorpholine. *Ann. trop. Med. Parasit.* **61**, 15–20.

Boyce, C. B. C., Crossland, N. O. and Shiff, C. J. (1966). A new molluscicide N-tritylmorpholine. *Nature, Lond.* **210**, No. 5041. 1140–41.

Boyce, C. B. C., Tyssul-Jones, T. W. and van Tongeren, W. A. (1967a). The molluscicidal activity of N-tritylmorpholine. *Bull. Wld. Hlth. Org.* **37**, 1–11.

Boyce, C. B. C., Tieze-Dageros, J. W. and Larman, V. N. (1967b). The susceptibility of *Biomphalaria glabrata* throughout its life history to N-tritylmorpholine. *Bull. Wld. Hlth. Org.* **37**, 13–21.

Boyd, C. E. and Ferguson, D. E. (1964). Spectrum of cross resistance in the mosquito fish, *Gambusia affinis*. *Mosquito News* **24**, 19–21.

Breitig, G. (1966). The necessity for the standardization of toxicity tests. *Verh. Int. Verein. theor. angew. Limnol.* **16**, 979–98.

Brooks, G. D. and Schoof, H. F. (1965). Simulated field tests of new insecticide formulations against *Aedes aegypti* larvae in 55-gallon water storage containers. *Proc. New Jers. Mosq. Exterm. Ass.*, 160–66.

Brooks, G. D., Schoof, H. F. and Smith, E. A. (1966). Evaluation of five formulations of Abate against *Aedes aegypti*, Savannah, Georgia, 1965. *Mosquito News* **26**, 580–2.

Brown, A. W. A., McKinley, D. J., Bedford, H. W. and Qutubuddin, N. (1961). Insecticidal operations against chironomid midges along the Blue Nile. *Bull. ent. Res.* **51**, 789–801.

Brown, N. C., Chadwick, P. R. and Wickham, J. C. (1967). The role of synergists in the formulation of insecticides. *Int. Pest. Control* **6**, 10–13.

Burdick, G. E. (1960). The use of bioassays by the Water Pollution Control Agency. *Trans. 2nd Semin. Biol. Problems Wat. Pollution.* Cincinnati, 1959, pp. 145–8.

Burdick, G. E., Harris, E. J., Dean, H. J., Colby, T. M., Shed, J. and Colby, D. (1964). The accumulation of DDT in lake trout and the effect on reproduction. *Trans. Am. Fish. Soc.* **93**, 127–36.

Burke, W. D. and Ferguson, D. E. (1968). A simplified flow-through apparatus for maintaining fixed concentrations of toxicants in water. *Trans. Am. Fish. Soc.* **97**, 498–501.

Burke, W. D. and Ferguson, D. E. (1969). Toxicities of four insecticides to resistant and susceptible mosquito in static and flowing water. *Mosquito News* **29**, 96–101.

Burmakin, E. V. (1968). Chemical methods of lake rehabilitation and preparation of new fish fauna in lakes. 1st and 2nd group fellowship study tours on inland fisheries research, management and fish culture in the Union of Soviet Socialist Republics, 1965–66. *F.A.O. Rome* No. TA 2547, 109–23.

Burress, R. M. and Luhning, C. W. (1969). Use of Antimycin for selective thinning of sunfish populations in ponds. *Invest. Fish Control* **28**, 1–10. U.S. Dept. of the Interior, Fish and Wildlife Service, Bureau of Sports, Fisheries and Wildlife, Washington D.C.

Burress, R. M. and Luhning, C. W. (1969). Field trials of Antimycin as a selective toxicant in channel catfish ponds. *Invest. Fish Control* **25**, 1–12. U.S. Dept. of the Interior, Fish and Wildlife Service, Bureau of Sports, Fisheries and Wildlife, Washington D.C.

Busvine, J. R. (1968). Design of tests for detecting and measuring insecticide resistance. Physico-chemical and biophysical factors affecting the activity of pesticides. *Soc. chem. Ind. Monogr.* **29**, 18–34.

Burton, G. J. (1964). An exposure tube for determining the mortality of *Simulium* larvae in rivers following larvicide operations. *Ann. trop. Med. Parasit.* **58**, 339–42.

Burton, G. J. and McCrae, T. M. (1965). Dam spillway breeding of *Simulium damnosum* Theobald in northern Ghana. *Ann. trop. Med. Parasit.* **59**, 405–11.

Burton, G. J., Noamesi, G. K., Zeve, V. H. and McCrae, T. M. (1964). Quantitative studies on the mortality of *Simulium* larvae following dosage with DDT under field conditions. *Ghana med. J.* **3**, 93–7.

Cabejszek, I., Luczac, J., Maleszewska, J. and Stanislawska, J. (1966). The effects of insecticides (aldrin, methoxychlor) on the physico-chemical properties of water and on aquatic organisms. *Verh. int. Verein. theor. angew. Limnol.* **16**, 963–8.

Cairns, J. and Scheier, A. (1964). The effect upon the pumpkinseed sunfish, *Lepomis gibbosus* (Linn) of chronic exposure to lethal and sublethal concentrations of dieldrin. *Notul. Nat.* No. 370.

Carlson, C. A. (1966). Effects of three organophosphorus insect on immature *Hexagenia* and *Hydropsyche* of the upper Mississippi River. *Trans. Am. Fish. Soc.* **95**, 1–5.

Chu, K. Y., Massoud, J. and Arfaa, F. (1968). Comparative studies of the molluscicidal effect of cuprous chloride and copper sulphate in Iran. *Bull. Wld. Hlth. Org.* **39**, 320–7.

Clarke, V. de V., Shiff, C. J. and Blair, D. M. (1961). The control of snail hosts of Bilharziasis and Fascioliasis in Southern Rhodesia. *Bull. Wld. Hlth. Org.* **25**, 549–58.

Cole, H., Barry, D., Frear, D. E. H. and Bradford, A. (1967). DDT levels in fish, streams, stream sediments and soils before and after DDT aerial spray application for fall cankerworm in Northern Pennsylvania. *Bull. Env. Contam. Toxic.* **2**, 127–46.

Cook, S. F. and Conners, J. D. (1963). The short-term side-effects of the insecticide treatment of Clear Lake, Lake County, California in 1962. *Ann. Ent. Soc. Am.* **56**, 819–24.

Cope, O. B. (1961). Effect of DDT spraying for spruce budworm on fish in the Yellowstone River system. *Trans. Am. Fish. Soc.* **90**, 239–51.

Cope, O. B. (1966). Contamination of the freshwater ecosystem by pesticides. *J. appl. Ecol.* **3** (Suppl.), 33–44.

Corbet, P. S. (1956). Some effects of *Simulium* control by insecticides on the feeding habits of insectivorous fishes. 2nd Symposium on African Hydrobiology and Inland Fisheries. Brazzaville. C.C.T.A. p. 81.

Corbet, P. S. (1958). Some effects of DDT on the fauna of the Victoria Nile. *Revue Zool. Bot. Afr.* **57**, 73–95.

Coutant, C. C. (1964). Insecticide Sevin: Effect of aerial spraying on drift of stream insects. *Science N.Y.* **146**, 420–1.

Craig, D. A. (1966). Techniques for rearing stream-dwelling organisms in the laboratory. *Tuatara* **14**, 65–72.

Cross, D. W. (1968). Stress as a factor in fish mortalities. *Yb. Ass. River Authorities*, 108–12.

Crossland, N. O. (1962). A mud sampling technique for the study of the ecology of aquatic snails, and its use in the evaluation of the efficacy of molluscicides in field trials. *Bull. Wld. Hlth. Org.* **27**, 125–33.

Crossland, N. O. (1967). Field trials to evaluate the effectiveness of the molluscicide N-tritylmorpholine in irrigation systems. *Bull. Wld. Hlth. Org.* **37**, 23–42.

Crossland, N. O. (1970). Personal communication.

Cushing, C. E. and Olive, J. R. (1957). Effect of Toxaphene and rotenone upon the macroscopic bottom fauna of two northern Colorado reservoirs. *Trans. Am. Fish. Soc.* **86**, 294–301.

Daniels, S. L., Kempe, L. L., Billy, T. J. and Beeton, A. M. (1965). Detection and measurement of organic lamprecide residues. *Tech. Rep. Gt. Lakes Fish. Commn.* No. 9, 18 pp.

Davies, D. M. (1950). A study of the blackfly population of a stream in Algonquin Park, Ontario. *Trans. R. Can. Inst.* **28**, 121–59.

Dawood, I. K., Farooq, M., Dazo, B. C., Miguel, L. C. and Unrau, G. O. (1965). Herbicide trials in the snail habitats of the Upper Egypt 49 project. *Bull. Wld. Hlth. Org.* **32**, 269–87.

Dawood, I. K., Dazo, B. C. and Farooq, M. (1966). Large scale application of Bayluscide and Sodium pentachlorophenate in the Egypt 49 Project area. *Bull. Wld. Hlth. Org.* **35**, 357–67.

Dazo, B. C., Hairston, N. G. and Dawood, I. K. (1966). The ecology of *Bulinus truncatus* and *Biomphalaria alexandria* and its implications for the control of bilharziasis in the Egypt 49 project area. *Bull. Wld. Hlth. Org.* **35**, 339–56.

de Araoz, J. (1962). Study in water flow velocities in irrigation canals in Iraq and their mathematical analysis. *Bull. Wld. Hlth. Org.* **27**, 99–123.

Deschiens, R. and Floch, H. (1964). Controle de l'action des molluscicides selectifs sur la microfaune et sur la microflore des eaux douce. *Bull. Soc. Path. exot.* **57**, 292–9.

Deschiens, R., Floch, H. and Le Coroller, Y. (1965). Les molluscicides cuivreux dans la prophylaxie des bilharzioses. *Bull. Wld. Hlth. Org.* **33**, 73–88.

de Villiers, J. P. and Rossouw, M. M. (1967). Structure and activity in molluscicides. *Nature, Lond.* **213**, 5082, 1208–9.

de Villiers, J. P. (1965). The development of molluscicides. *S. Afr. Indust. Chem.*

de Villiers, J. P. and Grant-Mackenzie, J. (1963). Structure and activity in molluscicides: the phenacyl halides, a group of potentially useful molluscicides. *Bull. Wld. Hlth. Org.* **29**, 424–7.

Dimond, J. B., Kadunce, R. E., Getchell, A. S. and Blease, J. A. (1968). DDT residues persisting in Red-Backed Salamanders in a natural environment. *Bull. Env. Contam. Toxic.* **3**, 194–202.

Doby, J. M. and Corbeau, J. (1962). Etude critique de la méthode standard de l'OMs pour la determination de la sensibilité des larves de moustiques aux insecticides. *Bull. Wld. Hlth. Org.* **27**, 189–97.

Doudoroff, P., Anderson, B. G., Burdick, G. E., Galtsoff, P. S., Hart, W. B., Patrick, R., Strong, E. R., Surber, E. W. and van Horn, W. M. (1951). Bioassay methods for the evaluation of acute toxicity of industrial wastes to fish. *Sewage ind. Wastes* **23**, 130–9.

Dugan, P. R. (1967). Influence of chronic exposure to anionic detergents on toxicity of pesticides to goldfish. *J. Wat. Pollut. Control Fed.* **39**, 63–71.

Dykstra, W. W. (1968). Some recent findings in pesticide–wildlife relationships. *Proc. N. J. Mosq. Exterm. Ass.* 24–9.

Edwards, R. W., Egan, H., Learner, M. A. and Maris, P. J. (1964). The control of chironomid larvae in ponds using TDE (DDD). *J. appl. Ecol.* **1**, 97–117.

Elliott, J. M. (1965). Daily fluctuations of drift invertebrates in a Dartmoor stream. *Nature, Lond.* **205**, 1127–9.

Elliott, J. M. (1967). Invertebrate drift in a Dartmoor stream. *Arch. Hydrobiol.* **63**, 202–37.

Elliott, J. M. and Minshall, G. W. (1968). A comparative study of invertebrate drift in the River Duddon (English Lake District). *Oikos* **19**, 39–52.

Elliott, R. (1958). A method for the investigation of susceptibility to insecticides in anopheline larvae. *Trans. R. Soc. trop. Med. Hyg.* **52**, 527–34.

Ellis, M. M. (1937). Detection and measurement of stream pollution. *Bull. Bur. Fish. Wash.* **48**, 365–437.

Elson, P. F. (1966). Aerial spraying of forests and associated abundance of young Atlantic salmon. Part I DDT. *J. Fish Res. Bd. Can.*

Elson, P. F. (1967). Effects on wild young salmon of spraying DDT over New Brunswick forests. *J. Fish. Res. Bd. Can.* **24**, 731–67.

Elson, P. F. and Kerswill, C. J. (1966). Impact on salmon of spraying insecticide over forest. *Adv. Wat. Pollut. Res.* **1**, 55–74. Water Poll. Control Fed., Washington D.C.

Eschmeyer, P. H. (1957). The near extinction of lake trout in Lake Michigan. *Trans. Am. Fish. Soc.* **85**, 102–19.

Fales, J. H., Spangler, P. J., Bodenstein, O. F., Mills, G. D. and Durbin, C. G. (1968). Laboratory and field evaluation of Abate against a backswimmer, *Notonecta undulata* Say (*Hemiptera: Notonectidae*). *Mosquito News* **28**, 77–81.

Farooq, M. (1967). Progress in bilharziasis control. *WHO Chron.* **21**, 175–84.

Ferguson, D. E. and Bingham, C. R. (1966a). Endrin resistance in the Yellow Bullhead, *Ictalurus natalis. Trans. Am. Fish. Soc.* **95**, 325–6.

Ferguson, D. E. and Bingham, C. R. (1966b). The effects of combinations of insecticides on susceptible and resistant mosquito fish. *Bull. Env. Contam. Toxic.* **1**, 97–103.

Ferguson, D. E., Cully, D. D., Cotton, W. D. and Dodds, R. P. (1964). Resistance to chlorinated hydrocarbon insecticides in three species of freshwater fish. *Bioscience* **14**, 43.

Ferguson, D. E., Ludke, J. L. and Murphy, G. G. (1966). Dynamics of endrin uptake and release by resistant and susceptible strains of mosquito fish. *Trans. Am. Fish. Soc.* **95**, 335–44.

Ferguson, D. E., Gardner, D. T. and Lindley, A. L. (1966). Toxicity of Dursban to three species of fish. *Mosquito News* **26**, 80–2.

Ferguson, F. F., Dawood, I. K. and Blondeu, Rene (1965). Preliminary field trials of acrolein in Sudan. *Bull. Wld. Hlth. Org.* **32**, 243–8.

Ferrigno, F., Jobbins, D. M. and Ruber, E. (1964). Practical aspects of mosquito wildlife investigations on Cumberland County marshes. *Proc. 51st Ann. Meet. N. J. Mosq. Exterm. Ass.* 74–84.

Floch, H., Deschiens, R. and Le Corroller, Y. (1963). Sur les proprietes molluscicides du sel cuprosulfitique de Chevreul en prophylaxie des bilharzioses. *Bull. Soc. Path. Exot.* **56**, 182–9.

Floch, H., Deschiens, R. and Le Corroller, Y. (1964). Sur l'action molluscicide élective de l'oxyde cuivreux du cuivre métal et du chlorure cuivreux. *Bull. Soc. Path. Exot.* **57**, 124–38.

Fredeen, F. J. H. (1962). DDT and Heptachlor as blackfly larvicides in clear and turbid water. *Can. Ent.* **94**, 875–80.

Fredeen, F. J. H., Arnason, A. P. and Berck, B. (1953a). Adsorption of DDT on suspended solids in river water and its role in blackfly control. *Nature, Lond.* **171**, 700.

Fredeen, F. J. H., Arnason, A. P., Berck, B. and Rempel, J. G. (1953b). Further experiments with DDT in the control of *Simulium arcticum* Mall. in the north and south Saskatchewan Rivers. *Can. J. Agric.* **33**, 379–93.

Frempong-Boadu, J. (1966). A laboratory study of the effectiveness of methoxychlor, fenthion and carbaryl against blackfly larvae (*Diptera: Simuliidae*). *Mosquito News* **26**, 562–4.

Frey, P. J. (1961). Effects of DDT spray on stream bottom organisms in two mountain streams in Georgia. *Spec. sci. Rep. U.S. Fish Wildl. Serv.* (*Fisheries*) No. 392, 11 pp.

Fukano, K. G. and Hooper, F. (1958). Toxaphene (chlorinated camphene) as a selective fish poison. *Prog. Fish. Cult.* **20**, 189–90.

Fontaine, R. E. (1968). Some recent developments and trends in vector control aspects of malaria eradication. *Mosquito News* **28**, 491–5.

Gahan, J. B., Labreque, G. C. and Bowen, C. V. (1955). An applicator for adding chemicals to flowing water at uniform rates. *Mosquito News* **15**, 143–7.

Garms, R. and Kuhlow, F. (1967). Empfindlichkeit von Simulien larven aus Norddeutschland gegenuber DDT und Baytex. *Zeit. f. Trop. Med. u. Parasit,* **18**, 119–24.

Garms, R. and Post, A. (1967). Freilandversuche zur Wirksamheit von DDT und Baytex gegen larven von *Simulium damnosum* in Guinea, West Afrika. *Anz. f. Schadlingskunde* XL.**4**, 49–56.

Gaufin, A. R., Jensen, L. D. and Nelson, T. (1961). Bioassays determine pesticide toxicity to aquatic invertebrates. *Wat. Sewage* Wks.

Gaufin, A. R., Jensen, L. D., Nebeken, A. V., Nelson, T. and Teel, R. W. (1965). The toxicity of ten organic insecticides to various aquatic invertebrates. *Wat. Sew. Wks.* **112**, 276–9.

George, J. L., Darsie, R. F. and Springer, P. F. (1957). Effect on wildlife of aerial application of Strobane, DDT and BHC to tidal marshes in Delaware. *J. Wildl. Mgmt.* **21**, 42–53.

George, L. F., Berry, R. A. and Mallack, J. (1968). Ultra low volume application with ground equipment for adult mosquito control. *Proc. 55th Ann. Meet. N. J. Mosq. Exterm. Ass.* 206–12.

Gildenhaus, P. A., Berger, B. L. and Lennon, R. E. (1969). Field trials of antimycin A as a fish toxicant. Invest. Fish Control **27**, 1–21. U.S. Dept. of the Interior, Fish and Wildlife Service, Bureau of Sports, Fisheries and Wildlife, Washington D.C.

Gillies, P. A., Womeldorf, D. J. and Walsh, J. D. (1968). A bioassay method for measuring mosquito larvicide depositions. *Mosquito News* **28**, 415–21.

Glancey, B. M., Baldwin, K. F. and Lofgren, C. S. (1969). Laboratory tests of promising mosquito larvicides. *Mosquito News* **29**, 41–3.

Gonnert, R. (1962). Bayluscide, a new compound for controlling medically important freshwater snails. Pflantzenschutz nachrichten, "Bayer", pp. 4–25.

Gonnert, R. (1961). Results of laboratory and field trials with the molluscicide Bayer 73. *Bull. Wld. Hlth. Org.* **25**, 483–501.

Graham, R. J. (1960). Effects of forest insect spraying on trout and aquatic insects in some Montana streams. Biological Problems in Water Pollution. *Trans. 2nd Semin. Biol. Problems Wat. Pollut. Cincinnati,* pp. 62–5.

Gras, G. (1966). Toxicite de fenitrothion pour *Aedes(O) detritus* (Haliday), *Gambusia affinis* (Baird et Girard), *Anguilla anguilla* (L) et *Pelodytes punctatus* (Davidson). *Bull. Soc. Pharm. Montpellier* **26**, 375–404.

Gras, G. and Rioux, J. A. (1969). Laboratory evaluation of some organophosphorus compounds against the larvae of *Aedes(O)detritus, Aedes(O)caspius* (Pallas) and *Culex pipiens pipiens, L. Mosquito News* **29**, 202–9.

Gretillat, S. (1965). Prophylaxie de la dracunculose par destruction des "Cyclops" au moyen d'un dérivé organique de systhèse, le dimethyldithiocarbamate de zinc ou Ziram. *Biol. Med.* **54**, 529–39.

Gretillat, S. and Lacan, A. (1964). Efficacite du zirame (dimethyldithiocarbamate de zinc) sur les gites a mollusques en riviere et toxicite pour les poissons. *Bull. Wld. Hlth. Org.* **30**, 413–25.

Hairston, N. G. (1961). Suggestions regarding some problems in the evaluation of molluscicides in the field. *Bull. Wld. Hlth. Org.* **25**, 730–7.

Hairston, N. G., Hubendick, B., Watson, J. M. and Olivier, L. J. (1958). An evaluation of techniques used in estimating snail populations. *Bull. Wld. Hlth. Org.* **19**, 661–72.

Harrison, A. D. (1966). The effects of Bayluscide on Gastropod snails and other aquatic fauna. *Hydrobiologia* **28**, 371–84.

Harrison, A. D. and Rattray, E. A. (1966). *S. Afr. J. med. Sci.* **62**, 238.

Hashimoto, T. (1969). Fish toxicity problems of pesticides in Japan: the present situation and the policies of the Ministry of Agriculture and Forestry. *P.A.N.S.* **15**, 325–29.

Hastings, E., Kittams, W. H. and Pepper, J. H. (1961). Repopulation by aquatic insects in streams sprayed with DDT. *Ann. ent. Soc. Am.* **54**, 436–7.

Hazeltine, W. E. (1963). The development of a new concept for control of the Clear Lake Gnat. *J. econ. Ent.* **56**, 621–6.

Heath, R. G., Spann, J. W. and Kreitzer, J. F. (1969). Marked DDT impairment of Mallard reproduction in controlled studies. *Nature, Lond.* **224**, 5214, 47–9.

Henderson, C. and Pickering, Q. H. (1958). Toxicity of organic phosphorous insecticides to fish. *Trans. Am. Fish. Soc.* **87**, 39–51.

Henderson, C. and Pickering, Q. H. (1963). Use of fish in the detection of contaminants in water supplies. *J. Am. Wat. Wks. Ass.* **55**, 715–20.

Henderson, C. and Tarzwell, C. M. (1957). Bioassays for control of industrial effluents. *Sewage ind. Wastes* **29**, 1002–17.

Henderson, C., Pickering, Q. H. and Tarzwell, C. M. (1959). The relative toxicity of ten chlorinated hydrocarbon insecticides to four species of fish. *Trans. Am. Fish. Soc.* **88**, 23–32.

Henderson, C., Pickering, Q. H. and Tarzwell, C. M. (1960). The toxicity of organic phosphorous and chlorinated hydrocarbon insecticides to fish. Biological Problems in Water Pollution. *Trans. 2nd Semin. Biol. Problems in Wat. Pollut.* Cincinnati, 1959, pp. 76–88.

Henegar, D. L. (1966). Minimum lethal levels of toxaphene as a pesticide in North Dakota lakes. *Invest. Fish Control* No. 3. U.S. Dept. of the Interior, Bureau of Sports, Fisheries and Wildlife Resources, Publ. No. 7. 16 pp.

Hickey, J. J., Keith, J. A. and Coon, F. B. (1966). An exploration of pesticides in a Lake Michigan ecosystem. Pesticides in the environment and their effects on wildlife. *J. Appl. Ecol.* **3**, Suppl. 141–54.

Hilsenhoff, W. L. (1959). The evaluation of insecticides for the control of *Tendipes plumosus* (Linnaeus). *J. econ. Ent.* **52**, 331–2.

Hilsenhoff, W. L. (1966). Effect of diquat on aquatic insects and related animals. *J. econ. Ent.* **59**, 1520–1.

Hira, P. R. (1969). Transmission of schistosomiasis in Lake Kariba, Zambia. *Nature, Lond.* **224**, 5220, 670–2.

Hitchcock, S. W. (1960). Effect of an aerial DDT spray on aquatic insects in Connecticut. *J. econ. Ent.* **53**, 608–11.

Hitchen, C. S. and Goiny, H. H. (1965). Note on the control of *Simulium damnosum* in the region of the Kainji Dam Project, Northern Nigeria. W.H.O./Oncho/7,65. Working paper for W.H.O. Expert Committee on Onchocerciasis.

Hoffmann, C. H. (1960). Are the insecticides required for insect control hazardous to aquatic life? Biological Problems in Water Pollution. *Trans. 2nd Semin. Biol. Problems in Wat. Pollut.* Cincinnati, 1959.

Hoffmann, C. H. and Droor, A. T. (1953). The effects of C-47 airplane application of DDT on fish food organisms in two Pennsylvania watersheds. *Am. Midl. Nat.* **50**, 172–88.

Hoffman, D. O. and Zakhary, R. (1954). A study of water temperature in a representative Egyptian canal in connection with Schistosomiasis control. *J. Egypt. med. Ass.* **37**, 963–7.

Holden, A. V. (1962). A study of the absorption of C^{14} labelled DDT from water to fish. *Ann. app. Biol.* **50**, 361–8.

Holden, A. V. (1964). The possible effects on fish of chemicals used in agriculture. *J. Proc. Inst. Sewage Purif.*, 361–8.

Holden, A. V. (1965). Contamination of fresh water by persistent insecticides and their effects on fish. *Ann. appl. Biol.* **55**, 332–5.

Holden, A. V. and Marsden, K. (1967). *Nature, Lond.* **216**, 1274.

Holland, H. T., Coppage, D. L. and Butler, P. A. (1966). Increased sensitivity to pesticides in sheepshead minnow. *Trans. Am. Fish. Soc.* **95**, 110–12.

Hooper, F. F. (1960). Population control by chemicals and some resulting problems. Biological Problems in Water Pollution. *Trans. 2nd Semin. Biol. Problems in Wat. Pollut.* Cincinnati, 1959, pp. 241–6.

Hooper, F. F. and Grzenda, A. R. (1957). The use of toxaphene as a fish poison. *Trans. Am. Fish. Soc.* **85**, 180–90.

Hopf, H. S., Duncan, J. and Wood, A. B. (1963). Molluscicidal activity of copper compounds of low solubility. *Bull. Wld. Hlth. Org.* **29**, 128–30.

Hopf, H. S., Duncan, J., Beesley, S., Webley, D. J. and Sturrock, R. F. (1967). Molluscicidal properties of organotin and organolead compounds. *Bull. Wld. Hlth. Org.* **36**, 955–61.

Hoskins, W. M. and Craig, R. (1962). Uses of bioassay in entomology. *Am. Rev. Ent.* **7**, 437–64.

Howell, J. H. (1966). The life cycle of the Sea Lamprey and a toxicological approach to its control. In "Phylogeny of Immunity". Vol. 25, pp. 263–70. University of Florida Press, Florida.

Howell, J. H., King, E. L., Smith, A. J. and Hanson, L. H. (1964). Synergism of 5,2′-dichloro-4′, nitro-salicylanilide and 3-trifluoromethyl-4-nitrophenol in a selective lamprey larvicide. *Tech. Rep. Gt. Lakes Fish. Commn.* No. 8.

Hubble, D. R. and Reiff, B. (1967). Reproduction of guppies (*Lebistes reticulatus*) after a single exposure to dieldrin. *Bull. Environ. Contam. Toxic.* **2**, 57–63.

Hunt, E. G. and Bischoff, A. I. (1960). Inimical effects on wildlife of periodic DDD applications to Clear Lake. *Calif. Fish. Game* **46**, 91–106.

Hunt, E. G. and Keith, J. O. (1963). Pesticide–wildlife investigations in California — 1962. Proc. 2nd Annual Conference on use of agricultural chemicals in California; Davis.

Hynes, H. B. N. (1961). The effect of sheep dip containing the insecticide BHC on the fauna of a small stream, including *Simulium* and its predators. *Ann. Trop. Med. Parasit.* **55**, 192–6.

Hynes, H. B. N. (1960). A plea for caution in the use of DDT in the control of aquatic insects in Africa. *Ann. Trop. Med. Parasit.* **54**, 331–2.

Hynes, H. B. N. and Williams, J. R. (1962). The effect of DDT on the fauna of a Central African stream. *Ann. Trop. Med. Parasit.* **56**, 78–91.

Ide, E. P. (1940). Quoted in Moye and Luckman, 1964.

Ide, F. P. (1957). Effect of forest spraying with DDT on aquatic insects of salmon streams. *Trans. Am. Fish. Soc.* **85**, 208–19.

Ide, F. P. (1967). Effects of forest spraying with DDT on aquatic insects of salmon streams in New Brunswick. *J. Fish. Res. Bd. Can.* **24**, 769–805.

220   BIBLIOGRAPHY

Jakob, W. L. (1968). Current status of mosquito research at the National Communicable Disease Centre laboratories, Savannah, Georgia. *Proc. 55th Ann. Meet. New Jersey Mosq. Exterm. Ass.* pp. 19–24.

Jamnback, H. (1969a). Field tests with larvicides other than DDT for control of blackfly (*Diptera: Simuliidae*) in New York. *Bull. Wld. Hlth. Org.* **40**, 635–8.

Jamnback, H. (1969). Bloodsucking flies and other outdoor nuisance arthropods of New York State. State Museum and Science Service, Memoir 19. The University of the State of New York. 99 pp.

Jamnback, H. and Eabry, H. S. (1962). Effects of DDT, as used in blackfly control, on stream arthropods. *J. econ. Ent.* **55**, 636–9.

Jamnback, H. and Frempong-Boadu, J. (1966). Testing blackfly larvae in the laboratory and in streams. *Bull. Wld. Hlth. Org.* **34**, 405.

Jamnback, H. and Means, R. G. (1966). Length of exposure period as a factor influencing the effectiveness of larvicides for blackflies (*Diptera: Simuliidae*). *Mosquito News* **26**, 589–91.

Jamnback, H. and Means, R. G. (1968). Formulation as a factor influencing the effectiveness of abate in the control of blackflies (*Diptera: Simuliidae*). *Proc. New Jers. Mosq. Control Ass.* 89–94.

Jamnback, H., Duflo, T. and Marr, D. (1970). Aerial application of larvicides for control of *Simulium damnosum* in Ghana — a preliminary trial. WHO/VBC/70.181, WHO/ONCHO/70.79.

Jensen, L. D. and Gaufin, A. R. (1964a). Effects of ten organic insecticides on two species of stonefly naiads. *Trans. Am. Fish. Soc.* **93**, 27–34.

Jensen, L. D. and Gaufin, A. R. (1964b). Long term effects of organic insecticides on two species of stonefly naiads. *Trans. Am. Fish. Soc.* **93**, 357–63.

Jensen, L. D. and Gaufin, A. R. (1966). Acute and long term effects of aquatic insecticides on two species of stonefly naiads. *J. Wat. Poll. Control. Fed.* **38**, 1273–86.

Jensen, S. (1966). *New Scientist* **32**, 612.

Jensen, S., Johnels, A. G., Olsson, M. and Otterlind, G. (1969). DDT and PCB in marine animals from Swedish waters. *Nature, Lond.* **224**, 5216, 247–50.

Johnson, W. C. (1966). Toxaphene treatment of Big Bear Lake, California. *Calif. Fish. Game* **52**, 173–9.

Johnson, D. W. (1968). Pesticides and fishes — a review of selected literature. *Trans. Am. Fish. Soc.* **97**, 398–424.

Johnson, W. D., Lee, G. F. and Spyradikis, D. (1966). Persistence of Toxaphene in treated lakes. *Int. J. Air Wat. Pollut.* **10**, 555–60.

Jones, J. R. E. (1937). The toxicity of dissolved metallic salts to *Polycelis nigra* (Muller) and *Gammarus Pulex* (L). *J. expt. Biol.* **14**, 351–63.

Keenleyside, M. H. A. (1959). Effects of spruce budworm control on salmon and other fishes in New Brunswick. *Can. Fish Cult.* **24**, 17–22.

Keil, J. E. and Priester, L. E. (1969). DDT uptake and metabolism by a marine diatom. *Bull. Env. Contam. Toxic.* **4**, 169–73.

Keppler, W. J., Klassen, W. and Kitzmiller, J. B. (1965). Laboratory evaluation of certain larvicides against *Culex pipiens*, Linn., *Anopheles albimanus*, Wied. and *Anopheles quadrimaculatus* Say. *Mosquito News* **25**, 415–19.

Kershaw, W. E. (1965). A report on the *Simulium* problem and fishery development in the area of the Kainji Reservoir. *1st Sci. Rep. Kainji Biol. Res. Team. Liverpool.* pp. 74–7.

Kershaw, W. E., Williams, T. R., Frost, S., Matchett, R. E., Mills, M. L. and Johnson, R. D. (1968). The selective control of *Simulium* larvae by particulate insecticides and its significance in river management. *Trans. R. Soc. Trop. Med. Hyg.* **62**, 35–40.

Kerswill, C. J. and Elson, P. F. (1955). Preliminary observations on effects of 1954 DDT spraying on Miramichi salmon stocks. *Prog. Rep. Atlant. Cst. Stas.* No. 62, 17–24.

Kimuru, T. and Keegan, H. (1966). Toxicity of some insecticides and molluscicides for the Asian blood-sucking leech *Hirudo nipponia* Whitman. *Am. J. Trop. Med. Hyg.* **15**, 113–15.

Klassen, W., Keppler, W. J. and Kitzmiller, J. B. (1964). Laboratory evaluation of certain larvicides against *Anopheles quadrimaculatus* Say. *Mosquito News* **24**, 192–6.

Knapp, F. W. and Gayle, C. H. (1967). ULV aerial insecticide application for adult mosquito control in Kentucky. *Mosquito News* **27**, 478–82.

Kuzoe, F. A. S. and Hagan, K. B. (1967). The control of *Simulium damnosum* Theobald (*Diptera: Simuliidae*) *Ann. trop. Med. Parasit.* **61**, 338–48.

Lagler, K. F. (1969), (Editor). Man-made Lakes. Planning-development. U.N. Development Programme. FAO. Rome. 71 pp.

Lauer, G. J., Nicholson, H. P., Cox, W. S. and Teasley, J. I. (1966). Pesticide contamination of surface waters by sugar cane farming in Louisiana. *Trans. Am. Fish. Soc.* **95**, 310–16.

Learner, M. A. and Edwards, R. W. (1963). The toxicity of some substances to *Nais* (*Oligochaeta*). *Proc. Soc. Wat. Treat. Exam.* **12**, 161–8.

Learner, M. A. and Edwards, R. W. (1966). The distribution of the midge *Chironomus riparius* in a polluted river system and its environs. *Int. J. Air Wat. Pollut.* **10**, 757–68.

Lennon, R. E. and Walker, C. R. (1964). Investigations on fish control. I. Laboratories and methods for screening fish-control chemicals. *Circ. Fish Wildl. Serv. Wash.* No. 18.

Lemke, A. E. and Mount, D. I. (1963). Some effects of alkyl benzene sulphonate on the bluegill, *Lepomis macrochirus*. *Trans. Am. Fish. Soc.* **92**, 372–8.

Lewallen, L. L. (1964). The effects of Farnesol and Ziram on mosquito larvae. *Mosquito News* **24**, 53–5.

Lieux, D. B. and Mulrennan, J. A. (1955). Mayfly control. *Mosquito News* **15**, 156.

Lieux, D. B. and Mulrennan, J. A. (1956). Investigations on the biology and control of midges in Florida (*Diptera: Tendipedidae*). *Mosquito News* **16**, 201–4.

Lindquist, A. W. and Roth, A. R. (1950). Effect of DDD on larvae of Clear Lake Gnat in California. *J. econ. Ent.* **43**, 328–32.

Lindquist, A. W., Roth, A. R. and Walker, J. R. (1951). Control of the Clear Lake Gnat in California. *J. econ. Ent.* **44**, 522–7.

Lockhart, J. D. F., Highton, R. B. and McMahon, J. P. (1969). Public health problems arising out of man-made fish ponds in the western province of Kenya fish culture. *East. Afr. Med. J.* **46**, 471–80.

Lofgren, C. S., Scanlon, J. E. and Israngura, V. (1967). Evaluation of insecticides against *Aedes aegypti* (L) and *Culex quinquefasciatus* Say (*Diptera: Culicidae*) in Bangkok, Thailand. *Mosquito News* **27**, 16–21.

Loosanoff, V. L. (1960). Some effects of pesticides on marine arthropods and molluscs. Biological Problems in water pollution. *Trans. 2nd Semin. Biol. Problems in Wat. Pollut.* Cincinnati, 1959. pp. 89–93.

Lowe, J. I. (1967). Effects of prolonged exposure to Sevin on an estuarine fish, *Leiostomus xanthurus Lacépède*. *Bull. Environ. Contam. Toxic.* **2**, 147–55.

Ludwig, P. D., Dishburger, H. J., McNeill, J. C., Miller, W. O. and Rice, J. R. (1968). Biological effects and persistence of Dursban insecticide in a salt marsh habitat. *J. econ. Ent.* **61**, 626–33.

McCrae, A. W. R. (1967). *Rep. E. Afr. Virus Res. Inst.* for 1966. No. 16.

McCullough, F. S. (1962). Further observations on *Bulinus* (Bulinus) *truncatus rohlfsi* (Clessin) in Ghana. *Bull. Wld. Hlth. Org.* **27**, 161–70.

McDonald, S. (1962). Rapid detection of chlorinated hydrocarbon insecticides in aqueous suspension with *Gammarus lacustris lacustris* (Sars). *Can. J. Zoo.* **40**, 719–23.

McDuffie, W. C. and Weidhaas, D. E. (1967). Current research by the U.S.D.A. of potential significance to world-wide mosquito control. *Mosquito News* **27**, 447–53.

McMahon, J. P. (1957). DDT treatment of rivers for eradication of Simuliidae. *Bull. Wld. Hlth. Org.* **16**, 541–51.

McMahon, J. P. (1967). A review of the control of *Simulium* vectors of onchocerciasis. *Bull. Wld. Hlth. Org.* **37**, 415–30.

Macan, T. T. (1958). Methods of sampling the bottom fauna in stony streams. *Int. Ver. J. Theor. Angew. Limn.* No. 8. 21 pp.

Macan, T. T. (1963). "Freshwater Ecology". Longmans, London.

Macek, K. J., Hutchinson, C. and Cope, O. B. (1969). The effects of temperature on the susceptibility of bluegills and rainbow trout to selected pesticides. *Bull. Envir. Cont. Toxic.* **4**, 174–83.

Marking, L. L. (1966). Evaluation of pp DDT as a reference toxicant in bioassays. U.S. Dept. of the Interior, Fish and Wildlife Service, Bureau of Sports, Fisheries and Wildlife Resources, **10**, 3–10.

Marking, L. L. and Hogan, J. W. (1967). Toxicity of Bayer 73 to fish. *Invest. Fish Control* No. 19. Resource Publication No. 36. U.S. Dept. of the Interior, Bureau of Sports, Fisheries and Wildlife Resources.

Matsuo, W. R. and Tamura, T. (1964). On the dispersal of the insecticide for blackfly control applied in running water. *Botyu-Kagaku* **29**, 21–4 (In Japanese).

Meehan, W. R. and Sheridan, W. C. (1966). Effect of toxaphene on fishes and bottom fauna of Big Kitoi Creek, Afognak Island, Alaska. *Invest. Fish Control*. No. 8. Publ. No. 12, 10 pp. U.S. Dept. of the Interior, Bureau of Sports, Fisheries and Wildlife Resources.

Meeks, R. L. and Peterle, T. J. (1967). Quoted in Ware *et al.*, 1968.

Mellanby, K. (1967). Pesticides and Pollution. In "The New Naturalist". Collins, London.

Merkens, J. G. (1957). Controlled aqueous environment for bioassay. *Lab. Pract.* **6**, 456–9.

Merryweather, Judith (1970). Personal Communication.

Meschkat, A. and Dill, W. A. (1961). Onchocerciasis and fisheries in Africa. Afr/Oncho/32.

Metcalf, R. L., Georghiou, G. P., Schoof, H. F. and Smith, C. N. (1969). Screening and laboratory tests for stages I, II and III. *Cah. O.R.S.T.O.M.* (Ser-Ent. med. et Parasitol.) VII, 111–19.

Meyling, A. H. and Pitchford, R. J. (1966). Physico-chemical properties of substances used as molluscicides. *Bull. Wld. Hlth. Org.* **34**, 141–7.

Meyling, A. H., Schutte, C. H. J. and Pitchford, R. J. (1962). Some laboratory investigations on Bayer 73 and ICI 24223 as molluscicides. *Bull. Wld. Hlth. Org.* **27**, 95–8.

Mills, G. D., Fales, J. H. and Durbin, C. G. (1969). Comparison of the effect of six pyrethroids against a backswimmer, *Notonecta undulata* Say. *Mosquito News* **29**, 690–1.

Middelem, C. H. van. (1966). Fate and persistence of organic pesticides in the environment. Organic Pesticides in the Environment. *Adv. Chem. Ser.* **60**, 228–49.

Moffet, J. W. (1958). Attack on the sea lamprey. *Michigan Conserv. Mag.*, May–June, 6 pp.

Moffett, J. W. (1966). The general biology of the Cyclostomes with special reference to the lamprey. *In* "Phylogeny of Immunity". Vol. 24, pp. 255–62. University of Florida Press, Florida.

Moore, J. B. and Breeland, S. G. (1967). Field evaluation of two mosquito larvicides, Abate and Dursban, against *Anopheles quadrimaculatus* and associated Culex species. *Mosquito News* **27**, 105–11.

Mount, G. A. and Lofgren, C. S. (1967). Ultra-low volume and conventional aerial sprays for control of adult salt-marsh mosquitoes, *Aedes sollicitans* (Walker) and *Aedes taeniorhynchus* (Wiedmann) in Florida. *Mosquito News* **27**, 473–7.

Mount, D. I. and Stephan, C. E. (1967). A method for establishing acceptable toxicant levels for fish — Malathion and the Butoxyethanol ester of 2, 4-D. *Trans. Am. Fish. Soc.* **96**, 185–93.

Mount, D. I. and Warner, R. E. (1965). A serial dilution apparatus for continuous delivery of various concentrations of materials in water. *Publ. Hlth. Serv. Publs., Wash.* 999 WP-23, 16 pp.

Moye, W. C. and Luckman, W. H. (1964). Fluctuations in populations of certain aquatic insects following application of aldrin granules to Sugar Creek, Iroquois County, Illinois. *J. econ. Ent.* **57**, 318–22.

Muirhead-Thomson, R. C. (1957). Laboratory studies on the reactions of *Simulium damnosum* larvae to insecticides. *Am. J. Trop. Med.* **6**, 920.

Muirhead-Thomson, R. C. (1966). Blackflies. *In* "Insect Colonization and Mass Production". (Smith, C. N., ed.), pp. 127–44. Academic Press, New York and London.

Muirhead-Thomson, R. C. (1969). A technique for establishing *Simulium* larvae in an experimental channel. *Bull. ent. Res.* **59**, 533–6.

Muirhead-Thomson, R. C. (1970a). The potentiating effects of pyrethrins and pyrethroids on the action of organophosphorus larvicides in *Simulium* control. *Trans. R. Soc. Trop. Med. Hyg.* **64**, 895–906.

Muirhead-Thomson, R. C. (1970b). Unpublished data.

Muirhead-Thomson, R. C. and Merryweather, Judith (1969). Effect of larvicides on *Simulium* eggs. *Nature, Lond.* **221**, 5183, 858–9.

Muirhead-Thomson, R. C. and Merryweather, Judith (1970). Ovicides in *Simulium* control. *Bull. Wld. Hlth. Org.* **42**, 174–7.

Mulhern, T. D. (1968). A preliminary report on low-volume spraying for mosquito control in California in 1967. *Proc. N. J. Mosq. Exterm. Ass.* pp. 47–51.

Mulla, M. S. (1961). Susceptibility of various larval instars of *Culex p. quinquefasciatus* Say to insecticides. *Mosquito News* **21**, 320–4.

Mulla, M. S. (1966a). Toxicity of new organic insecticides to mosquito fish and some other aquatic organisms. *Mosquito News* **26**, 87–91.

8*+

Mulla, M. S. (1966b). Solution to the phosphate resistance problem. *Proc. and Papers of the 34th Ann. Conf. California Mosquito Abatement Assn. Inc.* pp. 73–6.

Mulla, M. S. (1967). Larvicides and larvicidal formulations for the control of *Culex pipiens fatigans. Bull. Wld. Hlth. Org.* **37**, 311–15.

Mulla, M. S. and Khasawinah, A. M. (1969). Laboratory and field evaluation of larvicides against Chironomid midges. *J. econ. Ent.* **62**, 37–41.

Mulla, M. S., Metcalfe, R. L. and Kats, G. (1964). Evaluation of new mosquito larvicides, with notes on resistant strains. *Mosquito News* **24**, 312–19.

Mulla, M. S., Keith, J. O and Gunther, F. A. (1966). Persistence and biological effects of parathion residues in waterfowl habitats. *J. econ. Ent.* **59**, 1085–90.

Mulla, M. S., Metcalf, R. L. and Geib, A. F. (1966). Laboratory and field evaluation of new mosquito larvicides. *Mosquito News* **26**, 236–42.

Mulla, M. S., Amant, J. St. and Anderson, L. D. (1967). Evaluation of organic pesticides for possible use as fish toxicants. *Progve. Fish. Cult.* **29**, 36–42.

Mulla, M. S., Darwazeh, H. A., Geib, A. F. and Westlake, W. E. (1969). Control of pasture *Aedes* mosquitoes by dripping larvicides into flowing water, with notes on residues in a pasture habitat. *J. econ. Ent.* **62**, 365–70.

Muller, R. L. (1970). Personal communication.

Needham, P. R. and Usinger, R. L. (1956). Variability in the macrofauna of a single riffle in Prosser Creek, California, as indicated by Surber sampler. *Hilgardia* **24**, 383–409.

Newsom, L. D. (1967). Consequences of insecticide use on non-target organisms. *Ann. Rev. Ent.* **12**, 257–86.

Noamesi, G. K. (1964). The tube bioassay technique in test evaluate entomologically the effects of *Simulium* control operations in north-west Ghana. *Ghana Med. J.* **3**, 163–5.

Novack, A. F. and Rao, M. R. R. (1965). Endrin monitoring in the Mississippi River. *Science, N.Y.* **12**, 1732.

Nugent, D. A. W., Scott, D. and Waddy, B. B. (1955). Effect of water point treatment with DDT on the incidence of guinea worm infection. *Trans. R. Soc. Trop. Med. Hyg.* **49**, 476–7.

Ogilvie, D. M. and Anderson, J. M. (1965). Effect of DDT on temperature selection by young Atlantic salmon, *Salmo salar. J. Fish. Res. Bd. Can.* **22**, 503–12.

Onori, E., McCullough, F. S. and Rosei, L. (1963). Schistosomiasis in the Volta Region of Ghana. *Ann. Trop. Med. Parasit.* **57**, 59–70.

Ovazza, M. (1970). Follow-up of a mission on onchocerciasis in the Sudan: onchocerciasis survey and control. WHO/Oncho/70.78.

Pal, R. and Gratz, N. (1968). Larvicides for mosquito control. *P.A.N.S.* **14**, 447–55.

Paperna, I. (1969). Aquatic weeds, snails and transmission of Bilharzia in the new man-made Volta Lake in Ghana. *Bull. I.F.A.N.* **31**, 487–99.

Patterson, R. S. and Windeguth, D. L. von (1964a). The effect of Baytex on some aquatic organisms. *Mosquito News* **24**, 46–9.

Patterson, R. S. and Windeguth, D. L. von (1964b). The use of Baytex as a midge larvicide. *Mosquito News* **24**, 393–6.

Paulini, E. (1965). Reports on molluscicide tests carried out in Belo Horizinte, Brazil, in 1964. Mol/Inf. 20.65. III, 1–23.

Paulini, E., Chaia, G. and de Frietas, J. R. (1961). Trials with the molluscicides Rhodiacid and Bayer 73. *Bull. Wld. Hlth. Org.* **25**, 706–11.

Pickering, Q. H. (1966). Acute toxicity of alkyl benzene sulphonate to the eggs of the Fathead minnow, *Pimephales promelas*. *Int. J. Air Wat. Pollut.* **10**, 385–91.

Pitchford, R. J. (1961). A review of the use of non-residual molluscicides in the Transvaal. *Bull. Wld. Hlth. Org.* **25**, 559–62.

Porter, C. H. and Gojmerac, W. L. (1969). Field observations with Abate and Bromophos: their effect on mosquitoes and aquatic arthropods in a Wisconsin park. *Mosquito News* **29**, 617–20.

Post, A. and Garms, R. (1966). Die Empfindlichkeit einiger tropisch Susswasserfische gegenuber DDT und Baytex. *Zeit. f. Angewandte Zoologie* **53**, 487–94.

Powers, J. E. and La Bastille Bowes, Anne (1967). Elimination of fish in the Giant Grebe Refuge, Lake Atitlan, Guatemala, using the fish toxicant, antimycin. *Trans. Am. Fish. Soc.* **96**, 210–13.

Premdas, F. H. and Anderson, J. M. (1963). The uptake and detoxification of C^{14} labelled DDT in Atlantic Salmon, *Salmo salar*. *J. Fish. Res. Bd. Can.* **20**, 827–37.

Prevost, G., Lanouette, C. and Grenier, F. (1948). Effect of volume on the determination of DDT and rotenone toxicity to fish. *J. Wildl. Mgmt.* **12**, 241–50.

Rathbun, C. B. (1966). The arsenic content in soil following repeated application of granular Paris Green. *Mosquito News* **26**, 537–9.

Raybould, J. N. (1967). A method of rearing *Simulium damnosum* Theobald (*Diptera: Simuliidae*) under artificial conditions. *Bull. Wld. Hlth. Org.* **37**, 447–53.

Research Committee Water Pollution (1965). A review of the literature of 1964 on waste water and water pollution control. *J. Wat. Pollut. Control Fed.* **37**, 887–979.

Reynolds, L. M. (1969). Polychlorobiphenyls (PCB's) and their interference with pesticide analysis. *Bull. Env. Contam. Toxic.* **4**, 128–43.

Rioux, J. A., Croset, H., Gras, G. and Juminer, B. (1964). Priorité aux méthodes anti-larvaires dans la lutte contre les Aedes halophiles en Languedoc-Roussillon. *Archs. Inst. Pasteur Tunis* **41**, 385–96.

Risebrough, R. W., Reiche, P. and Olcott, H. (1969). Current progress in the determination of polychlorinated biphenyls. *Bull. Env. Contam. Toxic.* **4**, 192–201.

Ritchie, L. S. and Berrios-Duran, L. A. (1969). Chemical stability of molluscicidal compounds in water. *Bull. Wld. Hlth. Org.* **40**, 471–3.

Ritchie, L. S. and Fox, I. (1968). Comprehensive laboratory evaluations of the molluscicide 2'5-dichloro-4-nitro-3-phenyl salicylanilide (PSA): time-concentration relationships and susceptibility of stage-size arrays of snails. *Bull. Wld. Hlth. Org.* **39**, 312–15.

Ritchie, L. S., Radke, M. G. and Ferguson, F. F. (1962). Population dynamics of *Australorbis glabratus* in Puerto Rico. *Bull. Wld. Hlth. Org.* **27**, 171–81.

Ritchie, L., Berrios Duran, L. A., Frick, L. P. and Fox, I. (1963). Molluscicidal qualities of Bayluscide (Bayer 73) revealed by 6-hour and 24-hour exposures against representatives stages and sizes of *Australorbis glabratus*. *Bull. Wld. Hlth. Org.* **29**, 281–6.

Ritchie, L., Berrios Duran, L.A., Frick, L.P. and Fox, I. (1964). Molluscicidal time–concentration relationships of organo-tin compounds. *Bull. Wld. Hlth. Org.* **31**, 147–9.

Rosen, P. (1967). The susceptibility of *Culex pipiens fatigans* larvae to insecticides in Rangoon, Burma. *Bull. Wld. Hlth. Org.* **37**, 301–10.

Ruber, E. (1962). Further studies concerning the effects of DDT on salt marsh Copepods. *Proc. 49th Ann. Meet. N. J. Mosq. Exterm. Ass.* 181–7.

Ruber, E. (1963). The effects of certain mosquito larvicides on microcrustacean populations. *Proc. N. J. Mosq. Exterm. Ass.* 256–62.

Ruber, E. (1965). The effects of certain mosquito larvicides on cultures of microcrustacea. *Proc. N. J. Mosq. Exterm. Ass.* 207–10.

Ruber, E. (1967). Some effects on microcrustaceans of coastal impoundments for *Aedes sollicitans* control. *Proc. N. J. Exterm. Ass.* 139–44.

Ruber, E. and Baskar, J. (1968). Sensitivity of selected microcrustacea to eight mosquito toxicants. *Proc. N. J. Mosq. Exterm. Ass.* 99–103.

Ruber, E. and Ferrigno, F. (1964). Some effects of DDT, Baytex and endrin on salt marsh productivities, Copepods, and *Aedes* mosquito larvae. *Proc. 51st. Ann. Meet. N. J. Mosq. Exterm. Ass.* 84–93.

Sanders, H. O. and Cope, O. B. (1966). Toxicity of several pesticides to two species of Cladocerans. *Trans. Am. Fish. Soc.* **95**, 165–9.

Schober, H. (1967). A study of the use of Abate in mosquito control in Suffolk County, Long Island, N.Y., in 1965. *Mosquito News* **27**, 100–4.

Schmidt, C. H. and Weidhaas, D. E. (1959). Effect of varying conditions in a laboratory testing technique on the mortality of mosquito larvae. *J. econ. Ent.* **52**, 77–979.

Shafik, M. T. (1968). A gas chromatographic method for the determination of low concentrations of Abate in water. *Bull. Env. Contam. Toxic.* **3**, 309–16.

Sharaf el Din, H. and El Nagar, H. (1955). Control of snails by copper sulphate in the canals of the Gezira irrigated area of the Sudan. *J. trop. Med. Hyg.* **58**, 260–3.

Shiff, C. J. (1966). Trials with N-tritylmorpholine (Shell WL 8008) as a molluscicide in Southern Rhodesia. *Bull. Wld. Hlth. Org.* **35**, 203–12.

Shiff, C. J. and Clarke, V. de V. (1967). The effect of snail surveillance in natural waterways on the transmission of *Schistosoma haematobium* in Rhodesia. *Cent. Afr. J. Med.* **13**, 133–7.

Shiff, C. J. and Garnet, Bridget (1961). The short-term effects of three molluscicides on the microflora and microfauna of small, biologically stable ponds in Southern Rhodesia. *Bull. Wld. Hlth. Org.* **25**, 543–7.

Shiff, C. J. and Ward, Denise (1966). Variation in susceptibility to three molluscicides shown by three species of aquatic snails. *Bull. Wld. Hlth. Org.* **34**, 147–50.

Shiff, C. J., Crossland, N. O. and Miller, D. R. (1967). *Bull. Wld. Hlth. Org.* **36**, 500–7.

Shinkle, M. P. (1968). The complexities of chemical evaluations for larval mosquito control on diked salt hay marshes. *Proc. N. J. Mosq. Exterm. Ass.* 180–203.

Sjogren, R. D. and Mulla, M. S. (1968). Drip application of three organophosphorus insecticides for mosquito control. *Mosquito News* **28**, 172–7.

Sjogren, R. D., Mulhern, T. D. and Coplen, R. R. (1969). A device for the drip application of insecticide concentrates. *Mosquito News* **29**, 22–5.

Smith, A. J. (1967). The effect of the lamprey larvicide 3-trifluoromethyl-4-nitrophenol on selected aquatic invertebrates. *Trans. Am. Fish. Soc.* **86**, 410–13.

Solon, J. M., Lincer, J. L. and Nair, J. N. (1968). A continuous flow, automatic device for short-term toxicity experiments. *Trans. Am. Fish. Soc.* **97**, 501–2.

Soper, F. L. (1966). Paris Green in the eradication of *Anopheles gambiae* in Brazil, 1940; Egypt 1945. *Mosquito News* **26**, 470–6.

Sprague, J. B. (1964). Avoidance of copper zinc solutions by young salmon in the laboratory. *J. Wat. Pollut. Control Fed.* **36**, 990–1004.

Sprague, J. B. (1968). Apparent DDT tolerance in an aquatic insect disproved by test. *Can. Ent.* **100**, 279–84.

Sprague, J. B., Elson, P. F. and Saunders, R. C. (1965). Sublethal copper zinc pollution in a salmon river — a field and laboratory study. *Int. J. Air Wat. Pollut.* **9**, 531–43.

Starkey, R. R. and Howell, J. H. (1966). Substituted nitrosalicylanilides: a new class of selectively toxic sea lamprey (*Petromyzon marinus*) larvicides. *Tech. Rep. Gt. Lakes Fish. Commn.* No. 11, 21–9.

Stevens, L. F. and Stroud, R. (1967). Control of mosquito adults and larva with ultra-low volume aerial applications of Baygon and Baygon-Baytex mixture. *Mosquito News* **27**, 482–5.

Stout, V. F. (1968). Pesticide levels in fish of the north-east Pacific. *Bull. Env. Contam. Toxic.* **3**, 240–6.

Strufe, R., and Gonnert, R. (1962). Comparative studies on the influence of environmental factors upon the efficiency of Bayluscide. *Pflantzenschutz Nachrichten "Bayer"*. 15/1962, 50–70.

Summerfeld, R. C. and Lewis, W. M. (1967). Repulsion of green sunfish by certain chemicals. *J. Wat. Pollut. Control Fed.* **39**, 2030–8.

Surber, E. W. (1936). Rainbow trout and bottom fauna production in one mile of stream. *Trans. Am. Fish. Soc.* **66**, 193–202.

Surber, E. W. and Pickering, Q. H. (1962). Acute toxicity of endothal, diquat, hyamine, dalapon and Silvex to fish. *Progve. Fish. Cult.* 164–71.

Suzuki, T., Ito, Y. and Harada, S. (1963). A record of blackfly larvae resistant to DDT in Japan. *Jap. J. Expl. Med.* **33**, 41–6.

Swabey, Y. H., Schenk, C. E. and Parker, G. L. (1967). Evaluation of two organophosphorus compound blackfly larvicides. *Mosquito News* **27**, 1.

Tanner, H. A. and Hayes, M. L. (1955). Evaluation of toxaphene as a fish poison. *Col. Cooperative Fisheries Res. Unit. Quarterly Rep.* **1**, 31–9.

Tarring, R. C. (1965). The development of a biologically degradable alkyl benzene sulphonate. *Int. J. Air Wat. Pollut.* **9**, 545–52.

Tarzwell, C. M. (1965). The toxicity of synthetic insecticides to aquatic organisms and suggestions for meeting the problem. In "Ecology and the Industrial Society" (Goodman, G. T., Edwards, R. W. and Lambert, J. M., eds.), pp. 197–218, Blackwell, Oxford.

Tarzwell, C. M. and Henderson, C. (1956). Toxicity of dieldrin to fish. *Trans. Am. Fish. Soc.* **86**, 245.

Teesdale, C., Hadman, D. F. and Nguriathi, J. N. (1961). The use of continuous low-dosage copper sulphate as a molluscicide on an irrigation scheme in Kenya. *Bull. Wld. Hlth. Org.* **25**, 563–71.

Terriere, L. C., Kiigemagi, Ulo., Gerlach, A. R. and Borovicka, R. L. (1966). The persistence of toxaphene in lake water and its uptake by aquatic plants and animals. *J. Agric. Food Chem.* **14**, 66–9.

Thatcher, T. O. (1966). The comparative lethal toxicity of a mixture of hard ABS detergent products to eleven species of fish. *Int. J. Air Wat. Pollut.* **10**, 585–90.

Thomas, V. (1965). Effects of certain extrinsic and intrinsic factors on the susceptibility of larvae of *Culex pipiens fatigans* Wied to DDT. *Mosquito News* **25**, 38–53.

Tomlinson, T. G., Grindley, J., Collet, R. and Muirden, M. J. (1949). Control of flies breeding in percolating sewage filters. *J. Inst. Sewage Purif.* **2**, 134.

Torblaa, R. L. (1968). Effects of lamprey larvicide on invertebrates in streams. *Spec. sci. Rep. U.S. Fish. Wildl. Serv. (Fisheries)* No. 522, 13 pp.

Travis, B. V. (1968). Some problems with simulated stream tests of blackfly larvicides. *Proc. N. J. Mosq. Exterm. Ass.* 129–34.

Travis, B. V. and Schuchman, S. M. (1968). Tests (1967) with blackfly larvicides. *J. econ. Ent.* **61**, 843–5.

Travis, B. V. and Wilton, D. P. (1965). A progress report on simulated stream tests of blackfly larvicides. *Mosquito News* **25**, 112–17.

Travis, B. V., Guttmann, D. and Crofts, R. R. (1967). Tests (1966) with blackfly larvicides. *Proc. New Jers. Mosq. Exterm. Ass.* 49–53.

Travis, B. V., Dewey, J. E. and Pendleton, R. F. (1968). Comparative toxicity data on pesticides used for mosquito control. *Proc. New Jers. Mosq. Exterm. Ass.* 122–9.

Unrau, G. O., Farooq, M., Dawood, I. K., Miguel, L. C. and Dazo, B. C. (1965). Field trials in Egypt with acrolein herbicide molluscicide. *Bull. Wld. Hlth. Org.* **32**, 249–60.

U.S. Dept. of Health Education and Welfare (1964). Pollution-caused fish kills in 1964. Division of Water Supply, Pollution Control, Basic Data Branch, Washington D.C.

Vinson, S. B. (1969). Insecticide resistance in non-target aquatic organisms. *Cah. ORSTOM. Paris.* Ser. Ent. Med. et Parasitol. VII. 23–7.

Vinson, S. B., Boyd, C. E. and Ferguson, D. E. (1963). Resistance to DDT in the mosquito fish, *Gambusia affinis. Science, N.Y.* **139**(3551), 217–21.

Visser, S. A. (1965). Molluscicidal properties and selective toxicity of surface-active agents. *Bull. Wld. Hlth. Org.* **32**, 713–9.

Von Windeguth, D. L. and Patterson, R. S. (1966). The effects of two organic phosphate insecticides on segments of the aquatic biota. *Mosquito News* **26**, 377–80.

Walker, C. R., Lennon, R. E. and Berger, B. L. (1964). Preliminary observations on the toxicity of antimycin A to fish and other aquatic animals. Investigations in fish control. *Circ. Bur. Sport Fish. Wildl.* No. 186, 1–18.

Ware, G. W., Dee, M. K. and Cahill, W. P. (1968). Water florae as indicators of irrigation water contaminated by DDT. *Bull. Env. Cont. Toxic.* **3**, 333–8.

Warner, R. E., Peterson, K. K. and Borgman, L. (1966). Behavioural pathology in fish: a quantitative study of sublethal pesticide toxication. *J. appl. Ecol.* **3**, Suppl. 223–47.

Warnick, S. L., Gaufin, S. L. and Gaufin, A. R. (1966). Concentration and effects of pesticides in aquatic environments. *J. Am. Wat. Wks. Ass.* **58**, 601–8.

Water Pollution Research Laboratory (1967). Water Pollution Research 1966. Control of aquatic weeds, pp. 40–4.

Waters, T. F. (1961). Standing crop and drift of stream bottom organisms. *Ecology* **42**, 532–7.

Waters, T. F. (1965). Interpretation of invertebrate drift in streams. *Ecology* **46**, 327–34.

Waters, T. F. (1962). Diurnal periodicity in the drift of stream invertebrates. *Ecology* **43**, 316–20.

Waters, T. F. and Knapp, R. J. (1961). An improved stream bottom fauna sampler. *Trans. Am. Fish. Soc.* **90**, 225–6.

Weaver, L., Gunnerson, C. G., Breidenbach, A. W. and Lichtenberg, J. J. (1965). Chlorinated hydrocarbon pesticides in major U.S. river basins. *U.S. Public Health Report* **80** (6), 481–93.

Webb, F. E. (1960). Aerial forest spraying in Canada in relation to effects on aquatic life. Biological Problems in Water Pollution. *Trans. 2nd Semin. Biol. Problems Wat. Pollut.* Cincinnati, 1959, pp. 66–70.

Webb, F. E. and Macdonald, D. R. (1958). Studies of aerial spraying against the spruce budworm in New Brunswick. X. Surveys of stream bottom fauna in some sprayed and unsprayed streams, 1955–57. Can. Dept. Agric., Forest Biol. Lab., Fredericton, N.B., Interim Report, 14 pp.

Webb, F. E., Macdonald, D. R. and Renault, T. R. (1959). Studies of aerial spraying against the spruce budworm in New Brunswick. XII. Surveys of stream bottom fauna in some sprayed and unsprayed streams, 1958. Can. Dept. Agric., Forest Biol. Lab., Fredericton, N.B., Interim Report, pp. 12.

Webbe, G. (1957). The action on fish of several chlorinated hydrocarbons when used as larvicides. *Ann. trop. Med. Parasit.* **51**, 264–70.

Webbe, G. (1961). Laboratory and field trials of a new molluscicide Bayer 73 in Tanganyika. *Bull. Wld. Hlth. Org.* **25**, 525–31.

Webbe, G. (1963). The application of a molluscicide to the Mirongo River in Mwanza, Tanganyika. *Höfchenbr. Bayer Pfl. Schutz-Nachr.* **16**, 244–52.

Webbe, G. (1969). Progress in the control of schistosomiasis. *Trans. R. Soc. Trop. Med. Hyg.* **63**, Suppl. 82–91.

Webbe, G. and Shute, G. T. (1959). A further note on the action on fish of chlorinated hydrocarbons when used as larvicides. *Ann. trop. Med. Parasit.* **53**, 47–50.

Weidhaas, D. E. and Schmidt, C. H. (1960). Toxicological action of DDT on three species of mosquito larvae. *J. econ. Ent.* **53**, 106–10.

Weidhaas, D. E., Schmidt, C. H. and Bowman, M. C. (1960). Effects of heterogeneous distribution and codistillation on the results of tests with DDT against mosquito larvae. *J. econ. Ent.* **53**, 121–5.

Wenk, P. and Schlorer, G. (1963). Wirtsorientierung und Kopulation bei blutsaugenden Simuliiden. *Zeit. trop. Med. Parasit.* **14**, 177–91.

West, I. (1966). Biological Effects of Pesticides in the Environment. Organic Pesticides in the Environment. *Adv. Chem. Ser.* **60**, 38–53.

Westlake, W. E. and Gunther, F. A. (1966). Occurrence and mode of introduction of pesticides in the environment. Organic Pesticides in the Environment. *Adv. Chem. Ser.* **60**, 110–23.

White, E. (1965). (Editor). The first scientific report of the Kainji Biological Research Team. Liverpool. 88 pp.

Whitsel, R. H., Vickery, C. A., Rogers, C. J. and Grant, C. D. (1963). Studies on the biology and control of chironomic midges in the San Francisco Bay region. *Proc. Pap. A. Conf. Calif. Mosq. Control Ass.* 83–94.

W.H.O. (1958). Insect Resistance and Vector Control. 8th Report of the Expert Committee, 1957. *Tech. Rep. Ser. Wld. Hlth. Org.* No. 153.

W.H.O. (1960). 2nd African Conference on Bilharziasis (WHO/CCTA). *Tech. Rep. Ser. Wld. Hlth. Org.* No. 204, p. 37.

W.H.O. (1961). Molluscicides. 2nd Report of the Expert Committee on Bilharziasis. *Tech. Rep. Ser. Wld. Hlth. Org.* No. 214, 50.

W.H.O. (1963). Tentative instructions for determining the susceptibility or resistance of blackfly larvae to insecticides. 13th Report W.H.O. Expert Committee on Insecticides. *Tech. Rep. Ser. Wld. Hlth. Org.* No. 265, pp. 107–13.

W.H.O. (1963). Insecticide resistance and vector control. 13th Report of the W.H.O. Expert Committee on Insecticides. *Tech. Rep. Ser. Wld. Hlth. Org.* No. 265, p. 227.

W.H.O. (1965). W.H.O. Expert Committee on Bilharziasis. 3rd Report. *Tech. Rep. Ser. Wld. Hlth. Org.* No. 299.

W.H.O. (1965). Snail Control in the Prevention of Bilharziasis. *Monograph Ser. W.H.O.*, No. 5. p. 225.

W.H.O. (1966). Molluscicide screening and evaluation. A memorandum by eleven signatories following an informal meeting of investigators on molluscicide screening and evaluation. 17–21 Nov. 1964. Geneva. *Bull. Wld. Hlth. Org.* **33**, 567–81.

W.H.O. (1966). Onchocerciasis: Epidemiology and Control. W.H.O. Chron. **20**, No. 10, 378–85.

W.H.O. (1966). W.H.O. Expert Committee on Onchocerciasis, 2nd Report. *Tech. Rep. Ser. Wld. Hlth. Org.* No. 335, 96 pp.

Williams, T. R. and Obeng, Letitia (1962). A comparison of two methods of estimating changes in *Simulium* larval populations, with a description of a new method. *Ann. trop. Med. Parasit.* **56**, 359–61.

Wilton, D. P. and Travis, B. V. (1965). An improved method for simulated stream tests of blackfly larvicides. *Mosquito News* **25**, 118–22.

Winchester, J. M. (1967). "Col" formulations— a recent development in pesticides. *Int. Pest Control* **5**, 23–5.

Wolfe, L. S. and Peterson, D. G. (1958). A new method to estimate levels of infestations of black-fly larvae (*Diptera: Simuliidae*). *Can. J. Zool.* **36**, 863–7.

Wollerman, E. H. and Putnam, L. S. (1955). *Daphnia* help to screen systemics. *J. econ. Ent.* **48**, 759–60.

Womeldorf, D. J., Gillies, P. A. and Wilder, W. H. (1966). Mosquito larvicide susceptibility surveillance — 1965. *Proc. Pap. A. Conf. Calif. Mosq. Control Ass.* 77–9.

Workman, G. W. and Neuhold, J. M. (1963). Lethal concentrations of toxaphene for goldfish, mosquito fish and rainbow trout with notes on detoxification. *Progve. Fish Cult.* **25**, 1.

Wurtz, C. B. (1965) in "formal discussion" to paper by Alabaster and Abram, 1965.

Yeo, D. (1962). A preliminary statistical analysis of snail courts. *Bull. Wld. Hlth. Org.* **27**, 183–7.

AUTHOR INDEX

Numbers in italics indicate those pages in the Bibliography where references are listed.

SUBJECT INDEX

A

Abate
  caddis- and mayflies, 174
  fish, 56, 57
  formula, 208
  formulation, 193
  gnats, 152
  impact, 165, 166–7
  microcrustacea, 176, 179
  mosquitoes, 122
    evaluation, 125, 127, 130
  persistence, 9
  Simulium, 136
ACP, 44
Acrolein, 65, 69, 210
Acroneuria pacifica, 158, 169, 170, 173
Aedes, 119, 120, 123, 125, 129
  A. aegypti, 130
  A. sollicitans, 131, 177
Akton, 165, 176
Aldrin
  fish, 72
  formula, 207
  impact, 162
  stoneflies, 169, 173
  temperature, 182
  Tilapia, 60
Alkyl benzene sulphonate (ABS), 45, 50
Ammonia, 18
Amphipods, 165, 167
Annelid worms, 164
Anopheles, 126, 129, 132
  A. albimanus, 127
  A. freeborni, 126
  A. gambiae, 1
Ant, fire, 54
Antimycin
  dispersal, 196–7
  fish, 74–80
  and hard water, 186
  temperature, 181

Antimycin A
  formula, 205
  toxicity tests, 21, 31, 37, 38
Acrolein (aqualin), 95, 97
Arctopsyche grandis, 170
Arochlors, 192
Arprocarb, 127
Arthropods, 166
Asellus, 89, 155
Australorbis, 92

B

Baetis, 136, 160, 166, 174
Barbus sp., 62, 64
Bass
  largemouth (*Micropterus salmoides*), 38,
    68, 77
  rock, 74
Bayer 29493, 169
Baygon, 202
Bayluscide (Bayer 73, niclosamine), 2
  bilharziasis, 93, 94–5, 97, 98
  evaluation
    in field, 109
    in laboratory, 101, 104–5, 106
    large scale, 113
  fish, 13, 63–4
  formula, 209
  formulation, 192
  and hard water, 185, 186
  impact, 116–18
  pH, 189
  sea lamprey, 85–6
  and silt, 191
  temperature, 183
Baytex (fenthion)
  Cladocera, 118
  in combinations, 202
  fish, 56, 62
  formulation, 193, 194
  gnats, 152
  impact, 164–5, 166, 167

INDEX TO SCIENTIFIC NAMES OF GENERA AND SPECIES